A Phantasmagorical Machine

David Law

Copyright © 2023 by David Law

Second paperback edition June 2025

ISBN: 978-0-578-49990-1 (paperback)
ISBN: 979-8-218-19823-7 (ebook)

Many thanks to all, especially:

Orlando, my love; Tom S., for believing in me always and your generous heart; Margaret, for a lifetime of love; Patrick and Don, Michael, Richard, David D, Shannon, Joan, Joe DAF, Justin, Nelson, Sally, Kennith; Don W; Peter and Larry. And of course, my family.

I

SOLID STATE

1

I saw the image somewhere, some place where it gets copied and reposted if people like it. An animation really, a two-second image that cycles. I stared at it, thinking how crazy it looked. That weird moment when you forgot something entirely, then your brain connects the unrecognized thing with the memory and you realize you know it.

The moment was an orgasm, and it was supposed to be funny. It took that action in life and made you watch it over and over. What was strange about it was that it happened so long ago, and back then you couldn't freeze time like this. It was an image on cheap film that passed in a few seconds, but here it was, cycling, and people adding their wiseass comments. Shot from below, his hair hanging in his face, mouth hanging open with that dumb, stoner expression, he closes his eyes and his head drops forward. In slow motion it might have looked like praying, but here, repeating in two-second bursts, it's just mechanical.

It felt uncomfortable to watch. Not because of the explicitness or anything. More like someone dug him up where he lay, peaceful and forgotten, and shook him for one last laugh. It made me sad as I watched it cycle. Those totally dated colors, the cool blue of the sky so true, the hot red, pink, brown spectrum of skin from shoulders down the arms to the giveaway white suburban legs, all so shockingly fresh. Colors we don't have names for anymore.

Some of the comments asked who it is, how he could be found by searching. But he's long dead, I know that. I was there when they killed him. Seeing this image now, so fresh and alive, is eerie.

The lips are so red.

■ ■ ■

Here's what happened: in 1981, April maybe, two guys rolled him into a Persian rug off the floor of this rich guy's house in Palm Springs. They had beat him to death and now they had to get rid of the body. They put the carpet in a car and drove it up into the dark hills. When they found a good a place to stop, the bigger guy hoisted it onto his shoulder and walked through the pitch black to a clearing. When they came to the sharp edge where it dropped into a canyon, he snapped it open like a bedsheet; the body came flying out and hit the ground with a thud, then rolled over the edge.

Then they waited, listening to the sound of leaves and branches as the body rolled down and down. When they couldn't hear it anymore, they went back to the car and drove away. At the bottom of the ravine, crickets stopped chirping as this thing came rolling toward them; when it came to rest and didn't move, a few moments later, they started up again like nothing happened. So that's that.

Meanwhile, back in the now, and a few days later, I found out why such a clear image existed. Because it really was new. Someone found Ray's movies, fixed them up and reissued them. Turns out they had a lot of them, the silent loops with guys who had no names, or names Ray made up that day and forgot. That animation I saw was a bit from one of the reissued movies. Amazing any of it existed, and more, how they even found them.

I stared at one of the pictures for a long time. I hadn't seen him in so long. A kid trying to look tough. People took it seriously back then, but now it just makes you laugh. Or cry.

■ ■ ■

I remember this one time when Eva was at our house and Kevin was there too. She gave him the hard once-over, this judgmental look she did so well onscreen. "Who's that?" she said, waving the back of her cigarette hand toward the doorway where he stood, like he wasn't there. I told her it was my friend, that she knew him. "Oh," she said, and blew smoke out the side of her mouth. "You grew."

This was 1977, so we must have been fifteen. She hadn't seen him since we were both ten or something. He looked back at her and grunted. Most kids our age would have said Hello ma'am, shown some respect to a grownup, but not him. If she was going to gesture at him with her cigarette like he wasn't worth speaking to, he would throw it right back at her, no matter how old or famous she was.

It was an odd moment. Two characters you don't see in the same scene, from two different movies: on the right, blonde longhaired teenager in warm saturated color; on the left, perfectly coiffed movie star in crisp Technicolor silver-blue suit. One hand holding a cigarette, the other under the elbow of the cigarette arm, crossed in front.

Kevin was tall now, not the pug nose kid. Wide shoulders and that gold hair parted in the middle; beautiful green, almond-shaped eyes, shirt unbuttoned three buttons too far. When we walked to school together, people in cars craned their necks to get a look. Once an old guy stared at him so long he crashed into the back of a station wagon stopped at a light. Like a vortex moving down the street, all air and light focused on the cleft between the muscles of his chest in the open shirt under the Levi's jacket. And he stared at Eva now, with those same almond eyes, taking no shit.

"How old are you?" she asked.

"Fifteen," he answered, flat.

"The same age? Huh. You look older."

Then nothing more out of him; his face said it all. *I don't care what you think*. Just perfect. One person, at least, not intimidated by all this. But there was one thing about Eva: no matter how cranky or judgmental, there was always a grain of truth in what she said. She was usually – infuriatingly – right. So, after he left that afternoon, and I heard her talking to momma in the kitchen, and Eva said, low and gravelly, "I don't like that kid," I was furious. Butting her nose into my business, telling me, any of us, who we could know and be in love with. "He'll cause trouble," was all I remember her saying. And maybe because she said it, and I was so mad, it turned out that he was.

2

But further back now. Say, 1970. Everyone still had cars like shiny dinosaurs. Cadillacs and Oldsmobiles, devouring the streets with growling engines sucking down five miles a gallon. Eva had a Fleetwood, long as a city block, crisp and sleek in ice blue. It might have been some custom color. They used to do stuff like that, come up with a color for some celebrity and give it to them for publicity. When Eva stopped in front of our house in North Hollywood, even indoors you could hear the growling V8 under the hood of the shiny spacecraft from Beverly Hills, so out of place in our neighborhood of brown stucco houses and cracked sidewalks.

Momma came into the livingroom, Alicia, probably five or six, playing with a dollhouse in the corner. Outside, in the shade of the car, Eva tied a scarf around her big hairdo, lit a cigarette, checked her lipstick, then got out and made her way down the walk to the front door, holding the cigarette to the side for balance like she's walking through a minefield. At the front door, she put the cigarette in her mouth and knocked with a gloved hand, the doorbell long broken. "Jesus, Carolyn," she said when my mother opened the door. "There's a car up on blocks in your neighbor's yard."

"That's Norman's house," momma said. "He's a mechanic. He fixes cars."

"What kind of a neighbor leaves an eyesore like that for all the neighbors to look at? It's disgusting."

"It's his work," momma sighed.

"Well, my God, you can store a car in your garage. Or your driveway. But up on blocks, flaunting it like that? It's disrespectful is what it is."

Nothing more from momma, Eva brushed past her, said to us, "How are my favorite grandchildren?" and gave us hugs and perfumed kisses. I couldn't understand how someone old could have such smooth skin. She looked around our livingroom with the perfect comic pained expression. "What say I take the boy over the hill for the afternoon? No reason to sit around here," she said, leaving out *in this dump*.

"No," momma said. "They want to watch TV and I bought the frozen dinners they like. So please, just stay here with them. Read the paper or whatever. I should be back by ten thirty."

"Oh, I see. An *assignation*."

"There's pizza in the freezer and snacks on the counter. You know where the coffee is."

"Mmmm," Eva said. To us, "You see what a good grandmother you have? With everything I could be doing, what do I do with my spare time? I'm here, watching my wonderful, beautiful grandchildren, that's what."

"And they appreciate it," momma said.

"No trouble. No trouble at all. I just hope it's worth it to you."

"Hhhm?"

"Well, who's on the dance card tonight, the goniff or the shlemiel?"

Looking for something in her big black purse, momma said, "You don't know him."

"Oh ho, I know him. I know them all."

Into the purse, momma mumbled, "Here we go."

"Yes, here we go. I mean, Carolyn, can you disagree with me? The bunch of sad sacks you manage to collect . . . I don't understand why you put up with them. Messy, sloppy, aimless . . . what was that one you introduced me to, with the sweater?"

"I don't know." The stuff in her purse seemed to be jangling and swirling around. Eva tilted her head slightly, and at moments like this, it felt like she was playing to me as well as the other person in the scene, her timing and elocution crystal clear. "A *sweater*," she said. "On a date. And not even a new one, it was all *pilly*. What did we call him?" I looked at the floor but couldn't help the smile. "The fuzzball," she said, nodding.

"He was a nice man."

"Oh, nice man. There's a good measure. What was his name again, Mervin, Merwin . . .?"

"Melvin," momma said quietly.

"*Mel*-vin. Sounds like vermin. Vernon. Something." She opened her own purse and pulled out a new cigarette.

"You didn't give him a chance."

"Some people don't deserve a chance. It's one thing to be trusting, Carolyn, it's another to be *gullible*. You can always tell. Pilly sweater and all. And suspicious! I remember he did something with money."

"He was an accountant, mother. He manages money."

"Ah, there, you see," and she pointed the unlit cigarette at her. "*Manages* money. What does that even mean? You put money in the bank, you take it out. Big deal. Who has to manage it? You can't trust people who give you double talk like that. I hope you didn't give him any of your money to *manage*. And certainly none of the money I give you. God forbid," which came out *fowid* as the cigarette went in and she lit the match. "So that's all I'm saying. Didn't like him a bit." She moved the cigarette to the side of her mouth while she fooled with a broach on her suit; when she did this, with the cigarette to the side, she always looked to me like a mechanic working to get something right.

"Well, anyway," momma sighed on her way to the kitchen. Eva followed and they talked some more, then momma kissed us goodbye and left through the garage. In the kitchen Eva turned on KNX, the news echoing off the linoleum. Alicia back at her dollhouse, me playing with Matchboxes on the carpet. I heard Eva set up the percolator and soon, the blup-blup and the smell of coffee. When it was done, she got a cup, poured it, sat at the kitchen table and the soft waves of turning newspaper pages. Slow exhales of warm, nutty cigarette smoke mixed with coffee and filled the air, and suddenly the house felt stable and solid and calm.

Los Angeles had this sense back then. I saw the words on the front of my clock radio, *Solid State*, and I asked momma what it meant. She wasn't sure but she thought it had something to do with it being always on but not on. And that was the way it felt; you had the sense, no matter where you were, of a wide, flat city of people eating in diners and cars moving slowly on bright concrete streets. AM radio reporting a pileup on the San Bernardino Freeway, some foot powder you can't live without. Smog alert for tomorrow. Everything in simultaneous, horizontal order, this solid, ongoing state of things, all around you.

Right then, in our kitchen, the zip-zip of legs in pantyhose crossing, uncrossing, crossing again. Impatience. I look low and see the foot of the crossed leg tapping the air under the table. Then, calling to me, "Sweetheart." I look up, try to look surprised. "We're not getting anywhere at all here," she said. "What say you and I go over the hill for ice cream and coffee." I didn't think I had a choice, but I liked ice cream and she liked coffee, so it had to be ok. "Good. Then gather up your sister and we'll drop her at that nice Mrs . . . uhm, that girl your mother has . . ."

"Mrs. Melendez."

"Melem . . . yes, then we'll skeddadle. No need to bring the baby all the way over the hill."

Alicia sat watching this with her mouth open. Sometimes Eva did this, spoke as though someone wasn't in the room who was. Also, she had a habit of still calling her the baby even though she was six.

Eva took us by the hands – cigarette in mouth just long enough before she'd need it again –- hustled us into the Cadillac and took off. When we got to Mrs. Melendez's, I sat in the front seat and watched in the side mirror while she went up the stone walk and knocked. They chatted while Eva pushed Alicia gently through the open door, Mrs. Melendez shaking her head, looking confused. But Eva smiled, kept her gaze slightly over Mrs. Melendez's head, and waved her hands, brushing away her words. She nodded and I could see her mouth saying, "Thank you dear, yes, yes, thank you, thank you," and gliding down the steps, waving behind her as she came up to the car. "Well now, wasn't that convenient?"

Then she started the motor, pulled the lever down so the red line pointed to the big D behind the little glass window on the steering column, brought all the horses under the huge hood to life and pulled away from the dead grass and broken-down cars on the front yards of North Hollywood.

3

In the movies, when you saw him, he always looked slightly stoned. But also, you bought it completely. It never looked phony, like he was being paid to fuck some guy on a dirty sofa. He *sold,* was how Ray described it. It didn't look like acting, it looked like life. And being lifelike was a skill, he said. And a gift.

Anyway.

To go from the valley to the city, you make a run for the hills up Laurel Canyon, hit the top, and depending on how fast you're going, bump up and over; then you fall down twisting, curving roads till you flatten out again at the bottom. It feels more like flying than driving, and in momma's convertible, when we went over the top, we put our hands up, yelled *Woooooooo!* and without seatbelts in those days, you could really fly into the air. In Eva's car, though, just the opposite: inside there, you were safe and sealed up, protected from the wilderness, the *wildness,* outside. Maniacs, robbers, rapists, lunatics – all those people who lurked on every street corner, waiting to rob and beat you – well, they would just have to rob and beat someone else, some foolhardy person who wasn't vigilant like she was.

She drove us over the hill, then down to Olympic, where we made a right. Most of the streets were still cement slabs then, they went ka-chunk ka-chunk ka-chunk when they disappeared under the front of your car. Eva reached into her pocketbook and pulled out the gold cigarette case, pushed in the silver button on the dashboard, and when it popped out, lit another cigarette. I watched her perfectly shaped mouth as it went in there, lipstick holding it on like pink glue.

"Can I have a cigarette?" I asked.

"Certainly not. Smoking is not for children."

"When can I smoke?"

She didn't move her head at all, kept her eyes on the road. "When you're sixteen. Then your lungs are fully developed and ready to deal with nicotine." The way she said *nicotine*, three sharp syllables, made it sound so snappy. Without a word, we turned off Olympic into the parking lot of the restaurant with the triangle soaring toward the sky at the top of a high pole. Ships – we called it Spaceships – and she knew I liked it. We found a spot by the door.

Soon as we walked in, everybody's head snapped around to look, even with her big sunglasses on. The hostess took us to a table on the left, under burnt orange lamps dangling from the high ceiling like droopy teardrops. I loved Spaceships because of the flying sign and the nice waitresses, but mostly, because they had toasters on each table and they brought a plate of bread you could toast yourself. Eva rummaged through her pocketbook. Our waitress came over, wearing the uniform they all had that looked like a cross between a farmer's wife and a nurse. She was around Eva's age but looked older. You used to see a lot of old ladies like her from Texas and Oklahoma working in restaurants. They were pretty; under the old lady's face you saw the shadow of something delicate and photogenic, and someone probably said, thirty years ago, You are so pretty, honey, you should go to Hollywood and be in pictures. This lady never did get in though; she ended up working in the commissary or craft services. Her nametag said *Irene*. They smiled at each other, Eva and Irene, did this nod that people who worked at the studios had. It meant they recognize who they are, the star and the server, and even though one is famous and the other brings the coffee, they both know they're there to do a job and they do it.

"Would you like menus over here?"

"Yes, that would be fine, dear," Eva said. "And could you bring some bread for the boy? He's eyeing that toaster with an itchy trigger finger."

"Right away, Miss Loesch," Irene said. And that's her name: Eva Loesch. Or, rather, that's the name on the credits and in magazines. She had another name, too, the same last name as ours, which was Esther

Goldberg, but really, there was no one who would turn around if you yelled it. Because to people in restaurants and movie theaters, on buses and Merv Griffin, there was only one person, and that was Eva Loesch. To us, Nana, and later, just Eva.

While I looked at the other tables to see what they were eating, Nana pulled the folded newspaper out of her purse. Irene brought the dish of bread and I put a piece in, pushed down the lever and waited, felt the red heat on my face. "Don't catch your hair on fire," she said. Our joke, what she said if I leaned too close. "I'll bring home a burnt grandson and we'll have to call you Crispy."

I watched and waited. The gray steel inside glowing a new color, tiny springs and levers turning a deeper orange; the soft white bread becoming hard on its skin, turning shiny, then brown, then the lines against the red metal, black. It knows when it's done and pops up, and just as quickly the red disappears, turns back to orange then gray then cool steel.

Nana said, "May I try some of your wonderful toast?"

I gave her one. She took the dish, spread jam on the toast with a spoon, held her cigarette away with a straight arm and took a bite. "Oh my *goodness!*" she said, so loud people at the other tables could hear. "That is the best toast I have ever tasted in my life! Did you make this all by yourself, sitting here just now?"

I was proud. "Yes I did."

"Well, this is best toast I've ever eaten. That's all there is to it. The best!"

Irene came back to take our order. I had a tall stack of pancakes; Nana asked for her usual, a pot of coffee, a hard-boiled egg, a dish of beet soup with no sour cream. When it came, she lit another cigarette, held that in one hand while she cut up the egg with the side of her fork. "How are the pancakes?"

I said fine, and she poured coffee, opened the newspaper. "Oh god," she muttered, *"The Sound of Music."*

"Momma took us two times," I said, through a mouthful of toast.

"I'm sure she did. I just can't bear it, I'm sorry. After everything else, I don't need that shoved in my face." She put down the paper and looked at me. "Did I tell you they asked me to come in for the one about Siam?" She had, but I liked when she told it. "Deceitful," she went on, "that's what it was, plain and simple." The ceiling was so high in Ships that it echoed. You could hear people across the room coughing and clanking their silverware. Eva slapped the paper for emphasis. "Come in, come in, they said, oh, it's the perfect thing. All set, the ink is dry, all we need is one favor from you."

There's a pause where I'm supposed to say, "What?"

"Just a look," she went on "that's all we want. *Ha!* What a boob. That's what I was. A big, dumb boob. I go in there, all gussied up, and what do you think they offer? Just guess."

"The supporting wife?"

She pointed with the cigarette. "Could not have been more embarrassed if they dumped a can of paint over my head. Deliberate and deceitful."

I kept chewing, just nodded here.

"Then," she said, "*then!* To make matters worse, I think about it. I really do. I'm not vain. You can't be arrogant, you have to consider your options. And before I can call them back, *they* call me. *They've* decided. They want someone more Oriental looking. Can you imagine it? They ended up with a girl in a black wig, that's all I remember."

"Lady Thaing," I said.

"Lady *Thaing.* Hmmmf. What I could have done with that."

"But you were in it someplace. I saw the pictures."

"That was a road show in Chicago. I wouldn't do that again. People only come to see how old you look. How badly you're falling apart."

"Your agent should have got you the lead."

She nodded. "But in this life, you don't often get what you want."

I asked why. "Because," and she put down the paper and took a deep drag. "Because no matter what anyone says, you're still a commodity. You know what that is? It's something you buy or sell, like oranges or a coffee table. In pictures, they cast you because they know how much the public will pay to see you. In my day, the studio knew how much I'd bring in so they put me in. When people stopped coming, they stopped putting me in.

Plus, they used to own you with a contract, so you had to do any picture they told you to. Nowadays it's different. They pay you for every individual picture, like some kind of a temp."

"How much?"

"As much as your agent can get. How much you're worth at any given moment."

"Do people still buy you?"

She smiled. "Not as much as they used to. And sometimes, just to bring in the blue hair crowd. Remember when I had to go to Barbados last year? They wanted an older lady who ran a bordell . . . well, not a nice place. But an older lady with class, not someone from TV."

"Did you make a lot of money?"

"No. But you have to do things like that to keep your face in front of the public. Show them you still look like yourself."

But this was a problem I had with her. She always looked like someone else, some other age and some other person. Sometimes she was big and in color with boobs like missiles; other times she was young and looked like my mother in black and white on TV. Sometimes she had girl voices and other times she had her voice now, low and gravelly. Once I turned on the TV and she was talking to Mike Douglas. I went into the kitchen to see if she was still in the house. She was, sitting at the kitchen table. "Nana, how are you on TV and here at the same time?"

"It's videotaped, honey. It's pre-recorded."

Pre-recorded, I thought. Meant you could be in two places at once. Right now, in Spaceships, she went on: "The trick is enduring. First you become a known quantity, then it's your job to endure. You try on a bunch of acts and eventually you find the one that people like. So you act the act and they like you, and you have to keep doing it so they keep on liking you. And you have to keep on being that person, even when you get old, because they won't accept you getting old. Oh no. If you dare change, heaven help you. They get furious like you've committed some crime against them. And that's when you find out what you're made of. You get up every morning and people who never even met you want to cut you down, but you go past them and you smile no matter what. You act the act and you endure." She touched the tip of her tongue with the end of her little finger to remove a fleck of tobacco stuck there. "Not easy, let me tell you. But remember that. You must endure." She pointed at me with the cigarette, and I knew this meant it was important. The glowing red end aimed right at me.

"I will," I said. Remember, I mean.

"Just sloppy," she said, slapping the newspaper. "Climbing an Alp, singing lousy songs. They should have known better."

By the time we finished, she said there would be too much traffic to go all the way over the hill and come back again. "So you'll have to come home with me."

4

Eva's house on Palm Drive was bright yellow, with white shutters and rows of very upright, proper tulips lining the walkway to the front door. Like all the houses in Beverly Hills, immaculate, with gardeners coming every other day to take old blossoms off the flowers and trim hedges that didn't have time to grow. You would never see someone leaving a broken car in the front yard here. Eva was proud, too, that her house didn't change with every trend; it was cheerful and solid, a two-story Cape with wood siding and a slate roof. While the neighbors put up pagodas and Mediterranean villas and French provincials, the yellow Cape never wavered. It was made clear to us that Beverly Hills was divided into two camps: the phony, temporary people who built some garish showplace then cavorted around town until their money ran out; and the real people, the industry workhorses who'd lived in the same modest home for thirty years, whose addresses the maps and tour buses knew, and who knew each other from poker and the delicatessen.

When she and I got back that afternoon, she took the big container of coffee ice cream from the freezer, scooped some into a bowl and handed it to me. Then she turned on the little TV, opened the paper, lit a cigarette and started reading it. Which meant I could sit with her and eat the ice cream – *silently* – or go off and entertain myself.

The house had two big floors and a wide staircase: on the first floor, the livingroom, kitchen, parlor and dining room; on the second, bedrooms and other rooms with names like the sun room and the pink room. Those rooms had cabinets and closets filled with stuff, which was organized and put away in news print and cotton batting, zipped neatly inside plastic bags. None of it said a famous person lived here. If you didn't know her, there were no awards or signed pictures on the walls; mostly, this was a big, plain, solid house with comfortable furniture, the hum of a refrigerator and the echo of TV, right now, the Million Dollar Movie. Back then only a few VHF stations showing sitcom reruns or old movies on scratched, blurry film. Watching them was like looking through a time machine: you could tell how long ago they were made by how badly they aged. This one was so scratched up it was hard to hear through the cracking and popping. It was a very quiet scene, a man and a woman in black and white, the man inside a big cage in a jail and the woman sitting next to him. In Nana's quiet kitchen, the film crinkling almost a tangible thing, floating in the air. On TV, the lady lit a cigarette and handed it to the man through the bars and spoke so softly. *What's a gun for, Earl?*

Nana was deep into the paper, nodding with her half glasses on as she turned the pages. I got up quietly and left the kitchen to explore.

The phone rang a couple of times but she didn't answer. I heard it, and the TV, from the blue room upstairs, which, aside from the blue walls, was lined with white shelves holding heavy art books. Under the shelves were rows of white cabinets, each with a brass handle, which I decided would be today's excavation. Behind the first door I found wicker baskets, glasses wrapped in plastic, a bunch of cardboard boxes. I put those back and went to another. More old stuff. Tarnished serving platters, a glass punch bowl in newspaper. Closed that, went to a third. This had a pile of yellowed newspapers, and behind, another cardboard box with the word COLE in neat magic marker. Inside, under a layer of old newspaper: a wood pipe, a razor with a bone handle in a fancy leather case, an old velvet box with two gold cufflinks shaped like seashells. A stack of manila envelopes, curled in the corners. I opened one of those. Inside, a glossy of Nana with long hair, the young her; another glossy of a man with soft handsome eyes and a wide forehead. More papers and notebooks, and on the bottom, a photo album with a puffy white cover with names embossed in gold. Stiff cardboard pages, on each the same black and white wedding scene but different poses, a man and a woman with smooth skin getting married. The girl, of course, was Nana; the man who played the husband the one in the glossy. They didn't look like studio stills though; some were blurred and nobody was made up right. This was a real wedding. I looked back at the picture of the man. He had the nicest face, a warm smile. Like he was talking to you right out of the picture, telling you something secret and funny but just a little too soft to hear.

I don't know why, but I wanted the picture. If I asked Nana, I knew she would be cross that I found this person she had hidden. So I put the box back and folded the glossy in quarters and slid it into my back pocket.

After it got dark, after rush hour, Nana called me into the kitchen and asked me to sit at the table with her. At first I thought she knew I stole the glossy, but that wasn't it. She had her stationery and pencils on the table. Cigarette in the ashtray, the smoke a fine wisp, like a genie about to materialize. She counted out some dollar bills, silently mouthing the amount, then stopped, looked at an accounting book, then the money, licked her thumb and counted out a few more. Without looking at me, she said, "This is for your mother," and kept counting. "By the way," she said, trying to sound matter-of-fact, "how is she doing?"

"Good," I said.

She nodded without looking up, considered a moment. "You're very observant. That's a good skill to have."

I shrugged.

"And discreet." She picked up the cigarette, inhaled, kept counting while the smoke swirled in front of her eyes. The fine-tuning mechanic. "So I'm going to count on you for something. Can I do that?"

I nodded.

"Your mother's a good girl. Very nice girl. But sometimes . . . she makes the wrong decisions about things. Goes off on flights of fancy. I need someone I can trust to be my eyes and ears and let me know if there's anything . . . funny going on."

"Like what?"

She shrugged. "You'll know it if you see it."

I didn't know what to say, but Nana was right about most things, so I thought to just agree and figure it out later.

"So is that a yes?"

I nodded.

"Good. Now, one more thing to ask of you." She put the money in an envelope and sealed it and handed it to me. "Give your mother a message for me, will you? I want you to tell her that people judge us by the company we keep. Say it after me," and we did. "Good," she said. "And tell her that when you give her this." She put the papers and the accounting book away, said to herself, to me and no one in particular, "There are consequences to our actions."

All during the afternoon, the phone had been ringing, echoing through the house, but she never answered.

■ ■ ■

When we got home momma looked *askew* – her hair, eyes, clothes. All messed up and out of place. Standing in the middle of the livingroom, holding Alicia's hand like she'd been waiting for us to walk through the door. "Did you take him to *eat?*" she shouted.

"A snack, sweetheart, that was all. We weren't getting anywhere sitting around here. I thought a little fresh air would do us some good."

"What did you eat? What did you eat?"

"Pancakes," I said, panicky.

"That was not what we agreed on," momma yelled, like she might cry. "You said you would come *here* and sit with the children *here*. That's what you said."

"I know, dear," Nana said, brushing her away. "But look, the boy had a very entertaining afternoon and it looks like, uhm, Alicia, had a fine time with that girl you have. So what's the harm?"

"It's my house, and you promised to do it this way. You promised."

Nana opened her purse, took out the cigarettes and lit one. "Look, sweetheart, they're at an important age. We talked about this. You can't keep acting like a child yourself, as though you're free of all responsibilities.

That's what the judge meant about a mature *attitude*." The way she said it, three distinct syllables, made me think of this comedy where a guy played a xylophone on someone's head.

"You said you would watch them here," momma said quietly.

Nana let out a long theatrical breath. "Oh well, fine then. I won't waste any more your valuable time. Personally, I think you blow everything out of proportion." She leaned down, gave us warm hugs enveloped in fur, and left. Momma just shook her head, looked at the floor in front of me. "I still want the frozen dinner," I said. "I only had pancakes." She looked hurt. "And ice cream." Her eyes remained focused on the space in front of my legs, but she came forward, slowly, put her hand on my hair; then she bent forward and kissed the top of my head.

"Oh, Harris," she said. Which is my name.

Leaning over like that, she must have seen behind me. "What's in your pocket?"

I forgot about the glossy and the envelope. I pulled out the envelope and handed it to her. She took it, squeezed it a little, and I remembered what I was supposed to say.

"What?" she said, with surprise. "What do you mean by that?"

"Nana said to tell you that when I gave it to you . . . there are consequences, uhm . . . to our . . . something."

"Oh," she said, softly, to herself. "Oh," she whispered again. Then she walked into her bedroom and closed the door.

Alicia was standing there the whole time, watching. Now the house was quiet. I looked at Alicia; she looked at me. I went to my room, silently, pressed the door closed as gently as I could so the latch wouldn't make a loud click and listened until I heard Alicia do the same.

■ ■ ■

In the night, momma came in. The bed creaked as she lay down next to me, her soft brown hair falling onto the pillow next to my face. Her hair smelled like honey.

"Sweetie," she said. "Sweetie pie." She hugged me close, I could feel her breasts against my chest, her arms around me. She snuggled my head into the space under her chin. "Sweetie," she said again. I thought she was going to sleep here, keep me wrapped in her arms all night. But in a while, she took in a big sigh. "That wasn't very nice."

"What?" I said, into her throat. I felt her voicebox vibrate against my cheek when she answered. "Making you her messenger boy. If you want to tell somebody something, you should tell it to their face."

"I don't mind."

She was kissing the top of my head now, I could feel the moisture where our skin touched. She moved a little, pulled me in closer. When she did, she felt the thick paper under the sheets, moved her hand, feeling for it. I pulled out the glossy, folded in quarters. Through the thin white curtains, just enough dim light from the streetlamp illuminated the paper as it opened. The man's smiling face, big dark eyes like momma's, the secret he was whispering.

She looked at it a moment with no expression. "Where did you . . .?"

"In Nana's house," I said. "I found it in a box."

"Did she give it to you?"

"No. I didn't tell her."

She smiled. "She doesn't know you found this?"

I was ashamed but I had to tell her. She spread the picture on the pillow next to us in the light, put her head down again. "There were some other pictures in a book, too. I think she got *married* to this guy."

Momma's eyes were closed now, she was smiling. Her arm came up from her side and stroked my hair. In a while, she said, "Yes," and that was all.

Once, in a museum, I saw a painting of a girl lying in a field of grass. She was turned away, looking at an old farmhouse in the distance under an ominous sky. It looked like she was trying to get to the farmhouse, but she was just lying there almost like she couldn't get up. Because of the shape of her body and the long hair I got it in my mind this was a painting of momma and I asked how come she was in this painting. She laughed, told me it wasn't her. Right now, lying next to me, I thought of that picture.

"Yes," she said again, sleepy. "Nana was married to him. He's my father. Uncle Ron's and mine. They got divorced a long time ago. Before you were born. Nana was mad at him. She told him he couldn't see us anymore and she made him go away. *Banished* him. We weren't allowed to talk about him or say his name."

"What is it?"

"His name? Robert Cole. Well. That was his stage name. There's a real one, but it was too German sounding."

"Was he bad?"

She laughed. "No. He was just himself. Too much for Nana, though." Even with her eyes closed, in the dark of the room, I could see the expression on her face, and it looked strange, like she was in a trance. "But when we got older, we found him. We didn't tell her."

"Is he dead?"

"No. That's the dumbest thing. He lives in Bel-Air. He's there right now." I didn't know what to say, so I just kissed her neck. It tasted salty. She laughed and pulled me closer. "Hey, would you like to meet him? Would you like to meet your grandfather?" I thought I would, so I nodded, in the dark. I wondered if this was part of being eyes and ears. "OK then," momma said, slurry like jam. "OK. Let's go, you and me, and meet your grandpa. What do you think about that?"

"OK," I whispered.

"OK," she said, and she kissed me again. But it sounded like a question.

5

Two days later, after lunch, momma took Alicia to Mrs. Melendez while I waited in the car. She decided Alicia was too young to keep her trap shut.

When momma came back to the car, she wrapped a scarf around her hair, put on big sunglasses and lit up her own cigarette. It felt like we were going to rob a bank. Driving in silence except for the wind, we passed all the same houses you pass to get to Nana's but kept going beyond Palm Drive and the Beverly Hills Hotel; then a little further, up another road, and into Bel-Air, which you knew because of the fancy sign and the security booth. The guards glare at you as you drive past, especially in an old Plymouth.

Momma turned after the sharp turn, up to a big white house with white roses lining both sides of the driveway. On the lawn, bushes cut into shapes of animals posing and playing. More flowers, the warm, earthy smell of jasmine, tidal waves of red and yellow bougainvillea rolling down the sides and front of the house. The driveway sloped upward so sharp, we were pressed against the back of the seat when the car came to a stop. Momma stepped an extra long crunch on the parking brake to be sure it stuck. The house was so white, the sky so blue, it seemed like the whole thing just continued up to the clouds.

The front door burst open and a man came charging out. "Sweethearts!" he yelled. Tall and barrel chested with wavy white hair, walking fast down the brick walkway, holding something white and furry under his arm. I thought it might be a present, but when he got closer, it snapped a little bark: a tiny furry dog. In the other hand, a cigarette in a holder; while he walked he took a puff off it. The dog barked again, its little face opening up just an inch to let out this yap.

"Darlings!" he said when he got to the car. He was as big and handsome as anyone old could be; he still looked like the man in the glossy, only now with white hair instead of black. The eyes from the glossy looked right at me, curious and delighted. The dog yapped again, and the man plopped his big hand on top of my head. From inside the house someone yelled, "Is that them?" He let out a breath, yelled back, "Get out here you old bag and say a proper hello!" He turned to me, rolled his eyes. "Nagging fishwife." Then, to momma, "Give your old daddy a hug." He walked around the car and opened her door, practically pulled her out of the seat. He hugged her so hard, the dog gave a scrunched *arp* from inside his armpit. He said, "You're not electrified, are you? She didn't booby trap you to put an end to me once and for all?"

Momma laughed inside his big arms.

"Well, we'll just see," he said. "Crossing enemy lines and all." The man gave me a big, exaggerated wink then came around again and opened the door. He took my hand, held the little dog with the other, and walked me and momma up to the wide front door. "Pull up your panties, here we come!" he yelled.

Inside, everything was doilies and frilly patterns. An explosion of flowers and color, a big room on the left, a staircase in the middle, a big room on the right, and another room, the kitchen maybe, behind the stairs. All the rooms looked like living rooms, with sofas and chairs and little tables and lamps, like a house full of fat, square ladies in fabulous dresses bowing to each other. The tall man guided us into the livingroom on the left, one hand on my back, the other on momma and the dog. "I know," he said, looking around with a sort of dismay, "and the answer is yes, it is a bit much. We call this the Marie Antoinette room, what with all the chintz." He picked up a little bell from a side table, shook it comically hard and called in a southern accent, "Oh Jezebel, we're in the parlor, dear, in need of *refreshment!*" On cue, another man came walking in fast. "Heavens, my god, what a racket!" This one carried a silver tray with a dish of cookies and a jug filled with glowing yellow liquid. He stopped suddenly in front of momma and me and shouted: *"Oh. My. GOD!"* I jumped. "Look at these two adorable creatures!" He screamed so loud it almost made me scream.

He was old, like the other one, but not so tall. The front of his gray hair was a widow's peak, going way back on the sides. He slammed the tray down so hard I thought the glass jug might shatter. He came right up to me and stuck out his hand. *"Pleased ta meetcha,"* he said and I put out my hand slowly, but he screamed again, grabbed my sides and tickled me. "Oh my god, I could eat them up!"

The big one sighed. "Please don't do that. Let them sit down, why don't you, and gain their bearings."

The smaller one let me go, stepped back to get a look and put his hand on his chin.

"Well now, who would I be to him?"

"Eh, what's that?"

"Who would I be to him? Godfather? Godmother? Fairy godmother?"

"Well, let's not confuse the poor lad right off the bat. We really do have manners, young man, it's just not often we get a visit as important as this one. Perhaps we should start with some introductions." He looked at momma and she shrugged. "Well then, how do you do, Harris?" He did give me his hand, and I was tentative, but he took mine, solemnly, shook it, and nodded. "I'm Robert Cole. I'm your . . . oh my god, I'm gaining twenty pounds just saying it . . . I'm your grandfather. You were probably told I fell off a cliff or something." I didn't want to say he was never mentioned. "And this old has-been," he said, nodding toward the other one, "would be . . . well now, that is a good question. Great uncle sounds a bit fussy. I know. What do we think of great aunt?"

"Oh gawd, how Victorian. I'll need a petticoat to play that one."

"Then Grandfather Robert and Great Aunt Phil, and we'll just leave it there for now."

Phil jerked his head back with mock astonishment. I would learn, in time, that his Bette Davis was one of the best. To me, momma said, "Now introduce yourself." Phil pretended to go for my sides again, and I jumped, but he laughed and took my hand. Then he went to momma, squeezed her face to make the fish mouth. "And look at this girl! She gets prettier every time I see her! Ali MacGraw has nothing on this punim."

"Will you stop embarrassing these two?" grandpa said, gazing up at the ceiling. "They're liable to bolt and never come back." He leaned down to me and whispered while he looked at Phil, "Right now, she's Glinda the good witch. Let's see how long before she turns cheeky and we have to drop a house on her." He winked at me, finger to his lips.

"Terrible, *terrible* man," Phil said. "Now, why don't we start things off with some drinks. I'm sure after your long trip, you must be tired and parched." He picked up the silver tray and put it on a coffee table between a large sofa and a smaller one. Momma and I sat on the smaller one, grandpa walking around to the other and settling into it. He was bigger than he looked, but he moved with a lightness that made him seem to float. He had very wide shoulders, his thick hair brushed back; a white sweater wrapped around his shoulders, tied in front. Phil was smaller and quicker, like a nervous bird; he sat next to grandpa then suddenly shot up again. "Oh, fuck a duck, I forgot the glasses," and he picked up the tray and ran out. Grandpa smiled, let out a big breath. The dog in his lap yapped again.

"So, here you are at long last," he said. "A secret mission, I understand."

"We wanted to come," momma said. "It's nobody's business."

"Hear, hear," he said. He had this pleasant, open expression, as though you were saying something very interesting, and he was listening to you, enjoying everything you had to say, even if you weren't saying anything at all. "And the girl, she's doing well?"

"Alicia's fine," momma said. "She's six and going to kindergarten. I'll bring her next time. I couldn't risk . . . well . . ."

"Of course, of course," grandpa said. To me, "So, the mystery finally revealed?"

"I'm sorry, daddy," momma said. "He didn't know you were here until a few days ago." He brushed it off. "He found a headshot of you in some cabinet in Eva's house."

"Did he now? Of little old me? Well, isn't that interesting. I thought they'd all been burned at some midnight ritual with torches and pitchforks. Good to know I'm haunting a dark corner somewhere."

"I'm sorry we haven't been to see you sooner," she said.

"Oh stop. You have your own lives. We knew we'd see you eventually."

Phil came back with glasses on a tray, yellow drinks in sparkly crystal glasses and ice cubes tinkling. You could almost hear the thickness of the liquid by the muffled sound of the ice. He put a glass in front of us each, lay the tray on its side next to the coffee table and sat next to grandpa. "What are we talking about?" he said. "The battleaxe of the republic? I saw her on some talk show. Still using my eyebrows, I see. The cunt."

Behind the pleasant demeanor, grandpa stiffened, but his smile didn't waver.

"She's hanging in there," momma said. "It's not easy."

"Well," Phil said, "she's got a whole new bag of balls to bust. The face is holding up pretty well, I have to say. *My* face."

Grandpa said to me, "Phil was in makeup and styling many … *many* years ago, and I daresay he gave your grandmother a look that worked to her advantage." To Phil, "It's not *your* face, dearie. It belongs to someone else. You just brought out what was there."

"Balls," Phil said, too loud. "The fix-it man, that's what I was." He leaned forward, took a big swig from his drink. "My God, the shit they were painting on her then. When she walked in to my office, she looked like a fuckin' cigar store Indian."

Grandpa had this way of looking upward, the smile unwavering, scanning the sky from left to right while still talking to the people in front of him. "What say we change the subject to something more contemporaneous, eh?"

"Suit yourself," Phil said, sucking down half the glass. Momma took a sip of hers, and her ice cubes clinking sounded so good, I picked up my glass and took a sip too. It was very strong. It almost made me cough. I let it sit in my mouth a minute, burning, then when I was ready, let it in. It felt like warm potion, sharp and soothing. Like the stream Tinkerbell leaves behind her with stars and yellow rays.

"Now, what have you two been up to?" momma asked.

"Oh, we keep busy," grandpa said. "*Endless* people to see. Parties to attend, dinners, what have you. Though I have to say, so many of the old ones are kicking off. Far too many hospitals and funerals. But, knock wood, we endure. Phil keeps a few clients around town. He does them at home. Does quite well, too."

"They don't know how to cut hair these days!" Phil shrieked, finishing the rest of his drink. It startled me again, how he could just scream out of nowhere. "It's like a bunch of kids cutting with paper scissors! My God, the fuck-ups I have to repair."

Grandpa smiled, looked up again, in a little sing-song, said, "*Language . . .*"

"Yecch," he said, then to me, very direct, "Harris, does that bother you?"

No, I said. I thought he was funny. "See?" Phil said. "So shut the fuck up."

"Goodness, only ten minutes," grandpa said.

"Balls," Phil said, stood, went back to the kitchen.

"And you, my dear?" grandpa said to momma.

"It goes. I work. The kids go to school. Eva drives me crazy. But it's working. Things seem okay now."

"I'm glad of that. I . . ." He stopped then, went another direction: "I love the car. What is it, a Chevy?"

"A Plymouth I think. I do the books for a garage in Van Nuys. They had it cheap. It's a lot of fun. I feel like such a star driving around in it."

"Well, you are a star."

They talked some more, caught up on people I didn't know and boring things I didn't care about. Phil came back with the pitcher, filled his own glass, topped off momma's and grandpa's, sat down again. I leaned over, took another sip of mine, let it sit in my mouth before I let it down. I felt like a real grownup listening to them talk about grownup things in that colorful room. Although the colors and flowers on the furniture seemed a little too bright, swaying a bit.

"Mmm, they call me," Phil said, picking up where he left off. "They call me, plead with me. Oh, come over, you've got to fix this, you've got to fix that, some twenty-five-dollar-an-hour Beverly Hills *asshole* messed it up. And I go, I fix whatever they need. I'm one of the last ones too."

"What?" grandpa said. "Why, just the other day, you told that countess de whats-er-name what she could do with that very adorable shih-tzu she loves so much."

"It was ten o'clock at night!" Phil screamed. "For Chrissakes, someone calls in the middle of the night, what do you expect me to say? She wasn't *going* anywhere! That old cow just needed to cool her heels and wait for the morning!"

"*Tra la la,*" grandpa sang, "why don't we try one of these nice snacks, shall we?" He picked up the tray and offered it to Phil. "Oh, yum," he said, taking three cookies like a kid. Grandpa stood and offered it to us. I took one, momma too. And I had another sip of the drink.

"And you're doing all right, financially?" grandpa said to momma. His eyelids fluttered slightly when he said this.

"Well," momma said. "She helps us. So there's good and there's bad."

"Can I do anything for you?"

"No, no. Better to leave things the way they are."

"Of course. And you, little man?" Now he was looking at me directly. He seemed genuinely nice and interested in a way you never see grownups being toward a kid. I wanted to say something funny and grown-up, talk to them the way they talked to each other. But when I opened my mouth, I felt saliva, and then there were stars around grandpa's face and then I barfed onto the coffee table. Outside my head, I heard grandpa saying, "Did you give the boy a *drink?*"

"What?" Phil said. "We're having drinks. So what? You said we were having drinks."

Momma was over me, holding my shoulders and I heaved up again.

"Oh, you silly goose," grandpa said. "I set out that great big jug of lemonade on the counter! What did you think that was for?"

I puked another load, and another, and each time, the little dog yapped. He thought it was fun. Phil was moaning, "Ooooooh, yuck, that'll never come out," and I closed my eyes. All dark swirling and I fell sideways into momma's lap. The voices in the room seemed to echo and fade, swim around and flush down the drain until all I heard was grandpa's. "Good god, what kind of an *idiot* am I living with . . . you silly, silly, stupid thing, you."

6

I wasn't out long because it was still light when I opened my eyes and saw him looking down at me. I was on a bed in a room with bright blue walls. Grandpa sitting next to me, dabbing my forehead with a warm facecloth. I took in a big breath, looked around this room for momma or Phil but they weren't there. I had a headache.

"There now," he said. "Awake and sing." I tried to sit up. "Just a figure of speech. Stay a little, until you feel steady enough."

My throat felt inside out. "Can I have some water?"

He got up and went to a bathroom, came back and held my head as I drank. It was so cool and tasted better in a glass.

"I'm sorry I threw up on your table."

He chuckled, looked up at the ceiling like he did. "Oh my boy, don't even think of it. You have no idea the wonderful people who've puked in that very spot. I'm honored you feel comfortable enough to upchuck in our humble abode. I hope this means we're friends?"

I lifted my hand and he took it. "Thank you," he said, and put his big hand on the side of my face. He looked at me a long moment, like he was glad to see me. Like I meant something. "Well," he said, "seems you're coming around. I think your mother may be ready to go. Do you feel like sitting up?"

Downstairs momma was smoking, and it was late, and she was saying, "*We have to go! We have to go!*" Grandpa hustled us to the front door. On the way, I saw Phil passed out on the sofa, facedown on the cushions, snoring loud.

"Don't worry about her," grandpa said, "she'll sleep it off, and believe you me, when she wakes up, she'll get a tanning."

Outside, momma hugged grandpa, stood on tiptoes to kiss him. He leaned down, kissed her, kissed me, said, "Now off with you, before you turn into pumpkins." Momma took my hand and started down the walk; then she turned back, pulled me with her, hugged grandpa again, gave him another kiss, and he tried to keep smiling, but his eyes welled up. "Go," he said, "Go on now."

Momma started the car and the brake popped out like it does, then that desperate whining as it rolled backward down the hill. I waved at grandpa, standing outside his door, holding the little dog, waving back at us. The rest of the trip was a blur, momma flying down the Bel-Air hills to Sunset. On the way down Laurel Canyon, I sat up, leaned over the side and barfed again, spraying the air behind us.

We thought we got away with it. We thought we got Alicia home and started dinner and went to bed so everything looked normal, so on the next day, when we went to Nana's, nothing would seem out of place. Late in the afternoon, though, she put down her newspaper and stood up. She and momma were sitting in the kitchen and she said, "Carolyn, something odd is going on. I can't put my finger on it, but there's something *queer* about you and the boy today."

I was playing with cars on the living room floor, as quiet as I could be.

"I don't know what you mean, mother," my mother said.

"Well, obviously, you do. You've done something you don't want any-one to know about it. It's practically written across your face." She let this sit a good, long moment. "No, not anyone. Just me. It's something you don't want *me* to know about."

"Mother, I don't know where you're getting this."

"Oh, Carolyn, now I see. It's something very serious, isn't it? Your heart is beating a million miles a minute. I can see the pulse practically bursting in your neck."

Momma stood very slowly, put her coffee cup in the sink, tried to imitate the way she would put a cup in the sink if she wasn't lying. Even I could tell what a bad liar she was, and I was in the other room.

"Oh, mother," she said. "You're making things up. Honestly, you are."

"Now, what could it be? What on earth could it be? You're getting married to that pisher, whats his name . . . no, that's not it. One of the children is sick, someone is ill . . . no, no, that's not it . . ."

I tried to pay attention to the cars and the roads in the town on the rug, but Nana was closing in. She said, "It's something to do with me. Something you mustn't let me know."

"Mother! Stop this right now. You're being ridiculous."

I could hear Eva take a long, slow drag on her cigarette, pulling in air. I wondered if she could smell the top of my head, where grandpa put his hand.

"Oh my god!" she shouted from the kitchen. "You didn't ..."

"Mother . . ."

All I could see were legs coming down from skirts. Both standing now, cigarette smoke pouring out of the kitchen. Eva cried, "God in heaven!"

"Mother . . ."

"You went behind my back like a *spy?* Like a thief in the night?"

Momma tried to say something but Nana wasn't having it. She exploded. And when she got mad, it wasn't just yelling like most people, it was stage mad, controlled, directed exactly where she wanted it to go. And she wouldn't relent until she hit the mark and knew the blow landed. She told momma she was a disrespectful good-for-nothing, that she was selfish and two-faced and ungrateful and irresponsible. That she was a liar and a thief and conniving and weak minded and pathetic. And worthless, and then, no, worse than worthless. Stupid *and* worthless.

Momma took it all silently, then Nana shouted, shocked all over again. "You didn't bring the *children*, did you? Did you deliberately disobey me? *Is that what you did to me?*"

Silence first, then footsteps coming my way. She flew in, stood right in front, arms crossed. "Stand up, young man."

I didn't move.

"Stand up. Did you go with your mother to see a big, fat, phony old man?"

She leaned down, put her hands under my arms and lifted me so I looked her right in the face. Up close, I could see it really was drawn on beautifully – eyes, lips, eyebrows. She watched my eyes then let go; I hit the floor with a clunk and she bolted back to the kitchen. "Was that little weasel there too? The both of them? Carolyn, how could you do this to me?"

They went on for a long time, Nana getting crosser and saying things through gritted teeth that made momma cry. Finally, she had us both in the living room, against the wall. One last thing, and with the angriest voice she had: "Get out, the both of you. Get out of my sight." She spit out the last word like poison: "*Traitors.*"

Momma's face was a red blotch. We walked out, her holding my hand. The wood door slammed behind us, the heavy knocker knocking when it closed. We got in the car and drove out of the driveway, onto Sunset and turned left, and drove all the way out to the ocean. Stopped at a gas station while the sun disappeared behind the purple smog. We didn't say anything to each other. Momma paid for the gas and we drove out, us both thinking the same thing. Now we're banished, too.

7

There must have been some popular book about John Henry back then, because everyone talks about it now. I don't remember much about it except for these illustrations, all impressionist and dark. Like falling into some dream of screeching locomotives, sweating men and dark skies. So much going on, so much power and strength, and something else too; warm and arousing but not said. Like a lot of things, the story being about one thing, but the pictures, the feeling, about something else.

There was something in the way the painter drew the rage in John Henry's face while he's fighting the locomotive that stuck with me. The last picture is him on the tracks in front of the train, this huge engine, puffing steam, staring with uncaring eyes at the man on the ground. I looked at that picture a long time. At John Henry's face, the crying shape of his mouth as he lay sprawled with his shirt open, his chest big and powerful. And even though he was a strong man, he seemed so vulnerable; the strongest man you could imagine, torn open and helpless in front of this terrible machine. I traced the outlines of his chest with my eyes.

Outside, in our own real world of things, we were now officially on the outs from Beverly Hills. Momma kept to herself behind the closed bedroom door. It was never a good sign when she didn't come out of there. But dinners were made and we got to school and since there wasn't much I could do about things beyond my control inside the house, I spent more time out.

As dark and big as John Henry was, Kevin was the opposite: bright, blond, compact. Not a normal person like the rest of us; he was lit from inside. Illuminated. Even when we were kids, women made a big deal about him, with his devils-green eyes and long eyelashes. And he knew how to get what he wanted from people. He bargained like a grown-up for candy at the store, convinced neighbors to let us play in their yards, got anyone to be his friend just by smiling at them. The only person who didn't do what he wanted was his mother, because she was the original: once you saw her you realized where the high cheekbones came from. Mrs. Harmon wore tight V-necks and Capri pants and flat shoes because she was so tall. Most nights after dinner, she took a slow walk around the neighborhood, smoking, with her little dog Boojie, this fluffy Pekingese thing. He looked so small and silly next to her with her long legs and swirling honey-blonde hair piled high. If they were in their front yards, the husbands on our street stopped what they were doing, smiled big and waved; standing at the kitchen window, their wives came all the way out of the house, walked down the walk, said "Hi there!" too loud, and glared at their husbands.

My mother and Mrs. Harmon were friends, I think because they were the only women without husbands on the block. Also, momma recognized that inside those rolling hips and big boobs was a nice person who most people didn't see. One time I heard one of the neighbors say *hooker*, and I didn't know what it meant but I knew it wasn't nice. Momma didn't care about gossip like that. She and Mrs. Harmon drank coffee and smoked together and laughed about the same things; she had this laugh that came from inside, deep and golden like a pipe organ. She was fine that Kevin and I were friends, but she was also a tough, practical kind of person, and I think she thought I was a pussy.

A few blocks from our neighborhood was a park where the power lines come through. These are steel towers fifteen stories high that carry electricity from somewhere far away to somewhere else far away. The four huge legs of each tower anchor to the ground on massive concrete blocks, the size of a small building, and they sit in the grassy strip that cuts diagonally in a long, straight line all the way across the valley. You don't notice the towers until you look up at them; then you realize there's this endless line of silent giants with cords draped over their shoulders, marching through your neighborhood, over your house, miles behind and miles ahead. If you look up from the ground, the towers are skyscrapers, each one connected by wires to the others, and flowing through those wires are millions of volts of electricity that light the whole city. Sitting with your back against the concrete base, you feel like you're connected to everything.

There was a good spot near Verdugo where you could sneak through the fence and lie next to a tower without anyone seeing you from the street. Kevin and I took our bikes there after we got snacks from 7-Eleven. Maybe it was the electricity in the air, the disruption of molecules around us being so close to the towers, maybe the silence in my house. Whatever it was, one afternoon I decided to tell Kevin an important piece of information, something that seemed to come out of my mouth in that moment. Which was that when you grow up and get married, you have to kiss people, your wife and so forth, and it might be a good idea, us being friends and all, to practice for when that happens. I thought I was being very helpful telling him this and offering my assistance.

He didn't move, lying in the grass next to me, looking up at the tower. Then he sat up on his elbows. "Is that so?" he said. He chewed on the gum and my suggestion, for a moment. Cracked the gum in his teeth, blew a bubble. He was looking right at me now, then sat back and put his hands behind his head, devils-green eyes taking me in. "Is that so?" he said again. "What are we gonna do with you, Harris my man?"

I froze, held my breath. With that little smile coming up at the sides, he said, "Alright. But *not* on the lips." He turned a cheek to me and I leaned down and gave him one soft kiss. Like I thought: silky, perfect. He turned his head and I kissed the other side. Then he smiled, shrugged like it wasn't that bad and said, "OK. Now stop bugging me." He put his arm around my shoulder, pulled me next to him, and while my heart beat so hard I thought it would shake the ground, I could feel his own heart and his breath, going in and out so slowly like nothing had happened at all; so peaceful that soon enough he actually fell asleep.

■ ■ ■

It had only been a couple of weeks since Eva blew up, and momma stayed pretty much out of sight. So I was surprised one morning, coming into the kitchen, that everything was different. Instead of the lights off and the box of cereal, there were bubbling pancakes, the smell of butter and perfume, and momma standing at the stove with the spatula in her hand, hair up in a floppy bun with wispy bits floating around the back of her neck. In a very bright flower-print dress, she was singing this lyrical, bouncy tune to herself.

"Morning, shugah," she said, "rise and shine!" She came over to give me a kiss. "How 'bout a splash of orange juice?" She hummed and floated to the refrigerator, took out the juice, poured a glass for me and placed it in front of me with a flourish, then back to the stove, where more pancakes bubbled. Alicia came in. "What smells so good?"

"Pancakes, honeychild! All you can eat!"

"Oh wow." Her eyes big, she sat at the table, and momma put one of the dishes with a tall stack in front of her, sang some song in this falsetto, said, "But my, it's a glorious day!" Then she turned back to the stove, picked up a pan, and tossed the pancake in the air. It made a perfect flip and slapped back down. Alicia laughed and clapped her hands. "That one's for you, honey," momma said to me.

"I want it!" Alicia said.

"The next one, baby, the next one."

When she'd finished the pancakes, she kissed us both with smacks on the cheek and went to sit in the livingroom. I heard her light a cigarette, humming in that sweet, high falsetto. Didn't hear the TV come on, didn't know if she was reading the paper or just staring into space. All I could see, peering around the corner, was a leg, crossed over the other, tapping in rhythm to the song.

On my way to school, looking down at the sidewalk slabs of concrete lined up one after the other, I figured that was just something you do, becoming someone else. I saw Eva do it later on, sitting with her on a set; the bell rings and she walks to the stage and she is the character. But momma was better, she was much more real. The lady at our stove this morning *was* that person. The real artistry is becoming someone so fully that people don't know it isn't you.

■ ■ ■

Momma called her Ginger, as in, "Ginger knows what Ginger wants, honey." And Ginger was strong as an ox. She whistled while she vacuumed, mopped and swept, lifted the sofa with one hand while she pushed the vacuum underneath. With her high heels and flowered dresses, she looked much bigger than momma. On Saturday she made another big breakfast with sausage and waffles. She didn't eat any, just sat at the table and smoked, satisfied, watching us. "This is so good!" Alicia said, scarfing down another waffle, and Ginger smiled, taking a slow puff off her cigarette. "You know what we're missing?"

We looked at her and she squawked, made wings of her arms.

"Chickens?" Alicia said.

"Chickies!" Ginger said, and squawked right up closer to her face, right up close to my face. I laughed and felt scared at the same time. "What do you say we go and get us some chickies?"

Alicia's eyes got bigger. "Are you going to kill them?"

Ginger brushed her smoke away. "Why no, honey. They'll just be hangin' around, makin' eggs and such." This seemed to relieve her, so she went back to eating. I kept my eye on Ginger; she gave me a wink.

After breakfast we got into the car and drove north across the valley. The further you go, the houses and buildings thin out and you get to very dry, dusty roads and wide open fields. We arrived at a neighborhood with bushy trees and cool shade, dirt roads and a wood fence. A few cars were parked on the left side opposite a steep hill with a dirt driveway. Momma turned up that hill and gunned the engine. The tires skidded, threw rocks behind, the car swung side to side as we climbed the incline. She stopped just at the top, in front of an old wood house.

"Come on, let's go find us some chickens," she said. Alicia looked at the rickety house and the ancient rusted car in front and shook her head. "Suit yourself," Ginger said and slammed the door.

It was cool and moist here, like a forest, with pine trees and the smell of wet leaves. The coolness seemed to make everything quieter too; the sound of birds echoed and carried, chirps from under trees across the yard and behind this house that looked like an old prospector lived here. I heard a door slam around the corner, Ginger having gone inside. No chickens in sight, but the sound of horses behind the house. We sat in the car, Alicia and me, for what seemed like minutes on minutes. After a while I wondered if any kids were here, so I climbed out, over the door. "Where are you going?" she said.

"To look around." She tried to pull me back, her eyes wide, but I pulled away. Looking more carefully, I could see this was a really old house, this whole property sitting on a flat yard high above the road below. From somewhere behind trees we heard that braying again, and heavy feet stomping the ground. I thought the sound was bouncing off the trees and the horses were in the back of the house.

Behind me, I was only half aware of Alicia getting out of the car, but she didn't follow me toward the house. I heard her skidding down the slippery dirt driveway, down to the street. She probably thought that's where the horses were. I heard laughing and talking inside the house, and I wondered what hillbilly kids looked like, if they wore overalls and had missing teeth like on TV. I wanted to see.

Behind me was this crunching sound, soft and peaceful. For a moment I didn't pay attention, but when I did, and turned to look, it was coming from the tires of the Plymouth, falling slowly backward down the dirt driveway. Just beginning to pick up speed. It was eerie to see a car moving with no one in it. I watched as it slid backward and out of sight, like being pulled underwater. I scanned the path it would take, rolling, straight down and into the side of the cars parked across the street. And there, in the path, next to the cars, was Alicia, her back to me, listening for the horses beyond the trees. It happened so fast.

A flash of color shot past me. The print dress flying over the edge of the hill, the screen door slamming.

The Plymouth picked up its leisurely speed as it neared the bottom. Alicia took a split second to turn but my view was blocked by the cloud of dust and then *KA-LUNK*, the dead metal sound of car bodies crashing into each other. Then nothing. Only some dogs barking. Trees hissing in a gust of wind. Some people came out of the house near the parked cars, an old lady and old man. The old lady screamed, staring at something. It felt like a series of still photos, moving closer to the bottom of the hill in jerky stops. I couldn't get too close, but in my mind it seemed like I saw it with my own eyes.

Ginger stood at the back of the car where it was pressed into the side of the other one. She looked at it, hands on her hips. The old lady and the man were waving their arms, but Ginger looked sort of disinterested, like she found a stain on the rug and was trying to figure how to get it up. She reached down with her right hand and gently lifted the Plymouth by the bumper; with her left, she pulled Alicia out. She was limp like a doll. Ginger lowered the car and it made a gentle groan. She hoisted Alicia on her shoulder and pat her back like burping a baby. The old lady and the old man kept yelling in Spanish and the man pointed to their house, and the lady ran there. It seemed only a moment, but it had to be longer, when we heard sirens in the distance. They got louder, and the heavy grinding of a fire engine downshifting to make a turn. Dust in the air beyond the trees. Another moment and black and white police cars, a fire engine, a smaller red fire truck, all converged and skidded to a stop, encircling Ginger in the print dress. She seemed so relaxed. The medics took Alicia and laid her on a stretcher. Two policemen approached and started asking questions. Ginger answered, very nonchalant; pointed up the hill, then to where Alicia was standing, then the point of the impact. The police asked her something else and she shrugged, told them the same thing. The medic looking at Alicia said something to Ginger and the policeman and they all hustled toward the open back door of the ambulance. The medics slid the stretcher in and reached out to help Ginger, but she casually pointed to me, and the policeman came over and grabbed me, pulled me to the ambulance and Ginger took my hand and we both got pulled inside. The siren screamed and we took off.

Sitting next to me on the bench against the side of the ambulance, she held my hand. The loud siren and the bumping made it hard to hear anything. I thought she said something. I looked at her and I could feel the change; her hair falling out of the bun, the tall spine softening. I put my hand on her knee. The print dress was wet and droopy like a moist flower. She leaned toward me and pulled my head to her shoulder.

■ ■ ■

Not to leave you hanging: Alicia wasn't dead or even close. She broke a collarbone, one arm, a wrist and some ribs. She had a collapsed lung but that, and the bones, healed in time. The doctor said little kids are flexible.

The story was in the paper. Mrs. Melendez brought it over the next day. Alicia was still at the hospital, awake but in a big cast; they told momma to go home and sleep, which she did, and Mrs. Melendez, who was babysitting, showed her the newspaper. At the kitchen table, momma read the story, shook her head, got up and went to her room and shut the door. Mrs. Melendez left the newspaper and I read it. It said that an unoccupied car rolled down a hill on the something thousand block of a road in some town and pinned a little girl against another car. The girl's mother ran to the scene and extricated the child from the wreck. Accounts differ, it said; witnesses saw the mother lift the car off the child. Stuff about broken bones and injuries, and the girl would recover. Being treated at so-and-so a hospital and no vehicular charges were filed. The police officer on the scene said it was a miracle. The people in the story had our names.

An hour later our phone rang. From the other side of the hill, after coffee, a cigarette, and perusing the Metro section. Momma came out of her room and answered, spoke for a few minutes, went back to her room and got dressed. After she called the hospital, she took my hand.

It was strange walking up to the bright yellow house and ringing the bell like we were strangers. But that was just how it was, who we were at that moment. When the big door opened, Nana said, "Sweeties," like nothing was different at all. "Come inside, I have lemonade all made up." We walked in, the door closed behind us, and that was that. She wanted to know everything. How it happened, why the newspapers didn't take pictures. Especially she wanted to know what happened when momma moved the car off the baby, how she did that.

"I did not," momma said. "They made that up. I just pulled a little, that's all."

"But sweetheart, it says it right here!" Eva slapped the paper. "Why would they say it if it wasn't true?"

"I'm too ashamed. The whole thing is my fault. Driving around in a car with lousy brakes. They should have arrested me."

"Now, stop. Don't berate yourself like that. It was an accident, and accidents happen. It was no one's fault."

"Please," momma said. "Let it go."

But Eva didn't let it go. She told everyone about it, for months: waiters in restaurants, ladies at the supermarket. Even I got a part in the story. She took me to Spaceships soon after momma started leaving me off again. Our waitress's nametag said Madeleine, and she had stars in her eyes when Nana sat down with her tan cashmere coat and her fancy pocketbook and sunglasses. "I'm such a big fan," she gushed.

"Thank you, Madeleine," Nana said. "And this young man is my grandson. I'm sure you read all about his family in the papers."

"Why, *no*," Madeleine said, like she hadn't read about a war that just broke out.

"Oh, my dear, everyone in town is talking about it. My daughter is the girl who saved her child from a horrible automobile accident."

"No!"

"Yes," Nana said. "A car . . . a great, big sedan . . . fell *all the way down* a steep embankment, completely out of control . . . *pinning* . . ." she said this the same clear way each time, ". . . the child underneath."

"No!" Madeleine gasped, hand over mouth.

"Yes. My daughter *raced* to the scene, and with impossible strength . . . I don't know where she got it . . . *lifted* the car off the child and pulled her tiny, ravaged body out from under the wreckage."

Madeleine's eyes were huge.

"Just like that," she said, snapping her fingers. "Harris was there. He saw the whole thing. Isn't that right?"

"Yes."

"You see. You see that. I'm surprised you didn't hear about it, Madeleine. It was all over the papers. A miracle, right there, in the San Fernando Valley."

"That's amazing, Miss Loesch. A miracle!"

"That's exactly what it was," and she pointed the end of an unlit cigarette at her. "So there you are." Madeleine shook her head in wonder. Nana nodded as she lit the cigarette, took a quick inhale. "Now," she whispered, taking in the smoke. "I think the boy could use some bread. And coffee for me, please. Black."

■ ■ ■

It was strange for a while after we came back. The world as before but with two new characters floating at the edge. Nana knew we knew Phil and grandpa now, but I knew enough that we shouldn't tell her when we visited. If Alicia mentioned them, Nana put up the Stop hand, said, *It's not necessary to discuss it,* and that ended it. We only saw them every couple of months anyway, and we still belonged to Nana.

She never talked about us being banished, and as far as she was concerned, things went back the way they were before. She went on with her stories and expected us to listen respectfully, eat our ice cream and shut up. *The Sound of Music* was still around and Alicia wanted to see it again. Nana said she would cut her own hand off, then ours, before she took us. "Tell you what, though, there's another picture for kids, and it's written by the guy who did James Bond, so it can't be that bad. I'll take you to that one if you'd like." We said ok and she did.

This was about an inventor who lives in a windmill with his two kids, and they have these English accents so irritating you want to slap them. They find an old jalopy in a junkyard and the father rebuilds it. Then they meet this lady who wears fluffy white dresses and is very pretty. They go for a picnic and drive off a cliff but the car sprouts wings and propellors so they don't die. I sat there with my arms folded, thinking how it strained credibility that all these parts would be inside a car this guy actually built himself but didn't know were there. Still, I wanted a flying car like that one, and I tried to hide my face so Nana wouldn't see me cry when it saved them. There was a kingdom that looked like Germany and the King was Goldfinger and he was married to a fat lady. There's a very unsettling guy with a prosthetic nose who catches children, and the whole idea of using candy to catch kids seemed disturbing. The irritating kids get captured and the inventor and the lady save them by pretending to be toys. The lady sings on a music box and she moves so precisely with the music and the cranking sound. She says people think she's a just a toy but she wants to be free and have feelings. *Yearning* to have feelings. I bit my tongue harder and held my arms very tight.

"Well, what'd you think?" Nana asked when we walked out. I shrugged, said it was OK. Alicia said she wished we had seen *The Sound of Music*.

By this time, Alicia was out of the cast, and being wrapped in plaster had made her antsy. One afternoon at Nana's she was running the circle from living room to dining room to kitchen, the glasses in the dining room cabinet tinkling every time she went by. She did three loops. Nana tried to ignore it. I sat next to her at the kitchen table while she read the paper, but I could tell her patience was wearing thin.

"What the hell is that kid doing?" she said finally. "You never ran around like that when you were her age. What is she, a mongoloid?"

"She does it all the time. Momma says she has a lot of pent-up energy."

"Well, if she breaks my china running around like that, she's going to find out *I* have a lot of pent-up energy."

She held up the cigarette, waited for Alicia to make one more pass, and when she did, grabbed her by the collar like someone flying by on a merry go-round.

"Hold on there, partner," she said. "I want to talk to you."

"I wanna play," Alicia said, scowling.

"In a minute. Right now, you're going to sit at the table like a person and listen to what I have to say."

Alicia bit her lower lip.

"I've had enough of this running around like a banshee. There are consequences to this kind of behavior. Do you know what I mean by consequences?" Alicia was pissed off and crossed her arms. "Fine," Nana said. "In that case, I'm going to tell you a story. You ready to hear a story?" She shook her head, tightened her arms. Nana took out a new cigarette, held it a moment, then put it in her mouth, lit up and took a puff.

"Now," she said. "This is a story about the golem. Do you know what a golem is?" We shook our heads. "A golem," she said, "is a man made of clay. He was made by powerful rabbis in the old country." She said this in her deep, gravelly voice, and even though Alicia was mad, when you heard that clear, careful diction, you paid attention. "The way they made a golem was to dig deep into the soil for rich, heavy clay, and they formed this clay into the shape of a man. A giant, powerful man, two heads taller than any man in the village. The old rabbis used all their knowledge and wisdom to endow this clay man with life by writing a holy word on his forehead. That word," she cleared her throat ". . . is *emet*. Means truth. Can you say that?"

We did.

"Good," she said. "Now. Once they made this man and put the holy word right here," she tapped our foreheads, "they recited special prayers and incantations. These prayers said, Wake up! Wake up and come into life! And do you know what happened? The great, terrible giant stood up." Her movements showed this and we saw him in front of us. "He stepped out of the earth from which he'd been formed. He stood up with his fearful, dead eyes, and awaited the bidding of his masters. And do you know what it was they brought him into life for?"

"No," Alicia mouthed.

"They made him to avenge crimes against the good, honest people of the countryside. The golem lumbered across the land in the dark of night, and being made of clay, he could walk through streams and climb high mountains . . . *impervious* to the arrows and guns of his enemies. No one could stop him except the men who created him . . ." she took another puff, blew the smoke to the side, ". . . and they sent him to kill their enemies by crushing their throats with a single, deadly squeeze." She moved in closer. "When he completed his task, the giant, with its terrible, dead eyes, returned to the rabbi, who wiped one letter off the holy word, to spell *met* … means, he is dead … and *poof*," she snapped her fingers, "he turned back into to a lifeless blob of clay."

Alicia gulped. I took a swallow of juice.

"But then," Nana said, "the great power used to conjure the golem got away from even the wisest rabbi in the village. And when that happened, the giant wandered the countryside, out of the control of good men, wreaking havoc and terror on the simple country people."

She took a big, last inhale on the cigarette. "So. Now. The moral of the story," and stubbed it out in the ashtray. "The golem could visit anyone. He could visit you, or you, or me, under the cover of night, driven by the power of its terrible holy word. It has no rhyme or reason, but it knows about people who misbehave. It knows about people who tell lies, people who are rude, people who cheat their clients, but most important, it knows about children who disobey their elders. It knows about little girls who run around the house and break fine china. Any night, it could come and pay you a visit if it knows you were misbehaving. Do you understand what I'm telling you? Will you remember that?"

We both nodded. And for the rest of that day we stayed quiet, being good and obedient. When momma came to get us at the end of the afternoon, Alicia burst out crying into her arms. Nana busied herself washing a dish. Momma was surprised and said, "What is it sweetheart?" Alicia told her she was sorry for being bad and she didn't want the golem man to kill us because she was running around. Momma listened, stared right at Nana.

"What kind of a story is that to tell a child?" momma yelled. "How could you be so cruel?"

"Oh please. That girl was running around here like a wild animal."

"She's seven years old!"

Alicia was crying harder now, more scared by momma's yelling. "It's all right," momma said. "Old granny was just making up stories. She didn't mean to scare you like that, did you granny?" Eva said, "Poo."

"Nana's going to apologize, aren't you? It's not true about the golem man, is it?"

Nana stared at her.

"*Is it?*"

"Oh, all right," she said, sticking a dishcloth on a hook. "Yes, fine. I'm sorry, dear." She tried to take Alicia's hand, but she shrieked and hugged momma closer. "Well, I'm sorry," Nana said. "But you can't run around grandma's house and break things. I mean, Carolyn, those pieces are irreplaceable. Cesar Romero gave me that tea set."

Momma kissed the palm of Alicia's hand.

"Anyway," Nana said. "Grandmother is sorry, uh, Alicia. It's just a story. Really. Do you believe me, sweetheart? Do you believe Nana?" Alicia turned and looked at her. She sniffled and wiped her eyes. "Honey?" Nana said. Alicia nodded, holding tight to momma. "All right, well, there you go," Nana said. "No harm done."

Then they looked at me. Eva on my left, momma on my right, Alicia in momma's arms. Eva smiled at me with the same phony face. But I knew the truth when I heard it.

II

SOMETHING OUT OF NOTHING

1

In *The Ten Commandments*, the fog is a character. This scary green mist in the shape of God's hand reaches down to the land of Egypt, snaking along the ground, creeping under doors. In LA back then, smog was a character too. This gray blanket hanging over you all the time, a hot, lazy swirl that embraced you, surrounded you, reached into your pants and stroked you.

Maybe it was because everyone was so busy up to then, fighting wars and communists, that by the 1970s, the whole city felt done – worn out and burned out. There we sat, in the remnants of a former world, all these crumbling stucco palaces from the 1920s nobody wanted. Old men and women who used to be famous, thrown out of work, their studios closed and sold for condo developments, prowling the wide, smoggy streets in Lincolns and Rolls-Royces, their hungry eyes searching for something, some meaning. Later on I met some of these people, their gaunt faces behind tinted windows rolled down an inch.

The smog found me, fifteen, lying in my bed. Reached into my pants and whispered into my ear: wake up little man, wake up and come into life. The holy words, and I stood at attention. Outside, the air was the stagnant color of detective shows, the grimy landscape behind *Barnaby Jones* and *Mannix*. You'd turn on the TV and see the hazy hills beyond our house in some scene with a guy shooting another guy and chasing him in a big two-door sedan. Sometimes Eva appeared too. She often wore her own clothes, or she bought the wardrobe, so it was hard to tell them apart.

And now, in school, everyone was changing. It usually happened over summer. You left a kid and came back an adult, all boobs and muscles.

It felt like musical chairs, sitting down fast when you came to what you wanted to be. And the thing between Kevin and me had to happen. There was no other way, especially because of everything that happened later on. I still looked like a kid, but Kevin changed, without the awkward months of bad skin and cracking voices. Suddenly he was five-ten with wide shoulders and narrow hips. Girls giggled and ladies blushed. Cool guys wanted to be his friend, everyone gathered around him like he gave off heat. We still said we were best friends but that wasn't true.

Eva was at our house and she hadn't seen him for a few years. "Who's that?" she said when he came into the livingroom.

"It's Kevin, my friend. You know him."

"Oh," she said, and exhaled smoke. "You grew. How old are you?"

"Fifteen," he said.

"The same age? Huh. You look older." She took a puff, tapped it in the ashtray. "So, what exactly do you boys do for recreation, after school and so forth?"

"I don't know," I said. "Come home and hang out."

"And what do *you* do after school?" she said to Kevin. "You have a job or something?"

He said, "I keep busy."

"Mmm-hmm," she said, and stubbed the cigarette out. "Well, have a good afternoon you two," and walked out.

That night after dinner momma told me I shouldn't hang around him anymore. I asked why and she said Eva thought he was trouble. She said you have make something of yourself in this life and that was a kid who would never make anything of himself. Momma said she argued with her, said she didn't think Eva should decide other peoples' friends. Eva said momma was a fine one to talk, and momma said we were only kids and you can't tell anything about kids when they're young, and Eva said you can tell everything about kids, especially when they're young, and because of that, I was *forbidden* to see him anymore. That word, like a big wasp with a stinger in the middle. I was so angry. I said she can't tell us who we can be friends with. Momma sort of looked at me but her eyes were not really in focus. "I'm just telling you what she said."

"Well, screw her. He's my friend and I can do what I want."

She let out a sigh, sat motionless for a moment then just shrugged and turned on the little TV on the counter. "Do what you want," she said, to the TV. "I don't care."

As it turned out, I didn't have much choice. A couple of days later, we were supposed to meet after school and Kevin didn't show. I waited an hour then went home. I was mad; I knew he had a whole new life he wasn't telling me about. All his friends were seniors and he had a girlfriend and everyone said they were fucking. A couple of days later, walking home behind the ballfield and I saw him. He was waiting for something, sitting on a fence, smoking. When he saw me, he stuck out his hand with that sideways cool guy handshake. "My man," he said.

"Hey," I said.

"I missed you the other day. Sorry, I got tied up. We'll make it up, I promise."

"It's ok. You busy today?"

He squinted. "Ahh, no, no. Couple things I gotta do. Just some stuff, you know."

He sat higher than me on the fence, taller than me anyway. His legs were so long he could balance on the fence easily, holding the cigarette with one hand. He fit so perfectly inside his body. And I was this idiot, looking up at him, with my stupid kid backpack and stupid kid body that didn't fit anything.

"Well, when?" I said. Probably the tone in my voice. He blew smoke, hopped off the fence, tilted his head to the side. Took a good look at me with that same impassive expression. He stepped a half step closer, not right up to me but closer than you usually stand. His face filled my whole vision: green sphinx eyes, the wedge of nose, Mrs. Harmon's cheekbones. Just watching me, he flicked the cigarette away, glanced quickly left and right, put his hands on either side of my head. For a second I thought he was going to crush my skull, but he leaned in and pressed his lips against mine, his thick, spongy tongue coming all the way in and filling me. His mouth tasted like smoke and cold cuts, but a laser blast down my throat, to my balls. Then, with perfect timing, he pulled away, broke the seal.

Looked at me again and gave this nod. I wasn't sure what it meant: there, that's what you wanted; or that's all there is; or see, I can do anything I want. Anyway, that's what he did, and then the sound of a car coming up on us, a Camaro with a big engine. He stepped away, said, "That's my ride."

The car stopped and the door swung open. The driver was some high school kid I recognized and he popped the latch on the seat, pulled it forward for Kevin to climb in back. Other kids in there too, I didn't know them. They giggled at me. His gold head disappeared into the darkness of the cave, then the kid revved the engine and took off. And that was that, he was gone. No one else around at the back of the fields, no other people to witness. All I heard were the sounds of little kids playing in the far distance and the hum of freeways, always around all sides of us.

2

Eva always worked. Since she was teenager, she told us proudly. Getting a job was never a problem, never something she had to worry about. But when her movie career ended in the 1960s, like a lot of her friends, she was left high and dry. Her agents and the people she used to count on were outdated. They didn't know the new people who ran the studios and nobody wanted to hire old timers. For the last ten years most of her work was on TV, as a "special guest star." On these shows she usually played some steely authority figure – newspaper publisher, big city police commissioner, the wealthy boss of some foundation. Sometimes the character was good, sometimes evil, but always the same type. And she did all the shows, *Cannon, Charlie's Angels,* you name it. She was one of the actors everyone recognized but whose name they didn't quite remember. So when Alpine River Instant Coffee came along, she grabbed it. They wanted someone who resembled the picture on the label, and she had to wear a dirndl and a wig with blonde braids wrapped around the sides. Under the picture, in tiny lettering, it said Helga, so at the end of the commercial, they had her say, *Come to de Alpine River,* in a swiss accent, and it became a thing that caught on. Now people who never knew her recognized her on the street and yelled *Come to de Alpine River!* When the ads came on TV, she mumbled *whore.* If she came across an ad in a magazine she turned the page, mumbled *whore.* With strangers and fans always the same smile and polite thank you. Only we knew this was the smile she used when she hated your guts.

The other thing that happened was someone my mother knew before we were born came back into her life. A ghost from her past with a duffel bag and a scruffy beard, back from adventures in Europe and Asia, off a boat and up to our front door. It was after school, and Alicia answered the bell. I heard the voices from my room.

She was twelve now, tall and thin with long dark hair like momma's, but a cooler head than any of ours. The accident changed her; after she almost got killed, she decided she would take charge of her own life and not leave important decisions to any of us. Right now, this man stood outside the closed screen door, taller than momma, taller than me, with sandy hair, a sandy-colored beard, wearing clothes like an adventurer. I stayed far inside the hallway. He was framed in the doorway, the bright light outside and Alicia's slender shadow inside the screen door. He said, "I'm a friend of your mother, uh, Carolyn's. I was hoping to say hello."

Alicia scrutinized him a moment. "She's not home."

"That's all right," he said. "Will she be back later?"

"Are you a door-to-door salesman?" Alicia asked. There was some show about door-to-door salesmen, but we'd never actually seen one.

"No," he laughed. "Just an old friend." He squinted through the screen. "Harris, is that you?"

"Uhm, yeah," I said, surprised. I never saw this guy before. I stayed where I was. I couldn't see him very well. "Momma's not here."

"Yeah, I got that. Would you tell her I came by? I'll give you a number where she can reach me."

"I'm not supposed to open the door," Alicia said, but I told her it was ok. The man took a little pad out of his back pocket and wrote on it, tore off the paper. I walked up and he held it out when I opened the door. Alicia took it.

"Thank you," he said. "You won't forget?"

Alicia said, "We always give momma her messages." Then he turned and walked away. We watched him go down the street and climb into a green MG. He pushed the convertible top open and drove off.

"Let me see," I said. Alicia gave me the paper. *George*, he'd written, and a number.

Momma came home after work, went into the kitchen to make dinner. Alicia said, "A strange man came over today."

"What? You let a stranger in the house?"

"No," I said. "But he left a note for you."

Alicia gave it to her. She got the same pissed-off look she had when she forgot to pay the electric bill. She tore the note into pieces and threw it away. "Forget about it," she said. "If he comes back, don't let him in . . . in fact, don't answer the door. Just ignore him."

Alicia shrugged, went back to the other room and the TV.

■ ■ ■

By the end of the year, almost at Christmas, momma was going with a new guy named Ern. He looked like all the middle-aged divorced guys then: aviator sunglasses, mustache, Members Only jacket. Momma liked him because there was nothing obviously wrong with him. A lot of the guys had something bad going on; that other guy Melvin really did turn out to be a crook. He got momma to invest money and he took it and disappeared. Eva had the decency not to say I told you so, but she knew. Now momma was closing in on Ern, shoe-polish hair and all. She'd invite him over for dinner and he didn't talk to Alicia or me, just nodded as we sat down and his eyes went to momma and the plates she brought to the table. I don't think he knew our names. Whenever momma mentioned him, Alicia and I sang *Sergio Valen-tay*, the jingle for these designer jeans he was way too old to be wearing.

A couple of days before Christmas, momma and Ern decided to go to Palm Springs. She said Alicia and I would stay at Eva's and she took us to Beverly Hills to ask. I heard the TV in the kitchen, Mike Douglas telling Virginia Graham, "But they are lovely, dear."

Eva put down her coffee. "Palm Springs? I don't like the idea of you going out to the middle of nowhere with some strange man, especially now. I mean, for all you know, he could be the maniac, and we'll find you trussed up in a bag." The reason she said this was because, a few months earlier, the bodies of strangled women had begun turning up on hillsides all over the city, and everyone was pretty freaked out about it.

"Mother," momma said, trying to shoosh her so we wouldn't hear.

"Well anyway, it's a moot point. I'm doing a TV show in New York with Iris Costello. I'll be out of town, so you'll have to make other arrangements. Why don't you bring the children with you? Make a family man out of this molehill."

Momma said, quieter, "Ern is shy. He's not ready for the whole family yet. It's important we spend some time alone together first."

"Oh I see. Well, you know best." She let it sit a moment. "Say," she said, "while we're on the subject, I hear that Popeye the sailor man is back in town. Tell me, is your new fellow as good a catch as that one?"

All I heard in the kitchen was coffee percolating and soft whispers; then Eva saying, "All right, Carolyn, fine. But I think he's common. You should pack him off to Palm Springs with his *rich Corinthian leather* and stay with your children over the holidays."

"Well, that's what we decided to do, so we're doing it."

"Fine," Nana said.

"*Fine,*" momma said.

She tried everyone she knew, all the people in the neighborhood. No one had room, or they weren't home for the holidays. So she went with the last resort, and stood in our kitchen, holding the green wall phone close to her ear. I could hear his voice on the other end. "Of course, daddy," momma said, "that's fine, no problem. And only for the two days. I'll be back on the 27th." More hawhawing from his side. "And nothing," she said, seriously, "I mean, nothing, to mother." She put the phone back on the hook and caught me staring from the hallway. "Won't that be fun, sweetie?"

We took Eva to the airport on a Tuesday and stood by the window watching the plane take off to be sure she was in the sky and gone; from there, we drove directly to the top of the Bel-Air hill.

Grandpa and Phil came out to greet us, holding their drinks, skirting their way around white panel trucks parked in the driveway and delivery men carrying boxes out to the back. "Welcome, welcome, welcome!" grandpa said, kissing us, Phil standing behind him with a cigarette, looking dubious. Grandpa took Alicia and me up to the bedrooms he'd made up specially, laid out with white towels and mints on the pillows. "Suites for the sweets!" he said. Down in the driveway, a car door slammed and I looked out the window. Momma waved at me, then slung her arm around the seat and turned as she backed down and away. I sat on the window seat, breathing in the perfumey scent of the yard. Phil leaned against the doorframe, watching me, head cocked to one side. "So," he said. "Who will you be at the *bacchanal?*"

3

1998

OUTSIDE PALM SPRINGS

An Airstream looks so spooky, especially out here in the desert under the tense blue sky. It's a curved mirror, distorting reality. They always creeped me out with that 1950s atomic-age design, the polished metal skin, like it would cook anyone inside. And this one sure smelled it – sweat and rotten food and anything else that might have been in here with this guy. Plus, he died more than a month ago and it had only been aired out by police and vandals.

Under some of the junk, we found a box with his stash. A pile of well-worn magazines, their glossy covers torn and softened by years of use: reading, passing around, showing off, jacking off. In each of the magazines, somewhere, whether it was a photo spread or an ad, he appeared. This was his portfolio, his meaning and his life. And we were part of it now, sifting through it, exhuming this sweaty shrine for some answer, some explanation, for how this had all happened.

4

Phil asked me to come downstairs, for *libations*, and bring Alicia. I found her sitting in another bedroom off the hall, arms folded, scrunched in a white wingback chair. She looked like a mini-sized person inside it, in her blue Danskin pants and the shirt with a little pink flower with a face stitched on. The flower was smiling but she wasn't. She got up, grunted, and followed me to the livingroom; plopped onto the couch next to me, across from Phil and grandpa, the vast marble coffee table between us.

The dog Phil and grandpa had when we first met them had died, and in its place they got a white poodle named Piccolino. He sat on grandpa's lap now, his mouth open, tongue hanging out, breathing fast, every once in a while closing his mouth for a second to lick his lips. On the coffee table, grandpa and Phil's silver tray with the heavy glass pitcher, each of them holding the matching cut-glass tumblers, the alcohol so strong I could smell it from where I sat.

"Now, children," grandpa started, "we're so glad you're here with us for the weekend. I know we're going to have such fun."

"Mmmm," Phil said, taking an ice cubey swig. "Fun."

"No doubt you've noticed the activity in the yard. Well, I'll tell you what that's about. Every year, we have . . . at this time of the year . . . a gala . . . well, more than that, a spectacular holiday event, our premiere event of the season, you might call it . . . a grand Christmas *soiree* . . . one of the events . . . well, perhaps *the* event . . . that we're known for . . . and we're so . . . . *so* glad you're here to enjoy it with us."

"You said that," Phil said.

"And how true it is. But now. Just a few words about the event. A few things to review." His eyes scanned the ceiling, his mouth open in that wide expectant smile, like he's searching for something up there, a cue card or something. On his lap, with his little open mouth, Piccolino, a mini him. He went on: "We're delighted you're here with us, but if we'd known sooner that you were coming, we certainly wouldn't have scheduled a grand ball for the same weekend. Not that you're not *entirely* welcome. It's just that . . . well, this is a rather colorful cast of characters . . . wonderful people from all across the spectrum . . .. our old, old, *oldest* friends, as well as new ones . . .. top to bottom, soup to nuts . . ." Phil rolled his eyes. "Something to add?" grandpa asked.

"Me? Fuck no. I'm just listening to you ham and haw your way through this like some fuckin' Foghorn Leghorn."

I felt Alicia stiffen next to me.

"Uhm, yes," grandpa said. Phil took another swig and grandpa stared at him through the bottom of the glass. Phil held it a second then shouted into it, "Well go on already!"

Grandpa smiled back at us. "As I was saying. I'm sure you'll thoroughly enjoy the group of friends and acquaintances we'll be welcoming tonight. This is traditionally a costume event, so you'll see all sorts of wonderful people, dressed up in all sorts of colorful, exquisite outfits. Sailors, pirates, swashbucklers . . . and I daresay, you might even see some ladies dressed up as men and some men dressed up as ladies."

Now, as an aside, that was a pretty racy thing at the time. A drag costume ball wasn't the junior high prom event it is now. So when grandpa said this, Alicia twitched enough on the sofa to make it jerk. Phil put his heavy glass down, the wobbly route from his mouth to the table telling us this wasn't the first round of the day. "There'll be some crazy shit tonight, let me tell you," he said. Alicia's hand tightened around my leg.

"Oh dear me, no," grandpa said, his eyelids fluttering. "Nothing could be further from the truth. No, no, no. It's a very respectful crowd. In fact, this is one of the few events in town where the traditional can mingle freely with the bohemian. And as you'll see, in keeping with the spirit of the revelries, people are encouraged to be themselves. Or anyone they'd like to be. We pass no judgments whatsoever. So, children, you should be prepared for quite a spectacle. No telling who or what may show up."

"Amen," Phil said. Then suddenly, he almost screamed, "And the men! My god! Wait'll you lay your eyes on 'em! *Gorgeous!*"

"That is true," grandpa said. "We draw an attractive crowd. Old and young, they all come to Rick's."

"Gorgeous!" Phil said again. "Cowboys, Indians, muscle men. Hell, even the boys in drag." He leaned forward and whispered, *"You will come in public."*

Alicia slammed the table with her palm and stood up. "Can I have some juice?"

"Of course!" Phil shouted, and launched himself off the sofa and took her by the hand. "Let's you and me hunt down something *good* to drink," and they went off to the kitchen.

Grandpa smiled, let out a long breath. Took in another, enjoying himself and the silence for the moment. "Ah me," he said. "We really are very happy you two are with us." I smiled back. "Don't take anything the old grouch says to heart. Under all that swill and bile, she's very happy you're here too." Another smile, then after what seemed a momentary loss for words, "so Harris, you're, what now, sixteen?"

"Fifteen," I said.

"Fifteen. Goodness me. How can one even conceive of it?" He looked at me, anticipating. About to say something very witty, but waiting to see if I wanted to say something first. If not, he'd just go on. "Fifteen. My goodness. My goodness me. Yes." More smile. "Yes." It seemed he was looking for a way into something, moving around to get situated in the right position on the sofa. "Fifteen, hmm? Well, that's not exactly a child, is it? You're probably old enough to know something about world, aren't you?" I supposed I was. "And you wouldn't feel uncomfortable if I levelled with you then?" I said I wouldn't. "Well then. You can probably tell this is a gathering where all our friends can just . . . let down their hair a bit. Girls will be girls, boys will be boys, and boys will be girls." I nodded, hoping it looked like I understood. "It means being who they really are," he said.

"Who *we* really are. It's quite a crowd and I wouldn't trade one of them for the world. But the situation puts you in a rather precarious position, doesn't it? East is east and west is west. We have our world and you have yours, and unless I'm mistaken, your planets revolve around an entirely different center of gravity."

It must have been the blank look on my face.

"Oh, I am being obtuse," he said. "We've found ourselves . . . all of us . . . set up for a farce of sorts. You're here with us tonight for an event that I'm sure your grandmother would be none too pleased to find out you're attending. To keep the peace, you're going to have to pretend you didn't see any of this. Is that right?" I said it was. "I thought so. Well, I don't see any way out of it. Everyone had the best of intentions, but it's just one of those things we couldn't seem to avoid. I'm sorry if I had a hand in bringing about the current state of affairs." He sighed. "It's unfortunate really. That's not the way it should have been."

From the kitchen, we heard raised voices. First, Alicia, loud: "I said I don't want any!" and some clanking, a bottle against a glass; then Phil, angry but trying not to sound it, "It's an *aperitif*, honey, it's sweet. Like *punch*," then a refrigerator door slamming and footsteps storming out, stomping up the carpeted staircase. I met grandpa's eyes, and a door slammed upstairs. Grandpa raised his eyebrows. Phil came back in with a pitcher of something brown and three glasses, the cigarette in his mouth. He plunked the glasses down, one in front of each of us, poured out the drinks, splashing the coffee table, then plopped down next to grandpa. He noticed the two of us watching him.

"She wasn't thirsty."

"Did you give her some juice at least, you silly idiot?" grandpa said.

"Of course I did! I tried to pep it up a little and all I got was a big dose of fresh attitude for my trouble."

"Well, go and check on her in a bit, will you?"

"You go. I'm sure whatever I say will be wrong."

"I'm sure it will," he said, patting his knee. Then to me, "Where were we?"

"That's not the way it should have been," I said.

"Oh, not this," Phil moaned. "You're gonna pull *that* out? Mother fucker of god. Don't listen to him Harris. When he gets like this, he's liable to walk up and down Sunset Boulevard, flogging himself with a switch."

"I just want the boy to have some idea of what's going on here. What might have been."

"What might have been is you might have been a bar of soap in some Nazi's soapdish. But you're not, and you're here, so what's the point of beating yourself up? Jesus, what a waste of jizz."

Grandpa considered the inside of his glass a moment before he took another sip and let it settle. "I was only trying to tell Harris . . . well, let him know . . . that there was a time when Eva . . . his grandmother . . . would have enjoyed a party like this . . . would have reveled in it, in fact."

"Ah well, that is true," Phil said thoughtfully. I was amazed at his ability to fly up the scale into hysteria then descend just as fast. "She was one fun fuckin' broad when she wanted to be, I'll give her that. She'd dance on a table for a laugh."

"Harris and I were just discussing how he's going to have to keep this whole weekend on the QT. It'll cause them no end of trouble otherwise. It's a shame, really, she's not the same person she used to be."

Now I did have a question, and asked it.

"Oh, my, well," grandpa said. "The simplest answer is, everyone played their part but it all went kablooey. I'm sorry for my role in it. I still feel very guilty about it. The fact of the matter is, we were quite happy together."

"Oh Christ, here we go . . ." Phil said.

"Well, the boy ought to *know*," grandpa said, his cheeks suddenly red. "God knows what he must think of us."

"Of you, dearie. I'm just the other woman."

Grandpa nodded. "Well, it was a long time ago. A very different world. Back then, you had to be married, if you wanted to work. True, I had many friends who lived their lives loud and proud, as they say now. But not if you were a public person. The studios couldn't allow it. Hypocritical for sure, and they were happy to admit it. Get a woman, they'd say, any woman, and do what you like on the side. I'm ashamed of the whole business now. But in all honesty, I did love her, and I think she loved me. And besides, we were young and back then it was all about having a good time."

"Did she know how much *you* were having?" Phil said. "And with whom?"

"Oh, absolutely," grandpa said. "I never concealed my past. She knew about everything before we married. I tell you, when I met her, she was the smartest, funniest . . . *quickest* girl in this town. Too smart, though. They couldn't figure out what to do with her."

"Well, you got her a career."

"I helped."

"You did everything but break Harry Cohn's leg. Your grandpa knows all the secrets, Harris. Where the skeletons are buried and who buried 'em, and who fucked 'em before they buried 'em."

"Heavens," grandpa said, "what an agent of malicious intent you make me out to be."

"I've only seen him threaten to use the dirt once, and he did it for her."

"Well, she deserved it," grandpa said. "She'd done all the work. All she needed was that little push and she was on her way."

"And so were you. Is that when you turned into such a dirty bird? Job well done and all?"

Grandpa shrugged. "Perhaps. After that, she didn't need me anymore."

"Uh huh. And you got to missin' them franks and beans. Remind me now, what was the cock that broke the camel's ass? A band leader, something like that?"

"One of the boys from the NBC Orchestra. Clarinet player . . ."

"Woodwinds, of course. Perfect for you."

"Oh, it was a mess. In hindsight, I might have engineered it all, there was no accident. I was atrocious."

Phil nodded heartily.

"*Ostensibly*," grandpa said, "she was supposed to be out of town one night. I thought I'd have the house to myself . . . that is, just myself and the flugelhorn. But . . . very unlike me, I got the dates mixed up. And up she came, right into the bedroom . . ."

"God, if I could have been a fly on that wall . . ."

"And it wasn't pretty. She was very dignified about it. Left the room for a smoke while we put ourselves together. This poor fellow imagined we had some sort of open arrangement. On the way out, he asked her for an autograph."

Phil laughed into his glass. "Did she give it to him?"

"Well. No publicity is bad publicity. But clearly, that was the beginning of the end. She never spoke about it, but as they say, the train had left the station."

"And you drove it through every tunnel you could find."

Grandpa nodded. "I became quite a scamp."

Neither Phil nor grandpa said anything for a long moment, grandpa looking at the floor, Phil into his glass. It was the first time I heard them quiet together. I felt I was watching a private moment so I took another long, slow sip on the drink. After a moment, grandpa said, "Of course, things turned out for the best," and squeezed Phil's leg. "But there was . . . how would you call it? An alienation of affection." Grandpa looked up, his eyes moist. He tried to keep smiling. Phil looked at him surprised, almost understanding. "Well, Harris should *know*. If I don't tell him, no one is left. No one remembers this lovely, wonderful girl who just . . . disappeared. Ironic it should happen right then, the moment she hit it big. I don't like to think about what I did, but if I thought I was the cause . . . if I hurt someone so deeply . . ."

It was hard for me to picture who they were talking about. Imagining the person I knew the way grandpa was describing. Now it was my turn to feel uncomfortable, but the drink made me calmer. I said, "But if you didn't love her anymore . . ."

"Oh, but I did," grandpa said. "Perhaps we could have made it work. It's not what you'd think that tore things apart, you know, the, uhm . . .." Phil did the gesture, a pipe in his mouth poking out his cheek, but grandpa shook his head. "We let it get to a point where it was all too dishonest. That's a terrible thing to do to someone. Come home to a scene like that. She might have accepted it, too, a lot of women did back then. So I shook the tree harder, as it were . . . and finally we decided to call it a day. I simply couldn't put her . . . or myself . . . through that kind of disrespect anymore." He stopped and took a long breath. "Well anyway," he said, "Harris, it's not your problem. Just ancient history. But I did want you to have some perspective on the whole thing. Not just see us as a bunch of mindless hedonists."

Phil shook out the last drops from the pitcher. "What's wrong with mindless hedonists?"

Grandpa grunted, but looked downcast at the floor, emptied of something. They were quiet a moment more. Then, like the clasp on a silk purse snapping shut, his face came back on, the wide smile back in place. He looked up at me and said, "Well, enough of that. We have a dress-up party in a few hours and there's nothing more fun in this world than a dress-up party. Let's see what we can scare up for this young man, shall we?"

5

Upstairs, Alicia stared at it. "You can't wear that."

"It's a costume," I said.

"It's a pervy costume," she said.

What grandpa meant about scaring something up was for us to go through the little white door in the kitchen that I thought was a closet and down the rickety stairs to the basement – where, over some period of time, they had squirreled away the entire wardrobe departments of what looked like several different studios, all of it laid out on long rows of metal shelving that ran the full length of the house. One switch at the bottom of the stairs clicked on all the bulbs, hanging every few feet over the racks.

"Some of it we bought," grandpa said, surveying the inventory. "The rest, well, no one was looking and no one cared. So who better to have it than us?"

Row after row of dresses and hats, coats, pants folded on hangers, men's suits arranged by size and color. Suitcases piled with fake jewelry and feathered hats. Styrofoam swords, plastic shields painted gold; a whole corner like a shoe department, rows of 1940s-looking chunky women's shoes neatly lined up. It seemed endless. "Before we get too preoccupied," grandpa said to Phil, "be a dear and go get Alicia. She needs to pick something too."

"She's not coming," he said.

"I beg your pardon? I don't think it's up to you to decide . . ."

"I asked her. I went up there and she's shut up like a sarcophagus. She doesn't want to come to the party."

"Well," grandpa said, almost huffed. "I don't know whether to be insulted or relieved."

"Sorry," Phil said, shrugging, "Miss Otis regrets." He pushed a new, cold drink into my hand.

"Now Harris," grandpa said, "this is quite an opportunity. There aren't many collections like this in one place. After we're gone . . . if we're lucky, it will go to a museum. But for today, it's yours. The whole world, made manifest in silk and leather and chiffon. Take some time and consider what you'd like to be. Who you'd like to be."

It sounded an odd thing to say, at least to me. I wasn't used to people asking so bluntly. I felt my face get hot. I must have blushed because I saw grandpa blush as well, and he smiled, apologetically, almost bowed as he stepped a half-step back. He lifted his arm, gesturing toward the racks on either side of us. "Take all the time you need."

"We've got . . . ." Phil started, but grandpa shushed him.

I looked around. I knew they had to get things ready and I didn't want to hold them up. But more than that, having to make a choice. When you pick something, especially a costume, it's like saying who you are, who you want to be. And choices like that for me were unfamiliar. After a few sweaty minutes, I just grabbed something and said this would be fine.

"You're sure?" grandpa said, an eyebrow raised. I nodded and he and Phil exchanged some kind of glance; then, "So be it."

Back upstairs, Alicia said, "There's nothing there!"

I held the hanger with a pair of white shorts and a strap for the shoulder, tied up with a pair of sandals and a bow and arrow. "It's an angel or something." The drink made me confident, at least in arguing with Alicia. Her face rolled in on itself. "Oh, you're gonna get us in trouble," she said. "You're gonna get us all in trouble. When momma finds out . . . if you go down there . . . and what if Nana finds out? She'll kill us. Uh-uh. You have to stay up here."

"Come on, it'll be fun. It's a party. You have to come to a party."

"No," she said, eyes wide. "All we have to do is wait til Monday, then we can go home. You can't go. It'll be bad."

"Aw come on, don't be a spoilsport."

She smelled my breath. "Are you *drunk?*" She put her hands over her ears, walked to the window.

"Come on," I said. "It's just Phil and grandpa. They like to have fun. We can do what we want. It's a party. Besides, we never have any fun at home."

"No, no, this is bad, all bad." She curled up on the window seat. "Please just go in your room and stay there until momma comes back."

"You know, you're a real killjoy. Grandpa's nice. And his friends are nice. You're just being a crank."

"I'm not talking to you anymore." She pulled her knees up to her chin.

"Well, fuck you."

"No, fuck *you.*"

"Everything all right in there?" grandpa called from down the hall.

"Yeah," I yelled back.

She whispered, "You're gonna get in trouble. You're gonna get us all in trouble."

"You're just a chicken," I sneered.

"And you're a . . ." she said, but stopped. "You'll look like an idiot and everyone will laugh at you. *That's* what's gonna happen."

I stared at her a burning moment then went back to my room.

■ ■ ■

I could hear grandpa and Phil getting dressed down the hall; their muted shouting, glasses clanking, closet doors opening and closing. Grandpa's footsteps, heavy, making the walls quake, Phil's like a bird, so light they didn't shake anything. Outside, the catering people talking, setting up the tables and chairs and tents.

I sat on the bed and noticed this room had a full wall of mirrors over the sliding closet doors. It looked like another room, a reverse of this one, with another kid sitting in there. I stared at him. What I saw was a pasty, scrawny nothing with his shoulders hunched. Not big, not handsome, not talented. Just nothing. My mind went to the pitcher of drink downstairs on the coffee table. With everything going on in the house, no one would notice. I went down and it was still there. I filled one of the empty glasses; the ice in the pitcher had melted so the drink was watery but very cold. Soothing and pungent, I drank half the glass and refilled it, brought the full glass back to the bedroom. Now, with courage, I took off my clothes and put on the costume. Looked in the mirror. Even worse. Bones and ugliness. I turned my back to the mirror and breathed. Closed my eyes, and felt for something else.

For something.

Took another drink. The potion began to fill me with calm and confidence.

And I waited.

For something.

And with another glass it came. With my eyes closed, it made my skin tingle, my nipples hard. Power in my legs to jump, maybe fly; power coming up through my stomach, up my arms and shoulders. I turned back and looked in the mirror and there was that sad skinny kid again; but look away, and the power returned, in this world, in this room. I took another swig and realized that as long as I didn't see a reflection, didn't catch a glimpse, then whatever this is would fill me up and propel me through anything. It's there. It must be there for a reason. *What's a gun for, Earl?*

My hands were shaking. Not from cold or fear, but anticipation. My heart beating fast, ready to burn the alcohol like fuel in a jet engine. I drank the last of it, quickly. The tangy burn just perfect going down my throat, quenching thirst as it stopped my hands from shaking. I took long, slow breaths now, each one filling me more. I didn't need to look in the mirror again. Someone else was here now, taking over for us. Someone I could count on.

6

The back yard looked like a beautiful park. Gracious curves with soft, gentle rises, a kidney-shaped pool on the left, beyond that, tall trees lining the edges. Set up just off the back patio in the big white tent, an orchestra was tuning up, all the musicians in formal dress. The tent was open, flaps tied up in case of rain, but right now it was clear and dry. The transparency of the tent and the lights inside glowed as warm as the inside of my chest.

Floodlights at the corners of the house illuminated the yard. I wasn't keeping track of the time and I lost it completely; it seemed like dusk now, with cars pulling up in front, voices moving through the house below. I felt myself leaving the bedroom and descending the staircase, floating gently down and down. The sandals put wings on my ankles, and I could fly when I chose. The orchestra had started; they were playing waltzes and Christmas carols. I seemed to move an inch or two above solid ground, no effort on my part, through the living room, empty, to the kitchen, where an army of caterers and cooks in white, waiters in black vests ran around each other, hoisting trays of hors d'oeuvres onto shoulders. Out to the yard, and people greeting each other, couples and groups stepping off the deck onto the grass. No one notices me at all, and I wonder if this is a dream and I'm invisible.

I heard Phil behind me. "Oh good, there you are." When I turned, it was his voice coming out of a severe looking lady dressed in a plain gray skirt and jacket, round sunglasses and a black wig with bangs. Like the wicked witch of the west if she went to work as a secretary.

"Are you a teacher?" I said.

"No honey, it's Edith Head. She always stole my work so I get my revenge by stealing *her.*" He smoothed the skirt, turned around. "Fetching?" Actually, he could have gone out in the world dressed like this, it fit him perfectly. He looked at me then and stepped back, scrutinizing. "You know, I'm a little concerned about . . . this," he said, and made a circle in my direction. "We don't want to tempt the cannibals."

He looked at me a long moment more, waiting for a reaction, of which there was none.

"Well, I guess it's none of my goddamn business. Let's find the gasbag and get this show on the road." He took me by the elbow around to the side of the house where we found Santa, kneeling in the grass, gasping, trying to load a pile of wrapped boxes into his red bag. "No, please, don't bother yourself," he grunted.

"Good lord," Phil said, gathering up the smaller ones and stuffing them back. "Where the fuck are Donner and Blitzen?"

"They're upstairs, taking a shit on your bedspread. How on earth did I let you talk me into this?" Phil brushed off the costume, arranged the white trim, pulled down the back. "All in a day's work," he said, "but I think you better cut down on the pfeffernusse, dearie."

"I'll cut down *your* pfeffernusse," grandpa said. He got the bag balanced over his shoulder and caught his breath. And a look at me. "Well. That's certainly revealing."

"Uh huh?" Phil said, his head tilted and chin balanced gently on his thumb and forefinger. Then, a burst of laughter from the back yard, someone calling for them. "Oh dear, help me get situated," grandpa said. "Which way is the North Pole?" Phil straightened the Santa hat, cleared the hair from grandpa's eyes. Turned him by the shoulders and pointed him toward the back yard. "This way. And don't trip over the tannenbaum."

"I'll trip over your . . . oh, shut up." He closed his eyes, took a huge lungful of air, then in a much larger voice, "*Ho ho ho,*" as he took off around the corner. "Who's been naughty and who's been naughtier?" The crowd laughed and applauded as he made his entrance. I knew this was the part he liked the best, the part we all did. The moment the show begins.

■ ■ ■

There were knights and vampires, elves and fairies, pirates and gypsies. Several Glindas from the Wizard of Oz. One guy came as Little Bo Peep, with a long staff curved at the end, and three live sheep. Every few minutes one went *baaa-baaaa* and took off and someone had to herd it back. A big table in the middle of the tent with a fountain of punch, pink drink bubbling down a crystal sculpture into a glass bowl with plastic scoops around the edges. I took a glass and drank it. Sweeter than the brown stuff, but still strong.

I felt like I was looking at everyone through a screen. As I started to move into the groups of people standing around the yard, I nodded, smiled, watched their expressions. At first no one seemed to notice me, but slowly, as I lifted my eyes and watched them back, I saw some ladies smile and say hello. Some of the men looked like industry types, deep in conversation, but their eyes darted up and down quickly, pretending not to notice, but they do. Some did the once over but had no interest; one very old guy dressed like Sigmund Freud coughed on a cracker, and his monocle popped off.

Then the sound of the orchestra, Christmas carols interspersed with other songs – *Isn't It Romantic, Jingle Bells, On the Sunny Side of the Street.* Warm air scented by spices from mulled wine. And the famous dresses grandpa talked about. Shimmering material, thick, heavy silk and brocade in gold and silver, designed to reflect studio lights and sparkle on silver film. Tonight they wore them with tall wigs piled straight up, and thick white face powder, which made it hard to tell who were the men and who were the women. It didn't seem to matter, they were all so spectacular. They floated like ghosts, with elaborate frameworks underneath, mirages from some other time, over six feet in men's size high heels. They greeted each other and leaned forward for a kiss, and the dresses waved gently as they bowed, like graceful dancing mushrooms. The trees glimmered with tiny points of light. I felt lightheaded from the sweetness, the punch, the good nature of all these people. Maybe the drink did something to me because now strangers start talking to me and I answered back, and whatever I said seemed to be fascinating because they craned their necks forward and smiled and nodded eagerly. They laughed at whatever I said and shook my hand and touched my arm and I heard the music swell from the tent, and I felt like I was one of them. Like I belonged. My body seemed to fill the space where no one was before.

Maybe an hour later, at the back of the yard, I stood alone and looked up to try and see stars. Some lush waltz playing slow and mysterious. Behind me, a rustling in the bushes.

"Why hello there," someone said. When I turned, it was a man in a gladiator costume. He had a real southern accent that came out like, "Wah hullo there." But what he looked like was paralyzing. I couldn't believe anyone could be so handsome. Much taller than me, with black curly hair and big shoulders. Skin like milk, the clearest black eyes; arms as thick as my leg. He looked like a cartoon drawing of a prince if they drew muscles big and ridiculously sexy. "This is some crazy shin-dig, idn't it?" he said. I nodded, looking at his chin because I couldn't look in his eyes. It had a cleft in it that made a blip go off at the end of my dick.

"So'r you an actor or something? Everyone here seems connected to someone important."

"No," I said. "I mean, no, I'm not an actor . . ." I stopped and he waited. "Nothing. I'm just a guest." He laughed, said something like "Haw," and put his big hand on my shoulder. It felt like electric heat charging through my skin. "But look at this little thing," he said, and pulled at the costume. "This is the cutest damn thing I ever saw. Turn around, let me get a look atcha." I turned around and he made a soft whistle. "But you're a tiny strip of a thing, aint you?"

"I guess."

"Say, you wanna take a walk with me?" He smiled and it was like the sun looking right at me.

We walked under the trees at the edge of the yard, away from the music and people and lights. He told me his name was Everett Armstrong. He was 23, which seemed so mature. He said he wanted to be an actor, but right now he was a bartender at a place called Numbers. He said he met a lot of directors and important people there, but so far no one had given him a job. While he talked I watched the ground, lifting my eyes just enough to look at the silvery costume and the smooth skin. I felt him put his hand on my lower back. I hoped he couldn't feel me shaking. We kept walking, around to the pool shed. It had a farmhouse door, split in half, the top and bottom connected by a bolt. Everett held it open to me. His armor shined blue like the moon, and I didn't really think about what he was doing, whatever we were going to do next. Inside, in the dark, his hands were so big. His skin and sweat a fresh new smell; his mouth suddenly on mine, alcohol and sour. Arms wrapping around me, these big, muscular arms and chest, pulling me close. I thought this must be what love is, what it feels like to be wanted.

Everett acted like he was starving. His hand went up my leg, under the shorts. I let out a breath when he grabbed it, and he said, "Haw, you a horny boy." My knees almost buckled. I couldn't believe the feeling of someone else touching me. He pulled the shorts down so fast and kneeled and gobbled me up. I yelled something stupid, like *Og . . og .* . He reached up and put his hand over my mouth but kept sucking. It was happening too fast, like falling down a slide, but at the same time, I'm breathing air for the first time; this was what lungs were made for. Something I knew already, a full-sized person coming out of me. I closed my eyes and felt all of me coming loose, rushing down and out through my chest, stomach, balls, gathering all the energy from my legs, concentrated at just one point, and exploding. I heard him gulping and breathing hard down there.

Slowly, I opened my eyes. Took in a breath with new lungs. The air felt clean and the sound came up, the hum of the pool filter and a guy in armor, kneeling on the ground in front of me. "Jeej," he said, and spit it out. Then he stood and his big hands turned me around. I felt him push my head down toward the pool motor and my legs apart. I laughed, not sure what he wanted to do. I tried pulling my legs together and straightening up, but he was powerful. He stood over me, held me in place with his arms and I felt the soft head of something warm poking around my butt. I said no, trying to be cool, but he wasn't hearing. And I was thinking, well, maybe this is what you do, you're supposed to do this because this is what you do. But my voice said, "No, come on," louder, still a controlled whisper. "Everett . . ." is all I got out before his hand came around my head and wrapped my jaw closed. It was so big, it sealed my mouth. Just vocal cord vibrations muffled by thick flesh. The haze from the drinks began to clear, and I didn't want him to think I wasn't nice, but something else took over and I wanted to stop. And I realize that big muscles are there for a reason. They're no match for small ones. Huge arms and shoulders held me. I heard him spit a couple of times, and this object suddenly went fast, shocking, inside. And I'm ripped open.

I did scream and try to wriggle away, fight with everything, but it's not enough. The screams disappear in his hand. I hear him grunting and making these guttural noises, someone in another world moaning "Yeah, yeah, yeah, yeah." The taste of copper in my throat from screaming into a thick hand and thinking comes too fast, there being no way to get out, get off, get away.

He couldn't come fast; maybe being drunk it took him a long time. His hand was slobbery from snot and tears I couldn't see through, screaming to get him out of me. It didn't get better and I didn't pass out, and in the back of my mind I thought those might happen. But at the center of the white hot explosion was only one real thought and that was I had to do the thing I was told to do, which was endure.

I felt him finish. Then breathing. Then separating. I stayed upright a second before falling over like a folding chair, collapsing into a heap. I heard sobbing, but not connected to me; the cool dirt, my body pressing down on it. Dead weight, alive.

"God dayum," I hear him say, just as charming. "Dayum," he said again, amazed at the wonderful thing that just happened. "You are one sweet thing, you know that?"

I don't know if I answered or he said anything more. Only coming awake, a few minutes later, or an hour, and he was gone. The pool motor's deep hum woke me up.

■ ■ ■

In movies you see people struggle to get up after a fight, or old people groaning out of bed. I could only get as far as my knees. I reached back with my hand and there was blood on my fingers. I worried my heart beating would cause too much blood to gush out, so I used an old cloth from the ground to wipe back there. Then I looked at the cloth and there wasn't much, it wasn't pouring out like a water pipe. If I stand up and walk, I won't leave a trail of red on the ground.

But. But. But.

I'd like not to be here. I see the scene from an angle just above, someone on the dirt floor of this shed. I watch him brace his arms on the pool motor for balance; lift his body onto shaky legs. Pull up the pants, pull the strap around the shoulder, everything back like it was before. Besides the ass, the rest of me feels like quivering, stinging jelly. I have to think about how to walk, what to do: one foot on the ground then shift weight to the other. I don't seem to belong in this body.

Stepping outside into dark fresh air, I could hear the music and the murmur of people. It couldn't have been that long because everything out here was the same. Something happened that didn't happen, and I got sent to the moment before, alone now. I moved closer to the lights and the people standing around the lawn with their drinks. Phil was talking to a group of people and when he saw me, he did a double-take, left the others and came over, the gray skirt tightening around his legs as he took quicker strides. "Where did you run off to? We wanted to introduce you around." He looked at me and squinted. "Jesus Christ, you're white as a ghost." I looked at him too, felt his cool hand. The lady in the sunglasses scrutinized me carefully, eyes behind the lenses. "Did something happen? You're shivering all over."

My face is a poker face, I am sure. Nothing revealed while I hold her off. A moment to think this through.

And I do. And this is a bad thing. If I tell, he'll find grandpa and grandpa will go nuts. They'll call the police and all their friends and famous people are all having fun and being crazy, and I will interrupt it and cause a disaster. And much worse. What would they say? The police would see a kid in a sexy costume and all these men in dresses and it would be bad, it would be a catastrophe. They invited me to this party and I would destroy it. I would destroy them. And the police will ask me why I went into a room with a man, and everything will explode like Alicia said it would. I did something I shouldn't have done and it will be my fault. It will be all my fault.

So what do you do? What does one do?

I tried to say, "I'm fine," but my voice came out a croak. "Oh shit, you must be coming down with something," Phil said, and took my hand. "Come on, let's find Santa." He pulled me toward the house, all the lights around us brightening. Maybe he felt something through my skin, the cold jelly inside, because he turned and stopped, dead serious. "Harris. Did something happen?"

But there was nothing to be said. I had to contain it. "I'm fine," I said, and smiled, pleased that I could do it. He lowered his head and looked at me over the sunglasses.

We all have our parts to play. This is mine and nothing will be said. The party will go on, the weekend will go on, and nothing will be said.

And as soon as I decide this, I start to feel better. Something falling off and disappearing below the surface into the dark green opaque. The only thing I think about, much later, is not the physical pain or the moments themselves, which I cannot go back to, but the confusion. It felt so bad because he was so beautiful and I wanted him so much.

7

In the winter it rains.

Los Angeles gets cold, the skies turn gray, and solid sheets of water just fall, all day, all night, as though it's trying to make up for all the months that rain never came. It falls hard against rooves, on cars, on pavement, like something is wrong, like a water main exploded. Roads and sidewalks turn to rapids; suddenly there's a river tearing through someone's backyard in the hills, an angry lake forms at the end of a cul-de-sac. Hills collapse on neighborhoods, freeways buried under mud, sliding into the ocean. The empty concrete river beds and angled driveways make sense all of a sudden, put there just for that day, or week, or couple of weeks, when the sky floods the land and attacks us. At the top of the mountains that surround LA, the rain is snow, and we see the soft white caps like a matte painting in the distance. People who came here in summer are startled and they stare. They didn't know those mountains existed, hidden behind the wall of smog and haze. The mountains are there to keep the snow from getting in; the air in here is too warm, the storms over the desert too angry, so the best they can do is throw all that water at us in frustration.

■ ■ ■

Momma came back on December 27th, alone. She didn't say anything about Ern, just that he was staying in Palm Springs. After that, she never mentioned him again.

She picked us up from grandpa's two days after the party. She hardly said anything, her eyes dark, not really noticing us. Which was fine, because if she had pressed, I don't know what I would have done. I never felt out of my skin before, out of control of my insides. I was shivering and couldn't stop. Phil said he thought I caught a cold but I didn't have a temperature. They kept touching my forehead and I wanted to scream. Driving home, sitting in the front seat, I watched Alicia in the rear view mirror, her arms crossed, looking to the side but knowing I'm looking and she won't look at me. When we got home we all went into our bedrooms and closed the doors, all three latches clicking.

You don't know it, because no one knew anything then, but you could get away with murder. You're a kid, and it's 1977, and everyone is happy and stoned, but there is such a thing as too much to bear; things people absorb, what they call it now, *beyond endurance*. But of course, we must endure. That's what we do. Sometimes my mind went back but it was too confusing, like fireworks exploding in a closed room. I shake my head to shut it off. In bed, I reach down and grab my dick. Why is it so fucking hard? Why does it want trouble? After a couple of weeks, the pain inside is gone, not the ground beef way it felt before. I had no cuts on the outside, no visible wounds; whatever happened happened inside, and I imagine there must be a scab, and scabs heal over. It won't be skin though. It'll be scar tissue, something tougher, with less feelings when you touch it, and in a while, you forget it's there. I try to forget it. Make my mind go forward and think about what's next. That's all you can do.

After winter break, it felt like going back to school behind a sliding glass door. The same place but different. And sixteen, the year you can drive. I saw other kids getting bigger, kissing, falling in love. I watched them through the glass door while I forgot about doing things: momma had to remind me to get a haircut but I didn't care what it looked like; take a shower, but I didn't care what I smelled like; not wear clothes with tears in them because, you know. The year you look forward to, the first year of independence and adulthood, and I am perfecting the art of becoming invisible in front of everyone.

■ ■ ■

One day, I rode my bike to a Winchell's Donuts a couple of miles from the house. Opened the door and got hit with this blast of heat and the smell of frying fat. The air conditioning was broken, the glass walls steamed up.

Inside, the place was empty. No one there except the girl behind the counter, pissed-off, red-faced, fanning herself with a paper plate. I asked for a chocolate and a glazed, and she handed them to me on a napkin, soggy and wet. Whatever was wrong with the air conditioning made a loud grinding noise. It was so hot in there, it was almost unbearable, but for some reason I wanted to stay. As I turned the corner to find a place to sit, I saw something at the far end of the room. A person, alone, wearing a pink shirt and pink pants. All I saw was the reddish pink at first, but as I got closer, I realized it wasn't the clothes that were red, it was the skin. It was a woman, and her face and arms were bloated and bubbled that reddish color, like she was blown up from inside. It took my mind a second to figure out what it was seeing. She was burned all over, her face turned fat and round where it shouldn't be. Her mouth was over to the side, not really looking like a mouth, her arms too big and the wrong color. She turned her head and looked at me. I sat a few tables away, slow, so as not to scare her, and tried not to stare, but I did.

The way she sat there, so settled, I could tell she came here every day. This was her spot; the only place she went outside her house. She had six or seven donuts in a bag and she ate one, shoved it in her mouth, looking back at me like she was challenging me while she chewed. Something about how she pushed it in kept my eyes locked on hers. I knew it was rude to stare but I couldn't stop. I kept watching as she reached in and got another, slowly pushed it in and chewed that one slowly too. It went on for another whole donut, that one coming out of the bag, pushing in, chewing, and watching me watch her chew. And I knew what she was doing. She was trying to stuff them inside. They were the only thing she had, the only thing that loved her. She was trying to get them inside and as deep as she could.

My heart was beating so fast. I realized we weren't staring at each other because she was a burned woman and I was some kid; she was daring me to look at her. I could see myself sitting there through her eyes, this scrawny suburban jerk, hunched over his own donuts, scared eyes trying to keep level with hers. Two people staring at each other with the airless machine grinding out this terrible sound. After a moment, she lowered her glance, looked down at her bag, and started another. I got up and walked outside into the cool dry air.

My lungs opened, breathed again. As I walked away, I looked back through the foggy glass, but all I could make out was a blurry pink shape, the side of a face moving up and down slowly, and no one looking back.

■ ■ ■

In the meantime ...
Something Eva would say and move her cigarette in a horizontal line to demonstrate two things happening at the same time. *In the meantime*: this guy George had been calling, day after day, until momma finally answered. She chewed her lip while she listened, then pulled the long, tangled cord into her bedroom and closed the door.

A week or so later, she set an extra plate for dinner. He knocked on the door and she let him in, said, "This is George," and he said hi, and that was all either of them said. Then momma brought out dinner and we ate it. Momma talked, asked us all the same stuff, and we answered like he wasn't there. After dinner we watched some TV and George sat on the sofa next to momma. Not right next to her, but one cushion away. At about ten, he got up and said Bye, and momma mumbled something, and he was gone. Then he was coming over more often, walking in without knocking, like he had permission, and sometimes stayed overnight in momma's room. We got used to him at breakfast. This was different from Ern or Melvin, some new guy she was trying to impress. It was almost as if she was trying not to see him, let him in but turn away. She treated him like a ghost so we did too. He was certainly handy, though: he dug up the dead front lawn, turned over the dirt and planted grass. Fixed broken cabinets, put doors back on hinges. It sort of bugged me, to be honest, because I didn't know who this was or why he was there. I asked momma, finally, and she said, "It's just George. He's an old friend. Besides, he's a man, so you can ask him … I don't know … any *man* things you need to ask. Do you have any man things you need to know?"

I didn't and wouldn't. But there were a couple of things going on, and none I'd ask anyone about. For one, riding around the streets now, I noticed people looking at me. Men mostly, in cars. Pretending they weren't, while they were waiting at a light, or driving around the block, acting like they're looking for a street number. But I could sense how nervous they were by how the car moved. When I slowed enough for it to reach me, it was always some guy inside waiting for something from me. A signal.

■ ■ ■

Just before spring break Nana called. We were eating dinner and momma answered and handed the phone to me. I shrugged but she pushed it at me, mouthed, *Talk to her.*

"I've been thinking," Nana said. "I have a job coming up and I need a hand."

"Yeah?"

"Yeah. One of those *fekakteh* commercials. It's going to take a couple of days. Everyone has an assistant nowadays and I'm there all alone with a handbag and a roll of life savers. I need someone to help me out, and I think it would be a good idea for you to see how things work in a professional environment."

"Why?" I looked at momma and she badly pretended she didn't know what was being said.

"Because you're getting a little overripe there, buddy. The whole rangy look is not a good way to make friends and influence people. If you're getting that from George, let me tell you, that is not a good role model." I watched George across the table, wondering if he could hear. "I understand you have a school break coming up, so instead of lying around in your own stink, come with me and see how real people make a living."

"What if I have something to do?"

Intense silence on the other end.

"Well, what if I don't want to?"

"Listen, Charlie, this isn't a negotiation. You're doing it. And it's in Culver City, so you'll have to drive yourself. I'm not going back and forth over the hill every day."

"How am I supposed to get there?"

A sigh. "Put your mother on the line. You can borrow her car."

I held the phone to momma, shook it at her. At least this was going to cause her some inconvenience too. She took the phone and the little smile on my face sort of pissed her off.

That night she knocked on my bedroom door. I was about to start the night's marathon jack-off, so I told her to wait a minute. When it went down, I opened the door a crack.

"Do you mind very much?" she asked.

"What?"

"Helping out Eva."

"It's stupid."

"She'll pay you like a regular employee. Maybe it would be a good idea to get out of the neighborhood for a while. Besides, it would be fun to work at a studio, wouldn't it?"

"It's a commercial. How much fun is that?"

"I don't know. But maybe it'll . . . I don't know, maybe it'll help you come out of your shell . . ." and I slammed the door.

She waited a minute outside. I waited inside. She knew I wouldn't open it again. After another moment, I heard her walk away slowly.

■ ■ ■

Helga lived in some kind of weird Swiss fantasyland, so they shot the commercials on a studio backlot because they had those kinds of houses already set up. Of course I was late the first day. After the guard told me which stage they were using, I found Eva already in the makeup room.

"Sometimes people show up when the work begins," she said, and blew out smoke. I mumbled sorry. "Didn't your mother tell you when to leave to get here on time?" I said no. "Jesus," she said, "the two of you."

She was sitting in the chair with the mirrors, the hairdresser working to get the wig right. It took a while to unpin her own hair and flatten it down and cover it with a hairnet then lay the wig over that and pull it down as tight as he could. The braids were separate pieces that had to be wrapped around both sides. He tugged and yanked the wig so hard it looked like her neck might snap. "Jesus, Terry, my head doesn't get any smaller," she said. "Did you the bring the other one?"

"Yes, but I want to make this one work. The other one is too tight."

He was scrutinizing it from low angles, looking for ways to fold it down. "This one has the better color too," he said. She nodded and the makeup artist came in, introduced herself. "This is my grandson, Harris," Nana said, and they were polite, they nodded at me while they continued their work. Then the actor who plays her neighbor came in. He was a chunky older guy with dyed black hair. His voice went up and down, exasperated, and he played a lot of fussy clerks on sitcoms.

"Hello Eva dear," he said. He was already in costume, a brown pinstripe suit with a vest and a pocket watch. In the commercials he usually visits from some situation – a cooking class, returning from Italy – so with the snappy brown suit he was probably coming from a meeting or something. He looked me up and down. "Well he-*llo*," he said, dropping the second syllable the way his character spoke.

"This is my grandson," Eva said to the mirror. "Keep your pants on, Reggie."

"Oh Evie, what a fresh mouth. Never would I ever." He shook my hand. "It's nice to meet you, young man." He took another long look and winked, then went to sit in the chair next to Eva. "And how are you, swiss miss? Ready for explosive diarrhea?"

"Not this time. I made them put it in my contract. I spit it into a spittoon."

"Smart girl," he said, and twirled his necktie. Silence from them for a moment; they could see each other in the mirror and he gently lifted the edge of something silver from a pocket inside his vest. The makeup lady hummed, "I'm not seeing anything," and he slid it back, flushed. "I'll be sure to make it a twenty-take day," Eva said. "Heaven help us," he answered. "I didn't bring that much."

When they were satisfied with the makeup, we got into golf carts and drove out to the set. Rolling hills, Victorian mansions, Mexican towns, we passed them all and pulled up to the Tyrolean village. They had a camera setup facing one small house. The director looked like a middle-aged drunk, some blobby guy who hadn't shaved for a couple of days, wearing a safari jacket with the pockets all stretched out. It was still morning but he was already sweating and freaking out. Eva gave me a look.

They did the shoot in sequence: people outside first, then Reggie coming in with a fancy cane and acting British. He was coming from work, and couldn't survive another minute without a cup of Alpine River Instant Coffee, the heavenly aroma calling to him from across the street. It took half the morning to get the shot of him coming into the frame and seeing the house with Helga inside. Eva didn't have anything to do except sit near the window. It seemed like only a half hour into shooting when the director starting calling Reggie names under, and then over, his breath. Fuckin' idiot, stupid queer, goddamn fairy. Some of it he said loud enough for him to hear where he was standing. Each time they called for another take and the director cursed him out more, I felt bad for him. He had been in old movies, even before Eva, but people like him were contract players who never made enough money to retire on. Now he had to be funny and do precisely what this director was yelling at him to do, which seemed to me he was doing every time. After a while, it felt like watching someone hitting a dog with a stick, this director taking his frustration out on him because he felt like it. And Reggie had to take it. I guess that's why he brought the flask.

They broke for lunch and Eva and I sat at a picnic table in the middle of this village next to an empty lake. Even though it was a warm day, the phony snow on the buildings and the swiss landscape made it feel like we were on vacation in the mountains. Reggie took off as soon as they called time, and it was just her and me at the end of the table, eating our sandwiches. She was careful, wiping with a napkin, not to smudge the overdone lipstick.

"What do you bet?" she asked after a while. "You think he's gonna rip me a new one, or I rank too high on the totem pole?"

I didn't know.

"And by the way . . . that, young man, for your edification, is called an *asshole*." She nodded toward the director and crew arguing under an umbrella. "And you know what? This is the simplest goddamn setup I ever saw. This should only have taken a couple of hours. But this nasty bastard thinks he's Orson Welles or something." She shook her head. "I couldn't hear much from in there. Was it as bad as it sounded?" I nodded. "Poor Reggie. Sweet old fruit. He doesn't deserve that."

I drank my Coke.

"People can get away with all kinds of things," she said, shaking her head. Some birds chirped in the trees over us. In the distance the machine grinding sound of construction or a crane.

Movie sets were interesting. You had time to sit and talk between shooting because most of the time nothing is happening. A strange kind of reality; you have to be ready to jump up and perform, and you're sitting there in your costume, but for long stretches you're doing nothing. You find this specific rhythm, where you're talking, but not the way you would if you were yourself in the real world.

"Still, this is nothing new," she said, still watching the director yelling at everyone. "I was fired from a job once, did I tell you that?"

I didn't think she had.

"Only once. I'm a team player, you know that, I do what I'm told. But this job, what was it, 1961 or '62, just before you were born." She stopped a second, then went on. "This was in Spain, out in the countryside, and they had this one guy, a real piece of work. Someone new, not someone with any experience. Producer or something, I can't recall. I wasn't the star, I was playing the wise, older hussy, and for some reason, he didn't like me. Maybe because I had the name, or the salary. Whatever it was, he'd walk around and he'd give everyone his orders, and one day he came past me and said something, like, Hey baby, how you doing? and he slapped me on the ass, and I mean a real wallop. It wasn't nice. And I told him, I said, don't do that again, and he laughed and gave me this look."

She took a sip of tea, wiped her mouth.

"So a couple of days go by. We're working in this brutal heat and I'm in this big red barmaid outfit, with spangles and feathers and every stupid thing hanging off it, and he comes by again, and I can see it in his eyes, he comes right up and he honks my boobs . . . both of 'em . . . " She demonstrated this with her hands toward me and I had to bite my tongue because she did it funny. "And, yaha, yes, he thought it was funny too. So I slapped him right across the chops. Got him good, too. And he's got this look on his face" – she did it, also funny – "like he's so shocked, he can't believe someone would do that to *him*. He goes off and I go back to work, and in a few hours they call me in and tell me I'm gone. Get out, clear out this instant. Practically throw me into the street and my suitcases with me."

Another sip of tea.

"Now, of course, he's gone and I'm still here. But honestly." She looked back at the director shrieking at the crew. "I'm a hundred miles ahead of this clown. I know everything he's gonna do before he knows he's gonna do it."

She lit a cigarette and took a long breath, enjoyed it for a while. The trees made the nice, ssss-ssss sound with a breeze blowing through them. I didn't realize until I looked at her that she had been watching, and considering me. "These dumb commercials seem to be doing the trick," she said, "because I might have an offer coming my way. Pilot for a show. Which would be a big deal for me. For all of us."

"That's good?"

"It is good. Might be the last chance at the OK corral. Nobody's breaking down the door for fifty-seven-year-old broads these days. If I get it, and it gets picked up, I might ask your help now and then. You're smart and observant. I don't want you falling into the same mess your mother made of herself. Her and Captain Kangaroo down there."

I didn't know what to say, or what she was saying. But it didn't matter because they called us back to start the next segment.

■ ■ ■

I actually liked working with Nana. I grumbled but it was fun to watch everyone doing their job. I liked how everyone talked to each other, like a team working all together. Mostly it was interesting to watch her work. She walked onto the set and I could see her preparing herself without making it look like she was doing anything. She liked to joke about Method actors digging deep into themselves to figure out what an onion would do, but for herself, she knew she was hired to be someone like her, in this case, a character somewhere between Eva Loesch, the famous actress, and Helga, the picture on a coffee label. She just positioned herself and turned into the person they wanted.

I watched her with the asshole as well. He was coming unglued, blowing up at everything, sweating, wiping his running nose on his sleeve. Eva had this way of listening when he spoke to her, and speaking to him with respect, no matter how badly he acted or what shitty thing came out of his mouth. When he tore into Reggie again, she went up to him and touched his arm gently, nodded like she agreed and understood, but in her body movements, calmed him down and made him feel in control. The next day, when we were done, he even shook her hand and gave her a little head bow. Afterward, I walked her back to her car.

"Thank you," she said. She opened her purse and handed me some money. "This is your cut. You did a good job."

"I didn't do anything. It was fun."

"It was work," she said. "Remember it." Then she kissed me on the cheek and drove away.

8

School ended and the summer of sixteen began.

Eva got the pilot and they had to start right away. She came to North Hollywood to tell us.

"I didn't want to jinx it by talking too soon. It's a detective show with James Franciscus. They want a lady DA and apparently I'm just what the doctor ordered."

"That's wonderful news," momma said.

"We'll see. I gather I'm one of the selling points. They wanted someone with *weight and dignity*. That's what the network said. Weight and dignity. I told them I better start eating now."

"Do you know anyone working on it?" momma asked.

"I know everyone. That's how they got my name. For once, it sounds like a shoo-in. Although I know saying it out loud could scotch the whole thing. But what the hell, why not live dangerously?"

"When will it be on?" Alicia asked.

"If all goes well, they'll pick it up for the fall. If all goes well." She took another puff, glowing at the good news. Then she looked at me a moment longer, up and down. "Weight and dignity," she said, and tapped the ash off. "I'll know more in a few days." But we didn't hear from her for a couple of weeks. Momma said she must be working morning til night, because they have to work fast to make a pilot. And with momma at work and Alicia at camp, I was alone.

And suddenly it was quiet. And everything seemed to slow down.

The summer began with this haze that seemed to start something up inside of me. I went out looking for what it was, what it was asking for, but at the end of the day, all I saw was the sun sinking into a flat cushion of grimy cotton on the horizon. I had no money this year, no motivation to get any, and nothing to do. In the morning, a bowl of cereal and the box fan in the kitchen window, pushing hot air from one part of the room to another, its blades already thick with hairy dirt. The sound of traffic on four sides, giant rivers of freeway, trucks and cars all around. I had no ideas and no plan. Not like I even thought about it. Just floating, watching what I'm doing while I'm doing it. Outside, under the constant sun, you feel yourself cooking, changing color. I took my bike out and rode alone. Stopped, elbows draped over the handlebars, put a leg up on a pole while I waited for a light to change. Waiting for something. My hair was much longer now since I stopped giving a crap.

I rode out to Vineland, a very wide street. Down to the intersection with Lankershim, then back again. Over to a strip mall with a 7-Eleven and a Winchell's; bought a frozen fruit stick, sat on the dry-piss-smelling cinder block wall around the parking lot, sucking on it. Got back on the bike, rode some more down this busy street, listening to the traffic, the speed of the cars. Stopped at another light, stretched, pulled off my shirt and stuck it in the back of my shorts the way cool guys do. Guys who can say *man* and sound like they mean it. The light changed, but I didn't move. Just sat at this intersection, the sun warming my shoulders, cars rushing by. Another cycle, and I feel something pushing me when the light changes. You're supposed to go, to keep the traffic flowing; if you don't, you're breaking the rhythm. No one notices except the people who are looking for it. Just a tiny ripple, a difference, and you're aware of another reality. The same place but different, another world of language and signals.

I hear a car pull up in the parking lot next to where I'm waiting, a low brick wall between us. The soft crinkling of tires on pebbles, the car creeping slowly. I could feel how scared it was, the person driving. But I wait, I don't have to turn until I'm good and ready. My heart beating fast. The engine idling now, the car as far as it can go in the parking space. I'm high above it on my bike, outside under the brutal sun, waiting for whoever it is inside the faded green metal of the car's roof. Now I can turn, a moment, and look down.

It's a bald guy in a short sleeve shirt, peering out the open window. Scared, his eyes pleading. I never saw this guy before, just an ordinary old guy, someone's uncle. My heart is beating hard. He's asking something dumb and I answered, Yes, I know where the freeway ramp is. Yes, I can show him. And then it really is like *Barnaby Jones* or *Cannon*. I can see the angle from across the street, while the cars cross left and right in front of the camera's line of sight: this kid putting his bike behind the green dumpster where no one will see it, opening the passenger door of this nondescript sedan. The kid getting in, feeling the warm vinyl on his bare back and legs, and the car backing up and moving slowly into the alley behind the strip mall to the hidden parking lot. Watching while his shorts pulled down, the bald head going into his lap; in no time, squealing noises, grunting, this guy moaning when the kid comes in his mouth. In a quick moment, the man drives back to the dumpster and the kid gets out, gets on his bike and rides off. The sound comes back up as if nothing happened: street, bicycle, legs, hair. Ride around for the rest of the day, shirt back on, home in the late afternoon where Alicia's back from camp and Rice-a-Roni and momma asking how my day was. With the rice in my mouth, I said OK, nothing much, watched some episode of some TV show.

On Tuesday, more riding and listening and watching. It's hot so I stop for Gatorade. Ride across the valley, criss-crossing, sensing what each intersection feels like. Making some kind of mental map of intersections and energy. For one thing, I realize you can't spend too much time at the same spot. Someone you know will drive by and see you. You have to keep moving, but always aware of what's going on, feeling the eyes on you as they drive by.

A few days, a week under the smoggy valley sun, and my arms have turned the brown color. Someone different, not the scrawny nerd in the mirror. A couple more times when I'm still scared but trying not to show it, not doing anything except slipping down the shorts and letting the guy do whatever he wants. Whatever any of them want. The first time a guy opened his wallet I laughed, said No no, and waved it off. But I asked if

I could have his cigarettes and then I had my own pack, a prize to take with me. Put them in my back pocket, started down Vineland again with my shirt off and my cigarettes. I taught myself how to smoke right there, walking down the street that afternoon, letting the smoke curl into my eyes. Some of the guys wanted to see me again, asked to meet at a place at a time. I laughed, slid my pants on, lit a cigarette. Momma asked what I was doing all day and I said I hung out, bummed around with friends, with Kevin. She didn't know I didn't know him anymore. Alicia looked up at me from her bowl of cereal and didn't say anything.

And I went out again, under the burning sun, to the wide roads and the cars. It's so big and flat here, you feel you have no power, especially a kid like me who never had any. But overhead, the great, steel towers carry electric wires in their outstretched arms, fingers spread, marching all the way across our valley in straight lines. A chain gang of silent giants doing their job, carrying the power. And riding along the streets for hours, listening to the electric lines sizzle, the motor grinding in my groin, it came to me all of a sudden, like some superhero getting electrified – a three-way lightning bolt from power lines to balls to all the metal bodies of all these cars on the street, an energy only people brave or dumb enough to go outside alone and strip off their clothes can feel – which is this: all these people are hiding in their cars, in their shells, protected from the sun. But if you get past the fear of being exposed, you discover you control those cars. The street is yours. The great power lines are the reins, they're there for the taking, and if you do, then you control all this confusion and chaos. I can make the heads turn inside cars when they pass me. Whole lines of traffic slow when I turn a shoulder, turn a leg; I can make the cars stop, slow down, keep going, look at me or look away; I control the whole intersection. Suddenly, the power comes through me and I have control.

9

One afternoon, near the Taco Bell on Lankershim, I turned around and there was this dark green Grand Prix. A big car, filled with junk – candy wrappers and cans and trash on the floor – and a guy sitting in the middle of it. He stopped too fast and the tires squealed. I looked around, thinking, what is this idiot doing? He leaned out and asked one of the dumb questions, if I knew where the freeway ramp was. He was about 40 or 42, with a kind of green, gray, papery skin, little round glasses, and sweaty as hell. "Uhm, no," I said, looking at this collection of junk, trying to figure if it's safe to get in. I told him if he gave me a ride I could show him, and he said Okee dokee. In the car he opened his wallet, pulled out a twenty, showed there were more. I didn't want a discussion so I just took the one. Then like lightning, he's down there, and he starts this running commentary, saying *Oh hot* and *Scrumptious* and *Lovely*, through a mouthful of dick. I got a whiff of him and had to roll down the window. I looked out at the thick valley sky, the smoggy clouds, and went someplace else because I came without realizing it; he gagged and made this sound like a cat vomiting up a hairball. Then he pulled off and sat up.

"My goodness," he said, "that was a thirst quencher." Closed his pants, pulled himself together, sniffling and sweating. "So, uh, where was it you wanted me to take you?" I said forget it. I felt no rush so we talked for a while. I don't know why I was curious about this weirdo. Finally he said, "You know, I was hoping I'd run into you. To see for myself."

"Sorry?"

"What the hubbub was all about."

I lit a cigarette and stared at him.

"I was advised to cruise this stretch of Lankershim between eleven and three on a weekday afternoon, and here you are. In the very fine flesh."

"Somebody told you?"

"Heavens yes. You've got all the queens up in a froth."

That was enough. I pinged the cigarette out the window, zipped my pants. He got flustered and I pulled the door latch to be sure it was open. "But I'd like to talk to you . . ." he said. I was already halfway out. With my feet on the ground, I leaned back in. We both stared a second, then he pulled out his wallet and more money.

"You already gave me it," I said.

He waved the bills between his first two fingers. "Consider it a deposit."

I pushed the door shut hard.

■ ■ ■

Saturday.

The smell of coffee and bacon in the kitchen. Hot in there as usual, the dirty fan in the window. Momma standing by the stove, cooking, Eva next to her, George reading the paper at the table and Alicia, next to him, watching the TV on the counter. No one talking. When momma turned around, she seemed relieved I came in. "Good morning sleepy head! Who wants breakfast?"

Eva looked me up and down. "Good lord, what is that?" My hair had grown since she saw me last.

"Harris wants to be a cool guy," Alicia said.

"Jesus, I'm out of touch a few weeks and you all go native on me."

"Good morning Nana," I said, and took someone's undrunk orange juice.

"Tell me, Sabu, where's your elephant?"

"That's what all the kids look like," momma said. "Don't even start."

"Your neighbors are going to wonder what kind of a joint you're running over here."

"You know," I said, "a joint is what they call a pot cigarette."

"Is that so?" Eva said. "Well, thanks for filling me in on that. I won't ask why you thought that was important to share. Don't forget, you're talking to the DA here." That made me laugh, but she didn't. "Now, Carolyn, this shooting schedule is taking a toll," she said, lighting up. "I asked Harris if he might help me out from time to time."

"That sounds like a good idea."

"When?" I asked.

"Later in the summer. I'll know more in a few weeks." She twiddled her cigarette nervously. "See if we get picked up for another year before I start looking like an old lady who needs an arm to lean on. There's always that son-of-a-bitch Anne Baxter, sniffing around for my jobs." She stopped, looked me over. Bacon sizzling in the pan. Cigarette twitching. "And what is going on with you?" she said, quietly. For a second I didn't think she was speaking to me, a stage whisper for others not to hear.

"What do you mean?"

"First you look like you don't even shower, and now this whole . . . I don't know what to call it. Is this supposed to mean something?" She squinted, trying to see something not quite in focus.

"I don't know," I said. Tried to turn myself invisible the way it works with everyone else. But she wasn't fooled and I wasn't disappearing.

■ ■ ■

The summer went on that way in sort of sweaty slow motion – riding the bike, sliding into cars, hands sliding into shorts, pulling at me for something. When school started again, I felt bolder because I knew who I was. Someone who had a life outside. I had to look a certain way because that's what the guys expected, and it was a kind of confidence to play that role and be inside that person.

Some of the guys gave me pot. I tried not to smoke so much that my clothes smelled, but the cool people at school could tell. Sometimes they looked at me but they didn't talk. I'd see one of the girls about to, but then she'd stop and stay with her friends. I didn't care. It felt good to be scary to them. Fuck them.

Eva's show premiered in September and it was a hit. Suddenly she was everywhere – in TV Guide, doing interviews, talk shows. It was a detective show called *Bowman*, about a private investigator named Matt Bowman who grew up poor in the backwoods down south, and when he was a boy, he was a crack shot with a bow and arrow. Ha ha. The tagline for the show was *Matt Bowman always hits the target.* The characters were him, his beautiful, sexy assistant, the gruff, irascible police sergeant, and of course, the stern, officious DA. Eva wasn't in every show but she was in enough that she got the final title in the credits. It was one of the shows where the announcer read the actors names out loud in the opening: *"and Eva Loesch as District Attorney Margaret Lawson."* Momma said Eva was the happiest she'd ever seen. She finally had her own thing, and it looked like it was going to last. Even grandpa said so when we went up to their house for lunch. "I'm very glad. She's too talented not to have opportunities like this. I'm very happy for her. You can tell her I said that."

"I'm sure we won't," momma said.

"You can also tell her that hairdresser isn't doing her any favors," Phil said, far into his cups. "They're making it look like a *turban*, for Christ sake. People are gonna think she's hiding a gun up in that thing."

"It's only the first season," momma said. "If it gets renewed, they'll have money for better hairdressing next year."

"Hope so," Phil grumbled. "Goddamn turban."

"There, there," grandpa said, patting his knee, "I'm sure you'll survive."

But he really was happy for Eva.

10

I kept the money in a rolled up sock in the bottom drawer of my desk. I liked feeling it get thicker and heavier.

Some of the guys asked me to go places with them, and up to then I said no, it had to be in the car or somewhere close. But when some good looking guy who seemed decent asked to go to a motel or something, I said ok, but I was careful it wasn't too out of the way. The strangler hadn't strangled anyone in a while and the police thought he disappeared or moved away. Plus, they said he only went after girls. Sometimes the guy I was with was worried *I* was the strangler and I could see him watching everything I did very carefully; once we both said, at the same time, "only girls." But I did keep a Swiss Army knife in my pocket.

I liked learning what guys felt like. How their bodies moved, what they were like when they weren't putting on acts. Sitting down in their car, looking up at me on my bike, their eyes waited for me to say okay, and it seemed to open something in them. Mostly they did what I said and didn't give any trouble. Some of them acted hungry like they were never going to touch another human ever again. Some had wedding rings and looked like suburban dads; some were old or fat and it seemed like they saved up money or came from somewhere far for this one thing. What I disliked were guys who came and a second later threw you out, just blow and go. Because the best part was after you come, and there's this peace and warmth and everything feels right. The time you want to stay and feel connected, before all the bullshit comes back and fills everything up again.

■ ■ ■

The guy in the Grand Prix came back a couple of weeks later. I was on my bike, waiting at a corner near the airport. "Well, hello," he said. He was still in there with all the candy wrappers and bottles. "How have you been? You know, I've been looking high and low for you." Then he sang, "Where oh where has our little prince gone, oh where oh where can he be?" Just for that, more silence. "Cat got your tongue?"
I mean, you just had to stare at this guy.

"Well, as long as I've found you, let me state my case plain and simple." He pulled out a twenty. I shook my head, looked around to be sure no one was watching. "For your time. To hear me out." He held it out the open window. He didn't seem to have any intention to get out or get me in, so I took it, stuffed it in my shorts. "Thank you," he said. "I hope that buys me a few minutes. I've been thinking about you quite a bit since our last rendezvous. I wanted to find you again because, frankly, I believe you have something special." I stood up to start pedaling away, but he yelled, "Wait!" He pulled a card from his back pocket, held it out to me and I took it. "I own a production company here in the valley. We're always looking for new talent. *I'm* always looking for new talent. We're a legitimate operation, I promise you." Then, which I could not believe, he picked up an envelope from the seat and opened it to show me it was thick with cash. Just to fuck with him, I moved my leg on the bike seat so he could see into the shorts. His eyes went right there. "Alright then," he said, "if we're finished playing games, would you sit down with me for a few minutes to discuss a business arrangement? I'm sure there's a coffee shop nearby where we could speak." He pulled out another twenty and held it up. "For time and talk only." I sighed, said to meet at the Winchell's a couple of blocks away.

He was already inside when I got there. Standing up now, he was taller than me, but very skinny. The same pink, sweaty tank top he had on last week and these gray cotton pants. It looked like he never changed his clothes. We ordered donuts and coffee; at the table, he opened a napkin and spread it out before he put the stuff down. "A tablecloth for monsieur."

I took a donut and started eating.

"Well," he said, "isn't this nice? Much better than having to shout at the top of my lungs in a public right-of-way. And aren't you a fine looking fellow in person." He smiled this smile like it was something that he learned people do, but not something he knew how to do himself. Looking at him straight on, his eyes seemed magnified behind the gold-rimmed glasses, the lenses greasy so I couldn't tell the color. But the intensity was disconcerting, and they darted over my face, shoulders, arms. I looked at his shiny forehead, and pressed my chest against the edge of the table to control this trembling inside.

"Goodness me, you're wolfing that right down," he said. "Nice healthy appetite. Good for you." No answer out of me. "My name is Raymond," he said, but didn't extend a hand. He watched me, curious but wary, like I was some interesting animal in a cage. "And might I ask how your day is going?"

I just chewed, looking at the edge of the table where it met his stomach.

"Well, first, let me say, I don't ordinarily chase people down as I have with you. I'd only do such a thing for someone with a certain quality, a specialness . . . a *je ne sais quoi,* if you know what I mean."

I opened my mouth wide to show him the half-chewed donut.

"And as well," he went on, "the hubbub that preceded you. Here, I thought, is a young man with a built-in audience! What luck for a producer like myself. Did I mention I'm also a producer?"

Still no answer for this maroon.

"Our company is small but very agile. Production, distribution, we do it all."

I nodded, chewing.

"Well, I can see you're a man of few words, so let me get right to the point. Tell me," and he leaned forward, clasped his hands on the table, "have you considered a career in the entertainment industry?"

Now I did have to laugh. "You must be kidding. *That's* your opening line?"

He sat back, offended. "That's not a line. We're a legitimate business."

I had to shake my head, he sounded so ridiculous.

"As I've said, I respect your time . . . I'm paying you for it . . . we *are* an established company."

"Ya," I said. "So?"

"Would you mind if I asked about your background? Are you working full time? For yourself?"

I wasn't sure what he meant, but I had to look like I did, so I shrugged, like, of course.

"Well, I know a good thing when I see it. May I show you something?" He reached into a bag next to him, but the girl from the counter came by with a bucket and mop and started sloshing past us. I could smell the bleachy water. When she went around the corner, he pulled a magazine out of the bag. A nudie magazine. He put it on the table and folded the front cover over, opened to the back where there were ads up and down the side of the pages. They were small black and white pictures of good-looking guys, and blurbs about what sports they played and what they liked to do. They weren't naked, just shirts off. They looked like the handsome guys at school.

"We represent talent like this," he said. "Wholesome, athletic boys next door. Like yourself."

I snorted.

"What's funny?" he said.

"I'm not like them."

"Oh no? What are you, if I may?"

I shrugged, looking at them. "I'm just plain."

He stared a moment. "In any case, our work is very well known. Very important people buy from us." He folded the magazine so I'd only see the ads; the paper made this soft crinkling sound under his hands. "Imagine yourself right here. People all over the country, all over the world seeing you. Looking at you. Looking *for you*. Do you know what it's like to be known like that?"

They looked happy and carefree, their bodies strong and effortless.

"So, what are these?" I said. "What do you do?"

He leaned forward. "We have several lines. We do photo sets, artfully posed. We employ wonderful photographers who do very good work. And we do motion pictures. Shorts. Nothing complicated. Quick scenes one can do in an afternoon. We distribute through advertisements like this, and to theaters across the country. Our models do it for the fun, or the money, or both. And the exposure. And once you're known, well, there's no limit to what you can achieve. Or earn."

I looked at the ads. Didn't want to look at his intense little face. "I couldn't do this. No one could know."

"Goodness, there's no concern there. We're very discreet. No one sees anything except the people on our list. You can't imagine the number of young men I've helped buy a car or make a down payment on an apartment. And have a lot of fun doing it." He pulled out another magazine and pointed to another ad. "We pay on the spot, in cash, and very well. Makes things much easier. I mean, it beats pounding the pavement all day, doesn't it?"

When I sat back, I was still shivering.

"I'd have to think about it," I said.

He had this blank expression. "Well, consider the offer. You still have the card?"

I told him I did and got up.

"Would you call me when you think it over? If I'm not there you can always leave a message." I walked around the booth toward the door. "My name is Raymond," he said again, and stuck out his hand, which I avoided. "It's on the card. With the number. And call me even if you're not interested, just so I know." I was almost at the door; he had turned completely around in the seat. "We should stay in touch! I might have other opportunities!" And as I went out the door, "What's your name?"

11

There was this kid at school with a lot of pimples. His name was Christian. It was sort of painful to look at him because his face was so covered with these red bumps and pus, and he scratched them, and you could see how inflamed they were. He was also very gay. He talked with a lisp and walked pretty gay and nobody talked to him. He had longish hair in a Dorothy Hamill bowl (look it up), maybe because he thought it was stylish, or he was trying to cover his face with hair. Either way, it made him look even more gay. He walked around the school like he was in a different world from everyone else, just going about his business and no one talking to him, no one acknowledging he existed. Maybe that's why he talked to me. Because I could see him.

He started at lunch. I was sitting alone, reading some book, and he sat down at the long table across from me. Not directly across, but two seats away. He asked for the salt and I slid it over. Then what I was reading. I lifted the book, showed him the cover, went back to reading. Then, Is it good? And I had two choices. I could get up and walk away or I could answer. All the other kids got up and walked away from him. It seemed too cruel to do that, but at the same time, this was the gay kid nobody talked to. I sighed, said it was okay but not great. How come, he wanted to know. I told him, in a few words. So we had a conversation, even though his distance from me gave us cover. People would see us far enough apart and wouldn't think we were speaking.

Another time he saw me at a 7-Eleven and talked to me again. No one from school was around so I answered. And then another conversation.

And somehow we ended up being strange friends, as in, we would talk, but only when no one was watching: at the far end of the football field, in an empty classroom, very far after school. We exchanged phone numbers and talked at home sometimes. Since he sounded so gay, when he called, Alicia would call me, dangle the phone by the cord and let it swing, tilt her head to the side. I just grabbed it from her.

Christian and I lived in two different types of banishment. I was a mystery and I scared the other kids, but he was invisible and they didn't care about him at all. So he could sit near other people and since they didn't regard him as a person, he could listen to them talk. One time we met at a park with a kids' play area. We sat on a mini merry-go-round, the round plastic thing with four seats and a pole in the middle, and the round thing spins around the pole. As we talked, we moved the seat slowly around with our feet.

He said, "You know those two girls, Astrid and Bonnie? They were talking about you."

"Oh yeah? What did they say?"

"They thought you were cute."

"They did not say that."

"Yes they did. They were talking about guys in the class, and some other girl said your name and they said that. But they also said you were Paul Lynde's boyfriend."

"*What?* The guy on the Hollywood Squares?"

"Yeah. They said you were his boyfriend and you live with him and just come here for school." He turned red under his pimples, but he thought it was hilarious.

"That's funny," I said.

"I think they like you. I mean, the way they were saying it."

"That's funny," I said again.

What was good about Christian was he didn't talk a whole lot. You could just sit with him and do nothing and he didn't mind. Sometimes when we weren't saying anything, I would look at him. It was too bad he had all the pimples. He had a nice face and nice eyes and pretty lips.

Without all the pustules, he might have been ok. Looking at me directly, he said, "They're right. You are cute."

"Don't start." He just smiled and let it go.

I liked the handsome guys in cars, and I picked the ones I would go with, because they were sexy and desirable. Christian wasn't either of those, but he was easy to be with. And sometimes I thought maybe I'm wrong, maybe I should respond or give him something. We still didn't let anyone know we were friends, and I didn't want to kiss his pimply face.

There was a Wherehouse records we went to in Northridge. Christian's parents had a huge record collection and he knew all about music, so he told me what records to get for myself. He didn't have much money, so sometimes I bought one I knew he liked and gave it to him. And we were there one afternoon, looking in one of the bins, and across from us was this girl from school, a freshman or something. She looked up at us, looked down, tried not to show it. Looking at me really, not Christian. Finally she got the courage to ask if I went to North Hollywood and I said yes. She was nervous and giggling and kind of cute. We talked a little, then her mother came over with another lady. They seemed very charmed the girl was chatting with me, all smiles and kindness. The girl told them I went to her school, and the mother asked what my name was and I told her. The other lady looked at me, then leaned over and said something into the mother's ear and her smile disappeared. She put her hand around her daughter's arm and pulled her away to another part of the store. The other lady looked at me a hard second longer and went with them.

Christian thought it was funny. We joked about it, and went on looking through the bins. But after that, he must have found something out because he didn't talk to me anymore. When I saw him in school he averted his eyes, like everyone did to him. I thought about calling or going to his house, but I certainly wasn't going to chase after *Christian*, that pimply loser.

So fuck him. Fuck all of them.

12

I found that guy's card in a pair of dirty pants.

"Who?" he said, when I called from a payphone.

"From the donut store." Silence a moment, him repeating in a whisper to himself. "Oh yes, of course. Wonderful. How are you?"

I held the phone close to my face, covered the mouthpiece. I told him I was ready to talk.

"Superb!" he said, and gave me an address to meet him at. It was up in the hills, so I had to walk the bike halfway there. Which was good because it gave me time to think.

These guys can be weird. You have to keep aware, keep hands away from where you don't want them. At the same time, he's paying me to perform, and he should get some value for his money. You have to be a team player. Plus, I wasn't afraid of this guy. He was such a goon, I knew I could handle him.

When I got there, it was an ordinary brown wood house, like a cabin. The front faced the driveway, the back extended over the canyon on stilts. A Jeep was parked in the driveway next to the Grand Prix. I knocked on the door and the guy answered, smudged glasses and all. "Heavens to Betsy, I thought you bailed on us."

"No, it just took longer because I had to ... well, it just took longer."

"Well, no worse for wear. Come in, come in."

It looked like some kind of hippy pad inside, everything brown, orange and wood, with macrame plant hangers and ivy dripping over. Paintings of sunsets, an Indian praying to a horse flying into an orange sky. It smelled like stale incense over stale marijuana and cat piss.

"Glorious day, isn't it?" he said, and led me out to the deck. It over-looked this canyon and all the little houses sitting around and below us. It's really quiet in these canyons, so different from the valley. The silence seems to stop time. He pulled a plastic bag from his pocket, and inside it, a rolled-up tinfoil. Inside the tinfoil, some joints. He offered me one and pulled a lighter from another pocket. I smoked it and handed it back. "Oh no," he said, "must remain clear headed. I'm the technician today, *you're* the star." I scowled at him but the word seeped in. "Well," he said, "you look fine, just fine. So it's photographs we're doing, is that it?" He seemed to want me to answer, nod at least, and I did. "Lovely. Just some candid shots, I think. Nothing very elaborate. I only brought a camera, so we'll have to wing it with natural light. Will that work for you?"

He offered drinks and food but I couldn't have gotten anything down. I waited for the come-on, the flirty talk that would lead to the sex, but he didn't seem to be going there.

"Over on the sofa, I think, to start please."

I went over and sat there, with my jacket on. He lifted the camera and watched me for a moment. I looked at him, then looked away, pretended he wasn't there. "That's good," he said, and started snapping. "Turn your head a bit so I can see which side favors the light." He snapped away, stop-ping every once in a while and looking, pondering. "How about the jacket off now, yes?" I took it off and sat with my hands together. "Very nice. But it looks like you're waiting for the bus. How about putting your feet on the sofa and losing the shoes?" And I did that, and he snapped a bit more. "Very nice."

He asked a bunch of questions while he shot, dumb stuff to loosen you up. He stepped closer and reached for my pants. I pulled back. "I'm sorry," he said. "I thought we could just . . . open the top button a bit . . ."

"I'll do it," I said.

"I didn't mean to spook you."

"You didn't spook me. Just tell me what you want and I'll do it."

"Of course. You know, from what I recall, you have a very nice physique. Are you an athlete? A surfer or something?"

"Is that what they want?"

"Who?"

"The people who look at your pictures."

"Why don't you let me worry about that."

I lay my head over the back of the sofa.

"Did you grow up in the area? You a valley boy?"

"I've been around," I said.

"Around! Goodness. You don't look old enough to have been *around*. Not an old buzzard like me. Now I have been around."

"You don't say?"

"I do say," he said. "I do indeed."

"So, do you do a lot of these?"

"Photo shoots? Oh my yes." He kept snapping. "We're one of the oldest companies in the business. I actually started in retail, you know. Department store advertising. Photos of refrigerators and televisions. Very arousing, let me tell you. But then, when I was working for a mail-order catalog, I realized the potential in customer outreach. The power of a mailing list. The ability to offer people anywhere in the world something they might like. And I discovered we have a lot of things people might like right here in California. All it took was to put the two ideas together."

"So now you have this business?"

"I do," he said. I had already unbuttoned my shirt. I listened for the camera clicks and his breathing, which both seemed to come faster.

"That's awfully nice," he said. "I think we can lose the pants now, if you don't mind." I did. "You seem to have an intuition. You know right where the light is. Have you done this before?"

I shook my head.

"You know," he said, kneeling down, "I think these will come out very nicely. I think, for a test, these will be excellent. Of course I won't know until they're developed. But we have a very good lab. They work miracles. And we've needed it, let me tell you, with some of our models."

"Why's that?"

"Oh, a million things. Bad angles, acne, horrific tattoos. Gruesome scars you don't see until the clothes come off."

"Like what?"

"Oh, one fellow I recall. Had this huge indent . . . a hole really, in front, just above his left hip. Apparently one of his parents had shot him when he was very young. With a rifle, no less. Point blank range. He said he lost a few things, some organs and whatnot. But, my lord, I wouldn't have believed it if I hadn't seen it with my own eyes. A gaping hole in his abdomen, grown over with skin, like a cave."

"You took pictures of that guy?"

"Oh yes. Aside from the hole, he was very good looking. We had to cover it with props and clothing of course, but otherwise you'd never know."

"What happened to him?"

"I have no idea." The clicking continued.

"But you didn't see him again? I mean, he just disappeared?"

"Oh, a lot of them do. It's a tough business. The models come to me with all sorts of backgrounds. Some are reliable and we use them on a regular basis. Others are just in town on their way somewhere else. Some just disappear and there's no way to know what happened to them."

"But that guy. Could he eat and stuff? Like normal?"

He put the camera down. "I probably shouldn't have mentioned it at all. You asked about some unusual circumstances so I told you. I'm not the public services agency, you know. I pay good money for services rendered. Anything else is none of my business." He stopped and gave me a hard stare. "Look, I can't shoot this face."

"What face?"

"This judgment face. Let me tell you, that was good money I paid that young man, and the only money he'd seen in a while."

The energy had drained out of the room. I gave him a pouty face and pulled the front of my underwear a little. His eyes went there. He considered a moment, took a long breath, then lifted the camera and started again.

"It's just business," he said. "You should learn that straight away. You do good work and you get paid. And I can't think of anything more honest than paying people for the services they provide. I paid that fellow well, and whatever happened to him after that is no business of mine. And that's the only advice I have for you, my lad. Be sure and get paid. There are unscrupulous people in this industry who don't mean what they say. Unsavory people. They'd be out looking for someone like you. Like I said, you're something special. Not some trollop off Santa Monica Boulevard."

"Is that where you found him?"

"I don't recall. Possibly. Anyway, that's neither here nor there. Let's stay focused on the present, shall we?"

I thought about asking him what he was going to do with these pictures but I didn't care. He said it was just a test. After a while, he stopped, put the camera down.

"I think it's about time for the main course." He nodded at the underwear.

Once more, the sick feeling. And here it is, the doorway. This guy is taking pictures, and once they take pictures it's permanent. You're on someone else's pieces of paper, and you can't get them back. But I looked around at this dumb brown room, and the pot made me calm, and this guy was a weirdo, and who knows if this is all bullshit. And I could be scared and invisible my whole life, or I could be something, a real person. So I looked into his lens and his glasses and did what he asked. Did the poses he wanted, and did them exactly; gave him the finish he wanted, and it felt like nothing, like being inside a tube, taking directions from some voice out there.

When it was done, he gave me a towel and showed me where the bathroom was. I came out and he was putting equipment back in his bag. He seemed awkward and didn't look at me. His hands were shaking.

"Was that ok?"

"Absolutely," he said, to the bag. "You're remarkably easy to work with."

I waited another moment while he futzed around. He didn't seem to know what to do. Then he said, "Oh," and pulled out his wallet. Handed me a bunch of money. "I hope that will do." I didn't count it but it looked like a lot. Standing this close to him, I could smell his musty closet smell, his eyes watching me. We stood a moment, that close, and any fear I had was gone. Even though he was taller than me, I felt we were looking eye to eye.

"I'd like to be able to contact you when the shots are developed." I said no. "Well, how about a name? You can't begrudge me a name after all this now, can you?"

I stared at him. And wondered. What does he want? What do they all want?

"Kevin," I said.

His face broke out with this look of incredible pleasure and relief.

We said our goodbyes outside. I had hidden the bike behind a tree, so I watched as he backed the Grand Prix out, dust rising from the gravel into a cloud as he turned onto the street and drove away. I watched the cloud for a moment, listening to the quiet up here once more.

13

The second week of January, Eva asked me to help on the show. They were filming spring episodes now, with a good chance of getting renewed. One of the guests on that episode was a handsome dark-haired guy who was very tall and tan. He came up to me while I was standing at the craft services table. "What are you, the page boy?"

"Grandson. But assistant too."

"Aha. Double duty," he said and winked. The next day I made sure to wear my tightest jeans.

Eva only had one scene in that episode and another actor was out sick so they reshuffled what they were supposed to shoot. She and I sat on our folding chairs behind the cameras; the handsome actor sat across the stage from us, giving me these heavy-lidded looks every couple of minutes. I had one ear open for what Eva said, the other aware of him. Eva said something, and I didn't quite hear. Sounded like *earning.*

"What?" I said.

"What does it mean?"

"Making money?"

"No, *yearning.* It says it here. She looks at him with a sense of *yearning.*" She pointed to a line in the script. "Evidently Margaret and this fellow had a thing once upon a time. When he leaves her office, I'm supposed to look at him like that."

"Who?"

She tilted her head toward the man across the stage. "Mister bedroom eyes over there. He's a little young for Margaret, if you ask me, but I guess they need to spice things up for the blue hairs. Can you believe this clown with his polyester shirts? I'd have thought they'd find a classier beau for the old gal."

I shrugged. "I think he's ok."

"Well help me. You're the assistant, so assist. What does it mean?"

"I don't know," I said. "Wanting?"

"No, more than that. Wanting. Waiting. Hoping." She mouthed some words to herself, tried out different postures. "It's very odd. Margaret doesn't do much by way of asking anyone for anything. She's an independent kind of person, which is why I like her. Tell me, what do you yearn for?"

"I'm sorry?"

"I need a cue here. If this was a youthful fling, I need some kind of a story. You're youthful, what do you yearn for?"

"I don't know. Money? A car?"

"Those are just things, not what you yearn for." She stuck her chin out, trying to think of something. "Like leaning . . ." she said to herself. "Leaning. Learning. Wanting. Desiring something . . ." I thought of the photographer staring the other day. "*Looks at him with a sense of yearning*," she went on. "A fling . . . an experience . . . a youthful indiscretion . . ."

Now I did have an idea and started to say it, but stopped. She leaned down to her purse on the floor and pulled out a cigarette. When she sat up, she was smiling. "It's alright, you can say it," she said, and lit the cigarette. "I know you see them. Still in Bel-Air, in that hokey plantation?" I nodded. "Well, gold star for you. You're right. Dumb things you do when you're young."

She smoked in silence. I felt us in that half-real space again, inside this cavernous stage, waiting to be called to perform, or not. Talking to the person next to you, but not.

"What do they say about me?"

Had to stall here. "What?"

"Come on, you heard me."

"I don't know. I don't remember."

"Oh, Harris, you're not a good liar at all. I'm not afraid to talk with you about this. You don't air family grievances around children, but you're an adult now, and I'm sure you understand the complexities. What do they say?"

"Well, grandpa said he was happy for you, about the show and all."

"Did he? How many whiskey sours led up to that?" I did have to laugh. "Be careful," she said, "Those two get commission from Alcoholics Anonymous. What else did they say?"

"He wanted us to tell you that you should have had more chances" – she flinched on *us*; she knew we were all there – "and that they didn't know what to do with you in the old days."

"Well, that is true. It's all about types, and I didn't fit into one. Some of the idiotic things I did to please the bosses. You have to take a certain amount of crap. And the crap I took from that man." The way she shook her head made it feel to me like a cue.

"He was very sorry. He said if he caused things to happen . . ."

"If he caused things to happen!" she said, and someone nearby shushed her. "If he caused things to happen," she said, softer. "You've never met anyone so clever and diabolical . . . who could make so much mayhem when he wanted to. *Caused* things to happen! Jesus, Charlie, that's an understatement."

"He told me some things he did that were bad."

"I'll bet. Whatever you heard was the sanitized version. Anything else?"

To be honest, I didn't know what I should say. How much he wanted me to say and how much I was allowed to say. But the Eva talking to me now seemed different. In this on-set waiting space, we weren't related; I was a colleague and what you do with colleagues is be honest.

"He said he was sorry . . . he said that you changed, afterward. If it was his fault . . . he remembered you . . ."

The posture behind her face seemed to adjust, just the slightest.

"Well, that's very charitable," she said, and took a slow puff. "Nice to be analyzed and dissected in front of your grandchildren."

"He didn't mean it that way."

"You shouldn't be in the position of defending him. *I'm* your family. *I* took care of you. And your mother and your sister." But still, she seemed to think about it. Not denying, just digesting. "That's some nerve. *Changed*. Well, tell me this," she said, "do you think there are things you don't come back from? Things that change you so you can't go back to being the trusting soul you used to be?"

"Yes," I said, seriously.

"So, there you are. That's some nerve. Sticking the knife in, then complaining you're not the sunny girl he remembered." She caught my eye then, as if looking for something familiar. Then she tamped the cigarette on the floor. "You know, I think we ought to get back to the point here. We were talking about Margaret and what *she's* doing. What does she want?"

"Uhm, she likes the guy?" I said, switching the gear, "she remembers the guy, she wants the guy . . ."

"Nah, that's not enough."

"Maybe she thinks he's hot."

"Oh, Harris, please. Mister greaseball over there?"

I looked back and didn't see him at first. Then I saw he had moved against the back wall so that my body blocked Eva's view of him. He was looking directly at me, his fingertip moving slowly up and down his fly.

"Uh, Nana, I have to go to the bathroom."

"Fine," she said, paging through the script. "I'll figure it out myself. Maybe he had a dog she liked."

In the bathroom stall, he tore my pants down. I couldn't wait to get him inside me. He couldn't either. It was fast, hard, breathing, electric. Like real life, like how I hoped life would be.

Back at the folding chair, Eva coughed and waved the air. "My God, you smell like a perfume truck. What happened to you?"

"I think someone broke a bottle of cologne or something in the bathroom."

"Uccchh," she said, waving me away. "Go wash up. My god, death by Prince Matchabelli."

Later, when they finally did the scene and the two of them were standing close together on the set, I saw her turn and look at me. I don't know how she could see me in the dark, behind the lights, but it felt like she looked right at me.

14

So I really was curious and I called the photographer. He said to meet him at a diner on Saturday.

This was a diner like all the others, a long counter with stools, cushy booths along the front windows with brown and orange seats. The hostess gave us the once-over – this twitchy looking older guy and a scruffy kid, two people who don't look like they go together – and said, "Counter or table?"

"Table, dear, if you please," Ray said. "We have important business to discuss." She took us to the farthest booth at the end. "Capitol!" he said. When she was gone, he turned to me. "Well, *Kevin*. I've been so looking forward to hearing from you. I was afraid you'd gone AWOL on us. Such a mystery! No one has seen you in weeks."

I picked up a menu and glared at him over the top. Looked around this restaurant to be sure no one I knew was here.

"I wanted to tell you the photos came out just dandy. Everyone loves them."

The waitress came and brought waters. "Need some time with the menu?" She was older, and smiling. I like diner waitresses.

"Yes, dear, that would be fine," he said. "Start out with a cup of tea, if you don't mind, and a slice of lemon on the side."

"Doesn't that sound refreshing," she said, writing it down. "Right on that. Anything for you honey?" I shook my head. She waited a second, watching me carefully, then, still smiling, walked away. I looked through the menu and decided on a picture of an omelet with the Eiffel Tower behind it.

"Well, what a glorious day it is, especially getting to see you again," he said. "Naturally, this is on us. Expense account, you know!" He seemed so chipper and goony, it made me feel kind of queasy. He was prattling on, and I must have zoned out, because there was a silence after he said, ". . . so how have you been?"

"Uhm, ok," I said, into the plastic-coated pages.

"I must tell you, you have a fine relationship with the camera. The shots attest to that."

I shrugged, didn't look at him. Just turned the pages, looking at dishes with pictures of the coliseum, the Leaning Tower of Pisa, the Empire State Building. He was going on about photography and people he knew. I tuned it out, scrunching lower into the seat. ". . . and so," he said, "I suppose you could call me a jack-of-all trades . . . or a jack-*off*-all trades," giggling, "and that's about the long and the short it. And right now, perhaps, I'm sitting across from our next chapter." A pause. "What do you think?"

"Yeah, maybe."

He moved around in his seat. "You know, *Kevin.* Our talent usually demonstrate a bit more enthusiasm about working with us. You seem a circumspect young man, which is wonderful, but at the same time, you're the one who called me, and I rearranged my schedule to meet you. So I must admit, I'm not entirely clear on your motivation. Do you have an interest in working with us or not?"

"Yeah. Maybe."

The waitress put the tea in front of him. Despite her smile she seemed deliberate in her movements, watching us carefully. "Are we ready to order?" He told her what he wanted, with about five substitutions. I asked for the omelet and she smiled, holding for a second, but I think he picked up on it and said, *"Thanks,"* very curt, and she nodded and walked away. He considered me a long moment.

"Well, as I said, you take to modeling very naturally. Tell me, how does that come about?"

"I don't know. No one even sees me."

"What do you mean? You're very photogenic."

"No, I'm not. I'm ugly."

"Goodness, what to thing to say. You alluded to something similar when we spoke before. Could you elaborate on what you mean?"

"I'm invisible. People only see me when they want to. Or they're desperate. I'm nobody's first choice."

"I see," he said, and took a sip of tea. "Who is everybody's first choice?"

"I don't know. Those guys in your ads. Big blond guys."

"Well, that's certainly a type. But there are others too." He stirred his tea. "So those are your type? Big blond fellows?"

"Not really. I don't have a type. They're just . . . the ones everyone likes."

"And just so I understand, you're *not* the one everyone likes?"

I was about to say more, but someone came up to our table, a tall man who plopped himself onto the seat next to me. "Fucking hell Ray, you couldn't find someplace harder to get to?"

"I'm sorry Ozzie," Ray said. "I was trying to accommodate everyone."

"Well not me, that's for sure. And what's so fucking important you had to call me out on a Saturday?"

"I wanted you to meet someone very special."

The guy turned away from the booth. He was big and his twisting moved the seat like it wasn't attached. "Hey!" he yelled at the waitress, "some service please?" He turned back to us. "Yeah, ok, fine. So, who?"

I hadn't turned to look at him. I slid toward the window, trying to shrink into it. "This is the young man I was telling you about," Ray said. "From the shoot at Eddie's a few weeks ago. I showed you the contact sheets."

The guy looked at me. He was tall and it felt like he was looking down from a tower. He seemed very white and doughy, and he talked very bitchy. He turned to Ray and let out a breath. "Oh god. Not this again."

"Did you look at the proofs?" Ray said.

The waitress came and he asked for coffee and then he actually waved her away with the back of his hand. "Tell me you didn't get me all the way here out here for this."

To me, Ray said, "This is Ozzie, my chief cinematographer. He knows everything about the business. I'd be nowhere without him. Ozzie, this is a very promising young man I am sure . . ." but Ozzie put his hand up and shushed him.

"Give me your wallet," he said to me.

"Huh?"

"Give me your fucking wallet."

I pulled it out and gave it to him; he pulled out my driver's license, looked at it, rotated his wrist to show Ray, then slid it back and gave me the wallet back. "Uh huh," he said. "Every goddamn time, Ray."

"It's called talent cultivation. All the studios do it."

Ozzie picked up the menu, shaking his head. "You stupid prick."

"Well, let's not get bogged down with details. I just wanted you to meet this talented young man and welcome him into the family."

"Listen," Ozzie said, pointing a long finger at Ray, "I am not getting in trouble again over some trashy hustler you've fallen in love with this week. Or whatever the fuck *this* is. For Christ sake, Ray, what are you thinking?"

"Please excuse Ozzie," Ray said to me. "His talent, I assure you, is inversely proportional to his bad manners. And his bark is not as bad as his bite."

"Both backwards. But you got the last one right."

"Well, why don't we put business on hold for now and just enjoy a nice lunch, shall we? Now, uh, Harris . . . may I call you that?"

I nodded.

"Harris is a local boy, a valley boy if I'm not mistaken. And Ozzie, we know how popular they are." He shook his head. "And a very cagey young man. Rather hard to pin down. Tell us, Harris, what is it like to grow up here? Both Ozzie and I are transplants to California."

"It's nothing. Just like any other place."

"Oh no it's not," Ray said. "This is paradise. Especially compared to cold, miserable Michigan. What a haven it is to find a place like this with delights such as you, just hanging off the trees, ripe for the picking."

Now Ozzie and I laughed at the same time.

"I'm not joking," Ray said. "The two of you. I'm very serious. Why, drive down any street, any time of the day, and what do you find? Beautiful, sensual creatures, luxuriating under the sun. Nothing like it anywhere in the world. Beauty on every street corner."

"Whatever floats your boat," Ozzie said.

"Do tell us more about yourself, Harris. Obviously, you're an entrepreneurial young man. How does one so young come by such confidence?"

"I don't," I said.

"Savvy negotiating skills. Why just look, you've maneuvered two crusty old crones like us into a corner and hardly lifted a finger. I'd call that ingenuity."

Now I did feel my cheeks go red. "I'm not doing anything."

"Tell us a bit more. Do you have a girlfriend? Boyfriend? *Sugar daddy?*" I guess he thought that was funny, but I shrank further into the corner.

"Try another tack," Ozzie said dryly.

"Well then, what makes someone like you tick? You have an awfully cagey disposition. Makes it rather enticing to want to peel back the layers." He was staring at me through the lenses with this confident, alert expression, but behind it, a desperation.

"I'm just a person."

"Yes, I can see that. Well then, tell us what you look for. What turns you on? What *excites* you?"

"Professionalism," I said, evenly.

"How interesting. Could you say more?"

"I think you should be good at your job. You should be professional. Show up on time and not make a big deal about things."

"Well, that is certainly true. It is good to be professional. And are you?"

"Yes. But I need more discipline."

"You do?" Ray said, intrigued. "Well, in that case . . ." But Ozzie snapped his fingers in his face. "Leave it alone, will you? You're making a fool of yourself." He tilted his head in my direction. "Just let it go."

After the waitress brought the food, Ozzie looked at me really for the first time. I guess he figured I was there to stay. "Well anyway," he said, "pleased to meet you," and gave me a half-hearted handshake. "But if you want to use him," he said to Ray, "he's gotta pop more. Lift some weights, grow a mustache or something. I mean, honestly."

"Not everyone has to be one of the great big beasts you're so fond of," Ray said, and winked at me. "Some of us have more refined tastes." Ozzie sighed. "Now Harris," Ray said, "if we're going to have any working relationship, I do need a way of contacting you. I can't go on scouring the streets hoping to stumble upon you by chance."

I shook my head.

"You still have my card?" He went to pull another but I had the first one and pulled it out. The address was a long one on Burbank Boulevard. In gold italics at the top, *Nu-Man Productions,* and below it, *Raymond Cicero, Producer Director.*

"Will you?" he said.

"What?"

"Call me. This is a lucrative proposal. You have no idea the people who buy from us, the people on our customer list. Big names. Names that would make your ears fall off. The opportunities, Harris. They're limitless." He was about as convincing as a cartoon wolf with dollars signs in its eyeballs. But I listened.

Ozzie gave him a hard look over his coffee cup.

"Well then," Ray said, "we'll just leave it there for now."

■ ■ ■

I found it was helpful if you had a prop. That way, guys could tell you were looking and not just a person walking down the street. I found an old set of bulky headphones and carried them in my right hand, which was enough of a signal. And I had them with me, kneeling down to tie my shoelace, when I heard a car pull up. I began to stand up slowly to give the guy a good look, and when I did, it was Mrs. Harmon in her station wagon. She had a Vista Cruiser, one of those long wagons with windows along the top and wood on the sides. She stared right at me.

"Do you need a ride?" It sounded like a command. I dropped my cigarette, but not fast enough, and kicking it away drew her attention to it. "Get in and I'll take you."

On the way, she looked straight ahead. "Kev says he hasn't seen you in a long time."

"We're not really . . . well, we haven't hung out in a while. I think he has different friends now."

"He says he never sees you at school."

"I'm there. We probably have different classes."

She didn't ask anything more. When we stopped in front of my house, she pulled the transmission hard into Park. "Here you are," she said. I got out and leaned in to say thanks, but she kept looking straight ahead and drove away.

Oh boy, I thought. Here's some shit.

■ ■ ■

In the meantime ...

I thought about the things Ray said, especially about not walking around the streets all the time. In the beginning it had been really hot, but now it was starting to get tired. And the part about the magazines. Being one of the handsome guys on the side of the pages. It didn't seem possible that I could be one of those people, but since Ray really wanted a Kevin, I realized that guy could do it. That guy would like to do it.

I called and he said to meet him at his office. Which was hard to find, because it was this anonymous stucco storefront painted dark orange like all the other storefronts on Burbank Boulevard. It was the kind of block where people were doing things they didn't want anyone to know about. I found the right number and there was only a bell with *NM Productions* on a dymo label.

Ray opened the door, poked his head out, looking either way.

"It's just me," I said.

"Well, come in, come in."

He hustled me in and closed the door. "Welcome to our little empire. The nerve center, as it were."

It took a minute to get used to the dark. The place was broken up into two parts. The front, which looked like it used to be a hardware store, was where he had the desks; two picture windows were painted opaque dark orange so you couldn't see in from the street. The back, which used to be a storeroom, had long folding tables and packing materials. No one was working that day, and the tables were stacked with rolls of paper and bubble wrap, two large boxes stuffed with unopened envelopes beside them. "Orders," he said, and poked through them. "This is just one week's worth. I have the crew in on Mondays and Wednesdays, but at this rate, I'll have to bring them on full time."

I was kind of surprised actually. It looked like some dumpy office you would see anywhere: old office furniture with green vinyl seats and metal desks, on the walls only faded travel posters and clipboards. Something odd about there being nothing at all to show what was made here.

"Well now," he said, "what can we do for the mystery man? I was concerned we'd scared you off."

"Nah," I said.

He was quiet then, and I felt self-conscious. He looked at me, his eyebrows up, waiting for me to tell him what I wanted. There was a ratty green sofa against the wall. I slumped onto it, kind of loose, and let my legs fall apart. His eyes went right there.

"Would you like some refreshment?" he asked. "I have Cokes in the back."

I said sure and he said, "Back in a jif." When he came back, he handed me the Coke, rolled an office chair from behind the desk, and positioned it in front of me. "So," he said, "what game are we playing today?"

"I don't know. I just thought about ... what we talked about."

"About working with us?"

"Maybe."

"You know Harris, I have to say, you are an absolute master of ambiguity. I wonder, do you even know what you want?"

I had to shrug.

"Thought not. You know, everyone in this business knows exactly what they want. Money, money, money, sex, sex, sex. And I provide as much of each as I can. But I can't read you at all."

I shrugged again, spread my legs a little more. I could see he wanted to go for it, but at the same time he didn't. He moved around on his seat uncomfortably. It felt weird and exhilarating. Here was this guy with this whole business, these movies and magazines ads, and I had nothing except what was between my legs, but it felt like we were negotiating, that I had something to bargain with, and he wanted whatever it was.

He stood up slowly and walked toward me. He started to reach for my pants but I shook my head, said, "uh uh." He pulled back like I'd stabbed him, but he didn't take his eyes away. I started to unzip my fly.

"Let me get my camera," he said, breathlessly.

When he came back he started snapping away. He didn't have to tell me what to do, I knew exactly what he wanted now. He walked all around, and the snap of the shutter, the zip of the film winding after each shot, let something loose. I could hear him gasping and breathing heavy, and even though he didn't touch me, it felt like something connected and intimate. When it was done, we were both sweaty and catching our breath inside this dark orange room.

"My god," he said, and slumped into a chair. I didn't look at his pants, only his face, and the look he was giving me. Desire, satisfaction, hope. Something else.

15

Eva was friends with Merv Griffin. He'd had her on his show over the years, and they knew each other socially, but now that she was a big hit in *Bowman*, he gave her the full star treatment. His show was on in the afternoon, and momma, Alicia and I came home to watch it.

She got a huge welcome and came out like a victory lap, waving to the cheering audience. Merv gave her a kiss and a big hug.

"So," he said, when they sat down, "you've been discovered."

"*Re*-covered is more like it," she said. "Like an old sofa."

Big laugh.

"Well, the old sofa's doing just fine," he said. "You're at, what, number one, number two this week?"

"It's up there. I'm not sure exactly."

"And people are really taking to the show. It's something else, isn't it?"

"It certainly is. It's so good, and James of course, who's a wonderful man. Good writing, good directing. I'm very lucky to be part of it."

"But in a sense, this isn't anything new. You've been working steadily, haven't you? I mean, you never stopped."

"I have, Merv, yes. I've been doing films and television, commercials, really, all my life. I've been here all along, folks."

"Well, it's good to have you back. Now, let's talk about your career, shall we? You were with, what was it, Columbia, when you started?"

Alicia said, "This is boring. I've heard this all before." She got up and left. Momma shrugged and left too, but I stayed, lying on the floor.

"…and now jumping ahead," Merv said, "you did a big Technicolor musical …"

"Yes, *A Knight for a Night.* That was much later."

"That was what, nineteen fifty-four?"

"Fifty-eight, I think, when it came out."

"Was that a departure for you?" Merv asked.

"It was. I thought it was time for some comedy. I'd never done anything so outright slapstick like that, and I got the chance to work with Red Skelton. And singing and dancing."

"People still love it," Merv said. "They sing the songs."

"I know! Isn't that remarkable."

"Was it tough to do all that hoofing? If memory serves, you're doing a lot of jumping and pratfalls. Was that you or a stuntman?"

"Oh, that was all me. I was black and blue after *that* picture."

". . . and you came up with all that physical comedy. You and the director?"

"Yes, mostly, though I had some . . . well, I got some advice on how to do some of the routines. They were quite bawdy. We had someone who'd done burlesque sorts of things onstage."

"Why am I picturing people rolling around like bowling balls?"

"Oh yes, that was quite a bit. We had this musical number that was just falling flat. We needed something to punch it up, and someone came up with this idea. He said, look, we have me dressed up in these big, ridiculous hoop skirts, we have wizards and magicians, we've got a bunch of . . . not munchkins, but, uh, little people, midgets . . . and he said, let's throw it all together and see what happens. So, he had these little people come shooting out from under the hoop skirt, one after another."

"You mean … as if they were coming out of …"

She nodded, like, of course.

"Goodness," Merv said. "Was that difficult to pull off?"

"Not for me. All I had to do was stand there with my legs . . . well, in a wide stance. But the poor actors, they had to curl up tight, then these other fellows behind me, out of sight, kicked them out like cannon balls."

"That seems a bit risqué for 1958."

"Oh, sure. They had censors then, people on set who'd watch what you were doing. They were appalled. They told us to take it out, but we thought it would get a big laugh. And it did. Still does, when you see it in reruns."

"Who came up with that, the director?"

"You know, I can't recall."

She leaned down and took a sip from the coffee on the side table. She told me once you need a bluff prop, a thing you can waste time with to stop the action and let something land. By now I was thinking there was something strange about this interview. I knew how Eva liked to tell stories, but this was not one of them. It seemed like she was playing the part of someone on a talk show telling a story, but she was doing it for a specific purpose.

"Now, you're still in Beverly Hills, aren't you?" Merv asked.

"I am. Not a big fan of moving around. I'm still on the maps, I think, although most people know me now from the coffee . . ."

"Ah yes, Helga."

". . . so I don't get a lot of tour bus traffic. Which is fine by me."

"And your family is in the area?"

"They are. My son is in Washington but my daughter lives here, in the valley, with my granddaughter and my grandson."

A shot of something in my stomach.

Merv leaned forward and spoke in a lower, more gravelly tone. "Now, it was surprising nothing big came your way after *A Knight for a Night*. And then your marriage came to an end after that, didn't it?"

And now I sat up. I couldn't believe he would blindside her with a question like that. But she was calm and unruffled.

"Yes, it did," she said. She uncrossed her legs then crossed them the other way. "Robert and I had met soon after . . ."

". . . Robert Cole, the actor . . ."

". . . yes . . . soon after I began in the early forties. But by the time the Knight picture came along, we'd had two wonderful children and a good number of years together."

"That must have been hard, coming when it did."

"It was. But it was a mutual decision. The right thing for both of us."
She picked up her coffee and took a long, slow sip.

"And you two are still friends?"

"Oh, of course." She re-crossed her legs.

I stayed for the rest of the show but all they talked about after that was
diets and makeup. It still seemed strange, though, that she let him ask her
all those personal questions in front of a live studio audience. And that
she answered them.

16

I rang the bell at Ray's office and a guy who looked like a Teamster opened the door. Behind him, a bunch of guys in the back were sealing boxes with tape. He said Ray was out but to come back in a couple of hours. When I did, he opened the door himself. "What a pleasant surprise. Dexter told me you came by."

"Do they work for you?"

"Yes and no. Some of the fellows do machine work next door. They repair pumps and motors. When things are slow, they pitch in and help fill orders. They just don't look at the merchandise. You know – they have calendars over there with big titty girls in short shorts, holding wrenches. More their sort of thing."

We sat in his front office, him at the green metal desk, me on the ratty sofa. He had a bunch of papers and a desk lamp on. "So, what brings you around, young man?" He spoke in this chipper tone of voice, I guess, his attitude when there were Teamsters around.

"Nothing much. Just bored."

"Well, that's unfortunate. Though I imagine par for the course. Bleak midwinter and all. Not much I can do for you, I'm afraid. Bookkeeping is my life this time of day."

I stretched out on the sofa, put my arms over my head. Ray looked at me over his glasses, nodded toward the men in the back. I got it. No sexy bunny bullshit.

"But you know," he said, and took off the glasses and pinched his nose. He looked like a turtle without its shell. "We still haven't given you a proper test on moving film. Judging by the reaction to the photos, we'd make big bank with a loop or two." I wasn't sure what he meant. "A movie," he said. "A short. You paired off with someone else, or even a solo."

I didn't want to do any more than we already did. Right now this seemed like a secret I could manage, with this one weird guy that no one else knew about. "Well, it's there when you want it," he said, and went back to his paperwork.

He had one of those calculators with a roll of white paper. He could type numbers in with his right hand without looking, and keep entering numbers from a ledger book as the tape rolled out inch after inch. He didn't seem to want anything from me and didn't ask me to leave, so I lay back and looked up at the gray, smoke-colored ceiling. Nothing sexy here at all, just the sound of keys being pressed, the *ka-chong* of the calculator, the guys in the back room laughing, the smell of cigarettes. So that was what this was. Just a factory. Packing stuff, adding numbers, shipping boxes, and smoke.

After a while, Ray did look up at me. Even though it was day, the thick orange window paint made it feel like perpetual night inside, his desk lamp the only light on his face, a half-moon with smudgy, opaque glasses. "You know, Harris, it would be nice to have you around more often. Unfortunately, without a piece of work to pay you for, I'm hamstrung on my talent budget. However, we always need help around the office. If you had free time during the week, I know we could find things for you to do. Shipping and office work and so forth."

"Yeah, right. I'll tell everyone I work for a porno company."

He looked at me level. "Saxony Electric Motors." He nodded at the office next door. "They're on the lease. I could pay you off their ledger, then you can tell all the very important people you know that you're doing something macho like running heavy equipment. Something tells me you would enjoy getting *drilled* anyway."

"Ha ha."

But I liked it, and told him so. "OK," he said. He went back to his calculator and pretended he didn't care, but I could see how flush his cheeks had gone.

So that worked out fine. I told anyone who asked I had this job at a machine shop, and anyway, most of the time all I did was bring boxes to the post office, sweep up, and shuttle film cans. It was a good job for the spring, even kind of boring. Only a few odd things happened.

I was at the mall and a man came over. Regular looking guy, sort of balding with a comb-over, business shirt, pants and fancy shoes. He just walked up while I was eating an ice cream.

"Hello," he said, like he knew me.

I looked around, and no one else seemed to be with him. "Uh, hello," I said.

"Looks tasty," he said, nodding at the ice cream.

"Yeah?"

"Where'd you get it?"

"Outside the movie theater," I said, slowly.

"Well it looks good," he said. He seemed to be looking me over, up and down.

"You like movies?" he said.

"They're ok."

"I like movies too." He was breathing faster than there was reason to. "You work today?"

"Uh, no." I said.

"Day off?"

"I guess." Then nothing. It seemed like I wasn't saying what he wanted and he seemed to run out of stupid things to ask. He pulled a piece of paper out of his pocket, clicked a pen against his chest and while he wrote on it, he said, "Raymond Cicero is a creep. Call us when you're ready to do some real work." He pushed the paper into my hand. "You got a nice macaroni." Then he walked away.

■ ■ ■

I walked into the kitchen on Saturday morning. Momma was standing at the counter, reading mail. "Oh hello," she said, surprised. "You're up early."

"It's not that early."

"You're always out now and I don't get to see you anymore."

"Well, here I am." I got cereal and coffee. Sat at the table and started eating. The mail should only take a minute, but she stood there, unmoving, for much longer. "What is it?" I asked.

"I know it's none of my business," she said, to my back. "But, what do you do all the time?"

"What do you mean? I go to school, I go to work."

"Carla Harmon told me she gave you a ride a couple of weeks ago. She said you were just walking around the streets, looking aimless."

"Is that what she said?"

Momma sat across from the me. "So I'm a little worried."

"Well don't be."

She took a long sigh. "Harris, I know what pot smells like. A lot of kids are getting in trouble. It can really mess things up in school. With your studying . . ."

I gave her a hard look.

"I know you don't like me pressing you. You're a very private person. I just don't want to see you get into anything you can't get yourself out of."

"What does that mean?"

She shrugged. "I feel like I don't know you anymore. I don't know what you're doing and I'm a little scared."

"I told you. I go to school. I have a job. That's it."

She looked at me, so sadly. I knew she knew I was lying, but it was too late. I wasn't going to tell her anything now.

"You know, things can go very wrong, very easily," she said. "Especially around here. This world we live in, this city . . . there are a lot of bad people you can get mixed up with. And it may seem fun ... all the excitement, all the money. It's very seductive from the outside. And they're always looking for young people. For fresh meat."

That kind of startled me.

"And we're never as smart as we think we are," she said, "even though we come from this world."

"I don't know what you're talking about."

"Ok," she said. And I wondered what Mrs. Harmon really told her. "Maybe you ought to talk to your grandfather. He's someone with a lot more experience than the rest of us."

"Oh ho, that's a great idea. Alcoholics Anonymous up there."

She smiled. "Well yes, they do enjoy their cocktails. Phil is a handful. But he's not your grandfather."

"Grandpa's old. And rich. And he sits up in his house with his poodles and his martinis. He doesn't know what's going on in the world."

"So what is going on?"

"Nothing. I told you."

"I'm just . . ."

Then a latch came undone. I didn't realize it was closed until it popped open. Like with the guys, with Ray and his camera, I just let it loose. "Stop being so worried," I said, and felt this fury rise, "and besides, who are you to give me this whole worried mommy routine? Nana told me you got into all kinds of trouble with George when you were young, and now, with all this weird shit you do . . . like Ginger and her southern accent . . . Nana thinks you're completely nuts, do you know that? One time she asked me to *spy* on you and tell her if you did anything strange, and I didn't do it, so give me a little credit. At least I'm in the real world. I do things. I'm not pretending to be something I'm not."

Her face was a blotch of red. Stunned, frightened silence.

"So shut the fuck up and stay out of my business."

I shoved the chair at the table and left.

■ ■ ■

Ray said he had a piece of business to discuss, which was confidential, and *therefore,* he said, he wanted to take me to lunch. Which meant the chili dog stand a few blocks from the office next to a car repair shop.

We got our food and sat at a table under a metal umbrella. He looked around to be sure no one could hear. "Now listen," he said, "we've stumbled into an opportunity with someone who wields a good deal of power. Someone very important to the company. You've appeared on his radar, as it were, and I've been asked to bring it to your attention. Is this something you would entertain a conversation about?"

He seemed serious so I said of course.

"Good. I told you the snaps were a big hit. You have a fan base."

This surprised me only a little because I never heard anything about the pictures. I half thought Ray just kept them to jerk off to.

"This fellow, as I mentioned, is quite a big wheel. Apparently, you're just his cup of tea. He'd like to meet you for a private session at his palatial hilltop estate."

It took a second to take this in. "So, that's like, for money?"

"Oh my goodness yes. An order of magnitude you haven't seen yet."

My chili dog was the bluff prop. It was messy and cheesy, and I could eat for a while before saying anything back. Ray knew what I was doing and shook his head. "That's disgusting," he said when I slurped the chili with my tongue.

"How does that work?" I asked.

"He pays us – me – and I pay you. It's a straight date. However, because of who this is, the connections he has, he basically told me the company would get very favorable treatment in the form of loans and equipment for future work. This is someone who could help us very much."

"Why me?"

"Whatever you have is whatever he wants. I couldn't tell you more than that."

"What would I have to do?"

"Well, since he invited you up to the mansion, I assume he wants something up close and personal. Sometimes they want a piece of arm candy for an event, but I believe his interest in you is more visceral than visual."

But the way Ray was looking at me, his whole attitude, it seemed like something was not right.

"What is it?"

"I've worked with this fellow before. He's financed several projects and I have a pretty good idea where the money comes from. As long as we provide a good return, they're happy, and no questions asked. At the same time, he's not someone I want to run afoul of. And no matter what you may think, Harris, I do have some paternal feelings for you . . ."

"Oh my god . . ."

". . . *and* . . . let me finish . . . concern for myself as well. What this fellow could do for the business is incalculable. It's in my interest to solicit you to accept the offer. On the other hand, despite your bravado, I believe you're somewhat naïve in these matters, and I imagine our friend expects a *Kevin* who's not at all like your delightfully idiosyncratic self. I think the technical term for what he's looking for is a dumb horndog."

"I can act, you know."

"Yes, I do know that. But you're not hungry enough. To do these things, you need to need the money. Everyone who works for me needs the money, but frankly, I don't know what to make of you, except that you don't seem to need the money. If something doesn't suit you, you're likely to toss off some smart remark and disappear, leaving the rest of us holding the bag. I can't take that chance with this fellow. I need someone hungry enough to do what he's told."

I wanted to argue with him, but whatever he was telling me seemed to worry him. "So why did you bring it up?"

"Because I told him I would. And I wanted to see your reaction."

"So that's it?"

"For now. But this fellow doesn't take no very well. Let's see. Perhaps he'll move on and forget all about it." He watched me for some reaction, which I didn't have. "Wipe your chin, for God's sake, you have chili all over yourself."

17

When summer came, Ray asked me to help on the shoots. He said I should see how things work in a professional environment.

"And just what is *that* look for?" he asked.

"Nothing," I said. "It's fine."

He shot his movies in backyards around the west valley and cheapo studios in Hollywood. It was interesting the difference between TV shoots and these crappy porn loops. His movies didn't have sound – he added music and dialogue later –so he just talked to the guys on set and told them what to do. The concepts were simple: the poolboy and the rich guy, the salesman and the customer, whatever. Up to then, his movies were pretty low budget and he used guys he knew, regular looking guys off the street. But he had more money now, so he hired some real models who worked for Marvista, one of the big studios in town. These guys worked out and were well groomed, very tan and handsome. When they showed up to do the scenes, they were kind of cliquey and I felt like a dork standing on the side with the reflector, getting water, just being the runner. When one of the guys asked me to blow him to get hard, Ray yelled, *that's not the PA's job*, and had someone else do it. One night while we were doing equipment inventory, Ray asked, "so what does our esteemed critic think after a few weeks of production work?"

"It's hot," I said. Shrugged.

"Is that all? I believe I noticed a bit of excitement in the nether regions. Tell me, oh wise one, what could we have done to get more of a *rise* out of you?"

"It's fine, it's hot. What do you want me to say?"

"But you could have done better." He caught me and I laughed. "Well," he said, "soon enough. You and I know what you can do. Watch and learn, then we'll see what . . . develops."

■ ■ ■

During one of the shoots, this guy Kenny, who was one of the Marvista models, kept giving me the once-over. It wasn't a horny once-over, more like an assessment. Later on when we were breaking down, he invited me to a party. "You'll meet a lot of people," he said. It was the premiere for another film and Kenny was friends with the actors.

This was at a club in Hollywood. I didn't have a fake ID and I figured I'd get turned away, but the bouncer waved me in without even looking. Inside, they had a DJ and laser lights, lots of food and drinks; it was mostly guys, with some women, but everyone shiny and sparkling. They were showing clips from the movie on the wall, and the models looked so good, like real movie stars. A lot of the models were there, as well as older guys, rich looking guys, swimming around like sharks, but everyone having a good time, laughing, talking loud. And a lot of coke, which was not hard to spot.

Kenny saw me and nodded me over, introduced me to the group he was talking to. They were nice, they bought me drinks, asked a lot of questions. It was so loud it was hard to hear, and I couldn't tell if they heard what I was saying, but everyone was so happy, and laughing, and after a while I just talked and didn't care if they could hear me or not. I drank a bunch of drinks and that warmth of confidence came over me. Enough to do the coke they offered, which was mind-blowingly fantastic. I couldn't believe how aware I felt. How sensitive every inch of my skin was.

Those guys pulled me into their group and we danced for a while, and there were some speeches and other talking, and the alcohol and the coke seemed to sharpen everything, give me this total calm, horny energy. They pulled off their shirts, and I did too, and I danced harder, and they were loving it, and applauding me and hugging me. We ended up going to some guy's apartment, and I felt I was being carried along by this group of handsome, laughing men. There was a pool I could see out the window of the bedroom, glowing blue and green, but in my mind I was jumping off a diving board into this huge bed of swirling, glistening bodies, this perfect arc through the air from nothing and emptiness into the hot, sweaty surface below. Then I was one of them, and inside of them, and they were inside of me, and it felt like blasting into heaven. I couldn't get enough and they couldn't wear me out. Two and three and four guys around me, they laughed and kissed me, fucked me, I fucked them, then the next one and the next one and they loved it and they loved me. This is what love is, I said to myself. I felt drenched in pleasure, covered in it. And when I woke up the next morning, tangled in sweat-soaked sheets and arms and legs of all these naked, snoring guys, I felt worn out but transformed, vibrating with energy and excitement. This was life. I was in real life.

Somehow I dragged myself home and collapsed on the bed. In the afternoon, momma knocked on the door, opened it slightly.

"I didn't hear you come in. Were you out last night?"

"Oh yes," I said, to the pillow.

"Is everything all right? It smells like . . . chemicals in here."

Poppers probably.

"Pool," I said. "Too much chlorine."

"Ah." She waited another moment. "You sure you're ok?"

"Fine," I said to the pillow. And farted. She closed the door.

■ ■ ■

Kenny invited me to a few more parties, and I went, even though I knew there would be blowback. A couple of weeks later, it came. Ozzie leaned back from his editing station when I walked into the office. "You're in trouble," he sang, and tilted his head toward the packing room.

Ray was checking numbers on a clipboard as one of the guys loaded film into a box. Ray stiffened when he saw me and his face turned dark.

"Outside," he said. I followed him to the alley. "Had our fun, have we?"

"Uh, what do you mean?" Even I could hear the dumb high school moron.

"It sounds like you've become Marvista's new mascot. So glad you could stop by the business that's actually paying you. We're not taking too much of your time, are we?"

"I just went to a couple of parties . . ."

". . . behind my back and telling me *nothing* about it."

"It was just fun, it doesn't mean anything."

"*I* pay you. *I* found you. *I* get you dates that pay for your tight jeans and your gas and everything you need. And you do this to me? You betray me like this?"

"Jesus Christ, it was just some parties. I'm not working for them."

"Oh, bull shit. You're hanging around with all the boys who work in *direct competition* to me, and it slips your mind to mention it? Don't treat me like an idiot, Harris, really. You're smarter than that."

"Sorry. They just invited me so I went."

"Have you no loyalty at all? I thought you were a person of integrity. Then to find out you've gone and done this. Very insulting and disrespectful."

Now I did feel like a heel. "I'm sorry," I said, quieter.

He crossed his arms. "Well then, I have to ask … do you intend to stay with us or are you just planning to take my money and skip out as soon as you're able?"

"No. Of course I'm staying. It was just . . . nothing serious."

He kept staring. All his greasy little clothes and greasy glasses and greasy hair heated up and steaming. Fuming. "Alright. I believe you. I'm working on something for you. For *you*," he said, and jabbed me with his finger. "So when we're ready, we'll get you on the roster. Is that enough to keep you on our side of the fence?"

"Yes. Thank you."

"Alright." He started to go inside but couldn't help himself and turned back. "I found you! How could you *do* this to me?"

"I said I'm sorry."

The hurt kid looking up at me. He grunted and went back inside. I stayed to smoke a cigarette and tried to calm down.

■ ■ ■

What he came up with wasn't all that amazing.

"A locker room scene," he said, a couple of weeks later. "It'll be you and Joaquin. He's the champion wrestler, you're the attendant. He'll come in from a shower, find you sweeping the floor, then bing-bang-boom. How does that sound?"

Joaquin was a guy Ray used from time to time. He was hunky and squat, kind of cute, with slightly crossed eyes, lips as red as plums. I said it sounded okay.

But on the morning of the shoot it, I threw up. It came to me, all of a sudden, what this was. How different it was from everything else. I didn't have a name for whatever I did with Ray and his pictures, and anything I did with guys was my own business and no one was filming me. When I thought about it again, I threw up again, then sat on the toilet seat, my mouth dripping with puke.

"You alright in there?" momma asked through the door. I grunted. I felt desperate for something to calm this down. A cigarette, a drink, something. It felt like my skin was being peeled off. I hit myself in the forehead as hard as I could. I bit my hand so hard blood seeped out the pores in the teeth marks. "What do you do? What do you do?" I whispered. I looked at the clock. I had to do something. You have to do something. I took a long breath and told myself to stand up and move.

The crew was already setting up when I arrived. This was a warehouse in Panorama City. The set was built, a short row of lockers and a bench in front, the rest unlit because there was nothing there. The same crew Ray always used: Ozzie on camera, this guy Stuart doing lights and a girl named Violet on property and makeup. Just like any other setup, people moving sort of leisurely, bored, but with a sense of purpose.

"Very good, nice and prompt," Ray said. "How are you? Ready for the grand debut?"

I tried to smile but couldn't. He tilted his head, guided me off to the dark edge. "What are we thinking?" he said.

I retched again, put my hand over my mouth to make sure nothing came out.

"Oh god. You're not going to fold on me, are you?"

He took my other hand. I couldn't see his eyes in the dark. I know he could feel my shivering.

"Harris," he said quietly. "I've been very patient, showing you every aspect of this business and what really goes on here. You wanted to be part of it. I spent a lot of money on this shoot, and I did it all for you, and now you owe me. You have to pay the bill."

I nodded at the dark floor. I already knew this. I heard it all before. I swallowed back and looked at him. He smiled and put his hand on my shoulder.

"Alright people," he said, returning us to the light, "let's get ready to start. Joaquin, dear boy, how are you?"

■ ■ ■

And now this, and whatever this is, and whatever we're doing.

Eva steps onto her marks and *plants*. She has a costume and makeup and lighting to make her look like who they want her to be. But I have to be naked, and I have nothing, and they'll see all the pimples and spots and no muscles and hairs where I don't know they are. They'll see how ugly I am. Things only work in secret.

"Alright," Ray is saying, "now Harris, you're sweeping the floor and you come across the gym shorts Joaquin has left on the bench."

I can't move.

"Harris," Ray says. "*Kevin*. Sweep the floor."

I start sweeping.

"Very good. Now you see the shorts and you pick them up."

I pick them up.

"Now you sniff them."

I sniff them.

"My god," Ray says, "Ozzie, stop."

Ray walks to me. "It smells *good*, Harris. You look like you're eating liver and onions. It's supposed to be *intoxicating*. It turns you on." I nod, and we start again. I try to do what he says.

"Well, ok," Ray says, "not great, but we'll take it. Now you're getting turned on thinking about Joaquin, aren't you? Oh yes you are. That sexy wrestler you've lusted over so many times. Oh my goodness, you're thinking, how hot is that guy? Very hot, that's what he is. Isn't he, Kevin. *Isn't he?*"

I nod at Ray.

"No! Dammit ... Ozzie, just keep going, we'll cut it out. Now Harris, uh, Kevin, you're going to take those shorts and you're going to go around and you're going to sit down on the bench. You're going to sit down on the bench and when you do, you're going to smell those sweet shorts, and you're going to put your hand in your pants and start stroking. That's it. Sit on the ..."

And I trip over the bench.

"Stop!"

The lights and everyone's spirit come down.

Ray looked at the floor. Joaquin stood off set, opening his towel, checking his dick, not paying attention. "Five minutes," Ray said. "Harris, a moment please." He walked on, put his arm around my shoulder and walked me off. "I know you know how to do things, because I've seen you do them. Taking direction is not something new to you. So what, pray tell, is happening here?"

My mouth was dry as sand. I felt dizzy. He let out a long sigh, but patient. Interesting, how on set Ray had patience he didn't have anywhere else. "Maybe a quick joint might help?"

"I'll throw up."

He thought a moment more, his arm still around me. "Violet, dear," he called, "a soda if you don't mind." She brought one, handed it to Ray.

"Thank you, dear," and she walked away. Ray produced something from his pocket, an orange capsule, and pushed it in my hand. "Relax you," he said. "Give it a pop." I did, then we seemed to stand there for I'm not sure how long until, very confidently, he said, "alright now, ready to give it another go?" We walked back to the set. He took me to my entrance position, walked back to the camera, then calmly said, "All right, Harris, are you ready to start again?"

And somehow I was. I felt cushioned then. Floating slightly. None of this was as serious as before. In fact it seemed ridiculous how anxious I was. I nodded and Ray called action and I stepped on set and did it. I listened to what he told me and I could do enough that he didn't stop. I liked how calm I felt. Then Joaquin came on like he was supposed to and we did the dumb dialogue, and then I forgot about the camera and Ozzie and the crew. All I saw was Joaquin and his beautiful lips and his cute, crossed eyes. And then it was that guy again, who could do things. He had wings where there were none before. Everyone on set got quiet and we worked until Ray had what he wanted and very gently said, ok, hold right there. We changed setups and I stayed calm and turned on, and Joaquin was sweaty and turned on, and I could tell by how big his eyes were that he liked it, and we went on to the next setup. And as I let it go, let the power out, I turned it on more. Ozzie kept his fat fucking mouth shut, taking it seriously, taking me seriously; he and Ray consulted a couple of times on angles, but didn't stop us. We got through the whole scenario before the end of the day, and when we were done, they all broke into applause. Violet brought the horse blankets, put one over me, one over Joaquin. To me, she said, "Shit, I think I came in my pants about five times." I kissed her cheek.

Ray walked over and stood in front of me. I had not seen this look before. Pride, satisfaction, confidence. He put his hand on my shoulder, over the blanket. He didn't have to say anything at all.

18

And then, *The Tonight Show.* One night in March, during the second season of *Bowman*, there was Eva Loesch, in a stylish gray pantsuit, walking around the desk, waving to the cheering crowd. Someone Johnny Carson wouldn't have given a thought to in the past.

"But now," she said, "*they* invited *me!* Can you believe it?"

It was a Sunday cookout and she had agreed to come down to North Hollywood and sit in our dry backyard and eat hamburgers from the cinderblock grill George had arranged on the ground. "Oh, very nice," she said when she saw it. "Like beautiful downtown Beirut. Don't they have grills with legs nowadays?"

I was laying on the lounger at the end of the patio. Eva stood with a cigarette over momma and George, tapping her ash into the grill while they crouched over the coals. She was telling them where to put the newspaper and lighter fluid but they ignored her so she gave up. I heard her shoes clicking across the bricks toward me, then she shoved me over with her hips and sat down, positioned herself with her back to momma and George. She pulled the cigarettes out and offered me one, very matter-of-fact. I said no, she shrugged and put them away. Let out a long exhale. And sat there, not saying anything, while momma and George coughed and smoke blew in their eyes.

After a while, she said, "Carson show's just the beginning. They have me on everything the next couple of weeks. Newspapers, radio, the whole shebang."

"That's good?"

"That is good. A lot more attention. A lot more coverage. And a lot more scrutiny."

I mouthed the word Oh. She tapped her ash on the ground. "So, I'm a little concerned about the clown show going on down here. It all seems a bit hairy to me."

"What do you mean?" I realized we were speaking in low voices not to be heard back at the grill.

"I get a lot of questions now. Which is nice. But I don't have a husband to gush about. And as you can imagine, I don't want them crawling around Bel-Air. And there's only so much I can drone on about my petunias and my roses without sounding like a nitwit. So they ask about my wonderful daughter and my wonderful grandchildren. And I want to tell them how wonderful they are. But with your mother's friend back in the picture . . ."

"He's an okay guy."

She cleared her throat. "Do you remember the time you kids lived with me?"

I did; some vague memory of being at her house for a long time when we were little. I thought momma had gone away on vacation.

"That wasn't it," she said. "That was court-ordered custody. Your mother, and Soupy Sales over there, thought they were bohemians. *Thought*. They moved into some kind of a commune with a bunch of other losers up in the mountains. They had the idea they were going to bring two little children up there with them, but I didn't think that was such a good idea. And a nice judge agreed with me. Turned out there was lot of unsavory business going on . . . drugs and sex and bigamy and you name it. Some culty thing. Whatever it was, it turned into a big mess. So the deal was, your mother had to get herself straightened out and keep away from the merry pranksters if she wanted her children back. Obviously it worked out. But now, with Captain Crunch back again . . . and you getting a bit rank" – she flicked my hair – "it gives me cause for concern. If there are goings-on I don't know about . . ."

"You should ask them yourself," I said. She finished the cigarette and tamped it with her shoe.

"I mean it," she said. "This is not the time for funny business."

From across the patio momma yelled, "First course!"

■ ■ ■

George found this round table and bench made of poured concrete that looked like it was stolen from a Wienershnitzel. Now it sat in the backyard with a faded brown umbrella. We ate our corn cobs and hamburgers under it, the smoke from the grill drifting and making everyone's eyes water. Eva had another cigarette, but she put on a brave face and ate the sloppy burger and buttery corn as delicately as she could, trying not to spill on the expensive outfit.

"So when they called me up to the front office I was worried we were cancelled," she said. "But no. It was the Carson people. And they asked for me. I simply couldn't believe it."

"You looked very good," momma said.

"Thank you. For an old-timer, I was surprised how nervous I was. I never met him before. Nice man. And they take care of you very well. It felt strange to be treated like royalty at this point in the game. I asked if this was an interview, or a memorial. They got a big laugh out of that one."

We nodded and listened. And then, after she gushed a bit more, and momma asked all her questions, I felt a change in attitude; the heavy bench adjusted slightly as she uncrossed then re-crossed her legs, lit a fresh cigarette. I deliberately didn't look in case she was trying to catch my eye.

"So, George," she said. "This is quite a setup you've got here. This must have taken some manpower."

"I got some friends to help. We only set the grill up for today."

"I can see that. Very resourceful. Isn't he, Carolyn?"

Momma shrugged, grunted. Ate her corn.

"So, uh, George," Eva said, "tell me. Is this feast on you, or are we dining on Carolyn's dime today?"

"We split the expenses," he said, through a mouthful.

"I see. Very democratic. You know, though, I'm a little unclear. What is the arrangement here? Carolyn provides the grill and you provide, what? The meat?"

I looked down to stare a hole into the ground. But George kept eating, not taking any bait. "We share expenses in other ways. It all evens out."

"Ah. So, there are other things you do together. Tell me, are you living here?"

"It's really none of your business," momma said.

"Just a question. Nothing to get sensitive about. Unless there *is* something to get sensitive about. I mean, is there?"

"I live in Burbank," George said.

"George has his apartment and he lives there," momma said. "And that's all."

"I see," Eva said. "And what do the children think about that?"

"They're not children, mother, they're almost grown up."

"Well, they live here, don't they? They see comings and goings. It seems confusing to me, that's all. I mean, do the children go to your apartment?"

"No," George said. "I live there. They live here. They don't go there."

"Uh huh. Does Carolyn go to your apartment?"

"No," George said. "Well. Sometimes."

"Mmm-hhhm. And what do the children make of that?"

Alicia looked at momma, surprised. I guess she didn't know that. I didn't care, but momma seemed a little unnerved.

"It's nothing," she said. "It has nothing to do with them."

"Well George, how about you?" Eva said. "Where's your, uh, center of gravity? Your apartment or this house? Besides this . . . cement thing . . . I notice you did the front lawn over. Seems like you're making improvements here all the time."

"I like to be helpful."

"Always a good idea. But Carolyn isn't destitute, as far as I can tell. Are you, Carolyn? If you need things, you have the money to buy them, don't you?"

She nodded with closed eyes, chewing.

"She can make any improvements she wants. So George, it seems you're doing all this out of the goodness of your heart. Is that right?"

"That's what friends are for."

"Uh huh. Is that what you are? Friends?"

"You know, Eva," George said, "we can discuss this another time. We don't need to get into all this family stuff."

"Oh, are you a family? I thought you were friends."

"I meant," he said, "we don't need to get into some heavy discussion right this minute."

"Oh, ok, that's cool. I wouldn't want to get into anything *heavy*, baby."

"Can we just drop it?" momma said quietly.

The way Eva tapped off her cigarette, I could see it coming. Like loading the artillery.

"So George," she asked, "what are you doing these days? For work, I mean. Are you gainfully employed? You know how important that is. You know, where there might be questions or stipulations . . ."

"Mother, everything is fine," momma said. "It's water under the bridge."

"If you must know, *Eva*," George said, "I work at a marine repair yard in Malibu. Nice and steady, five days a week."

"That is good," Eva said. "Sounds like you've got everything ship shape then."

"Mother . . ."

"But, you know," she said, "I just have one more question." Momma's hands turned to clenched fists. "I've been the sole support for this family since the beginning, including the time you were off sailing the ocean blue. And here we are today, enjoying this smoky little feast. So can you fault me for asking questions? I mean, this *is* my family, isn't it? Is it unreasonable I should want to be sure everything is on the up and up? Because if there was anything . . ."

The table shuddered. Momma screamed, slammed her plate hard, sending corn and salad flying. "Mother!" she shrieked, and pounded the table again, then, sobbing, jumped up and ran into the house. "Carolyn," George said, and went after her. I heard their voices moving down the hall toward the bedroom and the door slamming.

Alicia and Eva and I just sat, not knowing where to look. The birds chirped, the sound of cars around us, the last clicks and snaps from the dying charcoals. Eva let out a smoky breath. "Now *that*, children, is called making a mountain out of a molehill. Ask a few simple questions and everyone goes to pieces."

Alicia let out a long sigh. "Nana, what's a center of gravity?"

"Well, dear," she said, "I'll tell you."

19

Maybe a month later, Ray called me to his desk. He waved a pink phone message, fanned himself with it.

"Big fish," he said. "Literally." He showed it to me:

From: *Charlie Salmon*
Re: *Business*
Message: *Please call at earliest convenience*
Below that, he'd drawn a fish with glasses and a hard-on, and underneath that: *Secret!*

"What the …?"
"I asked around," he said. "It's Gordon Booker."
"You mean *The Rangers* Gordon Booker?"
"The very one. I called back. Some woman answered. Stuck to the phony name. I didn't push, but she confirmed her client was *very eager* to meet Kevin. Your fan club awaits." I couldn't help myself, it made me happy. "Oh Harris," Ray said, shaking his head. But he couldn't keep from smiling too. "Such a whore. And only one film in the can." He knew this would be good money. And a big name. I could almost see the battle going on in his head: one of his models picked by one of the most famous guys in the world versus his weird possessiveness of what I did and who I did it with. I figured the money would win.

He lifted the phone off the cradle, turned it with his wrist. "Well?"

I nodded.

■ ■ ■

We set the date for a Thursday at the Beverly Hilton. This was a gleaming white building on the X-shaped intersection of Wilshire and Santa Monica where they filmed the Merv Griffin Show. Trader Vic's was on the first floor, and I knew it because Eva used to take us there for special celebrations with blue drinks. I had the room number on a piece of paper, and when I knocked, a girl's voice asked who it was through the door.

"It's Mister Pike with your rental car keys."

The door opened a crack and a pale girl with black hair and deep black eyes peered out. She looked maybe 25. "Come in," she said, checking both ways.

It was a big suite, with a living room and two rooms off it, one on either side; through the tall windows, the buildings of Century City beyond. "I'm Amanda," she said. "I help with all the complicated details of my boss's complicated life. He'll be out in a minute. Would you like something to drink?" She was casual but watching my every move. I asked for a Coke. She nodded at the huge white sofa and I sat; she brought me the Coke, then she sat on the other side of the L-shape, looking me over. She was simple and beautiful with no makeup, short hair, white t-shirt and jeans. She could have been a cute boy.

"Beautiful day," she said. I said yes it was. Had I met her boss before? No, I said, I didn't think I had. Did I know who he was? Yes, I thought I might have an idea. Obviously, she said, the need for confidentiality was essential. She had spoken to my manager about this, but she wanted to be sure he had emphasized it to me. Yes, I said, my *manager* made it very clear. That was good, she said. I thought the interview was going well. Then she came over and sat next right next to me, and stared, her eyes moving top to bottom, like a seamstress searching for loose threads. This close to her, I started to get hard. She tilted her head at me.

"What?" I said.

"Nothing. But . . . I hope you don't mind. No offense or anything, but I don't get it. You just look like some regular kid to me."

That made me laugh. "I don't get it either. I feel kind of dumb . . ." but I knew that was the wrong thing to say. "I mean, I haven't done this a lot."

"Aw," she said. Then she leaned forward and I thought she was going to kiss me, but I think she was smelling for something. The last test, maybe. Whatever it was, she sat back and let out a sigh. "Be good to my man, ok? He has a big heart and it's easily broken." She went to the bedroom door and knocked. "Olly olly oxenfree!" The double doors parted with a whoosh, and there he was, all six-foot-four, handsome, tan Gordon Booker. In a big white hotel bathrobe, black dress socks, and a cowboy hat.

"Well, hello young fella! Welcome to the roundup!"

■ ■ ■

Now, about Gordon Booker.

I don't know when he started, but I do know he was in a TV western in the '60s called *The Rangers*. He became America's favorite cowboy, the hot-tempered, dark-eyed young brother of a family of ranchers. As he got older, even though you could tell he was heavier and dyed his hair, everyone still loved him. Men, women, old people, young people – he was the kind of guy who, if you saw him on the other side of the street, you'd cross over to shake his hand and he'd make you feel he was honored to meet you. And now, standing there and looking at him, I felt that blip go off at the end of my dick. He was much older than me, maybe 55, and his skin looked sort of shiny, but I could see how handsome he was, once was, how him just looking at you could have blown your heart right out of your chest.

Amanda came back with a drink for him. He put his arm around her. "Isn't my girl something else? Good to meet you Kevin," he said, and took my hand, put his other hand over.

"Nice to meet *you*," I said, gushing.

"God, I haven't been to the Hilton in ages. I'd forgotten what a spectacular view this is." He let go of my hand, rubbed his own, a little nervous. "No trouble finding the place?"

"Nope." I was about to say I came here with my grandmother, but stopped before doing that.

"Well that's good," he said, "that's very good." Mouth open; seemed at a loss for words. "We validate?" he said to Amanda. She laughed. "Don't worry, I'll take care of it."

"All right, then. All the particulars taken care of. What next then? What do we think?"

"Dinner," she said, calmly. "You have a six-thirty reservation."

"Outstanding!" he said.

"So, you get dressed, and I'll have the car around in fifteen minutes. I laid out a nice pair of jeans and your houndstooth jacket." Gordon opened his mouth to say something, and Amanda said, "Not too flashy. And you have a private booth in the back."

"Hot dog!" he said. "See you in fifteen!" Then he moved back through the double doors – I wasn't sure if he actually backed out of the room to make the exit or I imagined it – and the doors seemed to close by themselves.

■ ■ ■

We drove out to Malibu in his silver Rolls-Royce. He turned off the PCH, down a narrow, dark driveway to this seafood restaurant on the beach, and parked in the big, mostly empty lot. You could hear soft waves rolling in behind the building. The waitress knew him and smiled, led us to a table in back, behind a half wall with a screen on the upper half. Gordon asked for a gin gimlet, I asked for a beer.

"Well, well, well. So, Kevin," he said, and rubbed his hands together, this gesture you'd see him do a lot. Kind of excited, kind of nervous. Funny to see him do it and say the name of someone I knew. "Here you are."

"Here I am."

"Exciting, huh?"

"I guess."

He smiled, took a sip of his drink. "You're, uh, pretty good," he said, and leaned forward, poked me in the chest. "Pretty hot stuff."

"Yeah," I said, and again, "I guess."

"Got all the moves," and he did this thing with his shoulders, pretending to punch me like a boxer. "Yeah, yeah, sure," he said.

It felt like he was dying on stage with no lines. I said, "I like your car."

"Oh, the Shadow. She is one sweet ride, isn't she? Only one of a bunch of 'em. Perks of being the big wheel. You can have any car you want and as many as you want. Got 'em in a garage in Encino. Full time mechanic, too." He took another long sip of his drink. I drank some of the beer. Tasted like piss.

Sitting this close I could study his face. It was very brown and broad, stretched tight in places. It looked like they had pulled the skin over each part of his face to keep that part looking like it always did. The waitress brought us the appetizers. Gordon had clams with breadcrumbs and started eating quickly, stuffing the breadcrumbs in. His hands were shaking. "So," he said, "pretty hot, doing what you're doing, huh?"

"I guess. It's just a job."

He lifted his glass. "Here's to that," and we clinked. He couldn't quite meet my eyes. To the table he said, "See a lot of action, do you?"

"Uhm, yeah."

"Quite the cocksman, that's for sure." His smile, his face a bit red, like he was trying to sell me on this, trying to sell himself on what he was doing. Maybe because of Eva and grandpa, I'm not as starstruck as other people, so it made me uncomfortable to see him this nervous. I knew Ray expected me to represent whatever his business was supposed to be, but I liked Gordon, so I dropped the posturing.

"Uhm, you know, I only did the one movie. I'm just some kid from the valley."

"Well, no matter, boy, you still got it going on. That's for sure." He looked up finally, meeting my eyes, and seemed to relax. It made me feel better when he started acting like you expect Gordon Booker to act. "I gotta say, it must be nice for you guys."

"What is?"

"To be young now, with everything that's going on. In my day, it was all about secrecy. Still is. All the mumbo-jumbo my gal Amanda put you through. Sorry about that. Comes with the territory. Got to keep the business going."

"I guess," I said, not understanding entirely.

"You know, the whole gay lib thing. You can be who you are and bone who you like and nobody gives a crap about it."

"I don't know …I mean, it's not like the old days . . ." I didn't want to offend him, ". . . but, you're famous, you can have anything you want. I mean, you called Ray's office . . ."

"Son, Gordon Booker don't call no one." At the same time, we both said, "*Charlie Salmon*," and laughed. "So, there it is," he said.

We ordered the rest of the dinner, and after another couple of drinks he loosened up some more. "So, tell me about yourself," he said. "How you got into all this. You want to be a movie star? Make it big in show business?"

"Oh god, no. I have no talent . . ." his drink stopped halfway to his mouth. ". . . for that," I finished.

"Ah, now, don't sell yourself short."

"I know actors," I said, "and I'm no actor." He looked at the glass, seemed to admire the assessment. "So you're not gonna hit me up for an audition? You don't want to be a million dollar movie star?"

"*No.*"

He raised his glass. "God bless you, son. Well I sure did, when I was young. Not much older than you. It's funny because I didn't start out that way. Just some beanpole of a kid from West Texas."

And here, remembering what Ray said about mouthing off, I told myself to keep my trap shut.

"I was a pretty shy kid," he went on. "Tall, skinny thing. Bad teeth, funny face. I looked like a pickle if you stretched him out too far. My folks had no use for me. I wandered around when I was sixteen, seventeen. Amazing the stuff you could do back then. I mean, ride the rails for real. Get on an empty train car and let it take you someplace. I had horse wrangling skills so I could do day work here and there. But they didn't like me."

"Who didn't?"

"The ranchers, the guys who did the hiring."

"Why didn't they like you?"

He smiled at his gin gimlet. "Cause I was too much of a sissy. A big, tall drink of sissy, that's what. The way I talked, the way I acted. Got dirty looks, people made fun of me. I got pummeled a couple of places too, beat up pretty bad. Then, *hello*, middle of the night, the same guys come in to get their nut. I tell you, for a while, I didn't know if I was coming or going. Or coming *and* going." That made me laugh, for real. "So I learned to be an actor, right there, in a boxcar in Missouri. Turned myself into a long, lanky cowpoke. Asked myself, how does that guy talk? How does he pick up a coffee cup? Had to figure it all out so I could stop taking the beatings. And sonofabitch, it worked. Got into a train one guy and came out another. *Well, how do, ma'am, just passin' through town.* Made him up and everything."

He drank the last of his drink, caught the waitress's eye, shook the empty glass.

"Once I got to LA, I did stunt work, wrangling, that kind of thing. And I could say my lines and mean them. A lot of the stuntmen couldn't, so I got bits and pieces, here and there. And I'd be in someone's house, I'd see these antiques and fancy cars, and thought, damn, I can do better than this tired old sack of crap. I'm better lookin' than him, better rider and everything. I will tell you, I was ambitious. The things I did." He took the new drink from the waitress, smiled at her. "But you know what it's like," he said, "you're the fresh meat now," and winked.

"My mom said the same thing."

That seemed to startle him. He looked at me thoughtfully. Reappraised. "When you first appear," he said, "you have some kind of a scent. Don't know what it is, but people can smell it. They want to sink their teeth into it, get a . . . *mmmm* . . . a good bite of that fresh, tasty sirloin. But then you stay, and you don't look so fresh anymore, and they move on to the next new thing. But I couldn't go back. There was no place in the world for someone like me, so I had to stay. And if you do, you gotta stake out your territory. So I became the cowboy who could talk and came cheap, and that was all. It's not like New York, you can't be a *thespian* here," he said, with a lisp. "They need a cowboy, so you're a cowboy. You show up and you're just what they expect. That's how I played it and that's how things worked out." He took a breather, said, "Now you talk so I can eat something. Tell me about yourself."

I shrugged. "There isn't anything. I'm just some kid."

He gobbled his food, shook his fork. "*Natrue*," he said, mouthful of clams.

I measured what I could say. "I'm from North Hollywood. I went to school. I have a sister. Uhm, I did that movie for Ray."

"You have a, uh . . ." and winked.

"Boyfriend? No. I'm just . . . I don't know . . . this whole thing is just stupid fun." Maybe that was too much. "I mean, it's interesting. You learn a lot. You meet a lot of people."

"You gonna stay with it?"

"I don't know. I haven't thought about it. It's just for . . . well. Nothing. But, can I ask you something?"

He shrugged.

"Why did you call us? I mean, Ray's stuff is pretty crappy. There are better studios with big, handsome guys. It seems like . . . I don't know . . . they would be the kind of people you'd call . . ."

He just smiled at the question. "Now, lemme ask *you*," he said. "Is that your real name?" I knew Ray wouldn't like it but I told him. "Much better," he said, and shook my hand. "Gotta be cautious. I had a good sense about you. And anyway, I'm just a horny old man, so what's the difference?"

Just then an older couple came up behind him. Gordon saw the change in my face and he straightened up. "Oh, Mr. Booker, we're such big fans . . ." the lady starts. They gush and fumble. He's gracious, turns sideways in the booth even though I can see it hurts his back. They go on for five minutes before the husband hustles them off, autographs on cocktail napkins, both of them delirious. They looked at me for a second but had no reaction to this scruffy looking kid in a hidden booth in a dark restaurant.

After they left, he did the curious laugh like before, silent, shaking his head.

"They love you," I said.

"Damn right." He went back to his dinner, chewing thoughtfully. "Made their whole day. Maybe their whole trip. Hell, maybe a story they'll tell the rest of their lives . . . meeting *Gordon Booker* in Hollywood. Jesus, even I'm impressed." Then he was quiet.

"What?" I asked.

"There's a world of good, honest people out there, and you gotta be there for 'em. You wouldn't believe some of the good old boys I've met. Big, tough guys who just break down 'cause of how much this fella Gordon Booker means to them. And I know for a fact, if they knew anything about me for real, they'd be the first one to put a bullet right through my skull. And yet, I gotta love 'em. They open their hearts to the man and he has to be there for them."

"That sounds tough."

"What's the alternative? Move to Paris and put on a beret? No sir. Gordon Booker's a creation of this town, and in this town he must stay."

That made me sad. He looked at me and smiled.

"You're a funny, weird kid. Don't know why I'm telling you all this. Not at all how I thought the night would turn out." Then he reached over and messed up my hair.

■ ■ ■

The house in Encino was hidden from the street by wall of hedges. We pulled into a round driveway with a lot of garage doors, and a house that seemed to ramble all around it. Back then, they still had set designers doing stars' homes the way their fans expected: inside, it was all burled wood and fireplaces and bear rugs and animal heads. In the bedroom, a gas fireplace on a light switch. In the middle of the San Fernando Valley on a hot summer night, you can have a fire crackling and the air conditioning cold enough to need it.

It seemed there was no one else in the house. The bedroom was surprisingly plain, with an ordinary beige chest of drawers and beige bed-spread and blankets. A few pieces of nondescript art on the wall. I guessed this wasn't his real bedroom.

He had taken off all the cowboy stuff and put on a thick purple robe. He was still tall but not as tall as before. He brought over two wine glasses and we toasted and drank, and he sat on the bed, groaning as he swung his legs up. I took out the joint I brought from my back pocket and lit it.

"Do you have to?" he asked.

"It helps me relax," I said, which was true.

"Stuff stinks."

He grunted and sat up, arranged a pillow behind his back. He finished his glass of wine while I finished the joint, then he turned the light off, and the fireplace turned the room to a dark gold. Loose from the pot, I stood over him on the bed and started doing a sexy striptease. He took my hand and pulled me down next to him. I tried to kiss him but he turned away. I went to open his robe, but he pushed my hand off. I looked for his eyes in the dark but he wasn't looking at me, so I slid my clothes off and waited.

It took a while, but slowly, he turned, opened his robe and brought me inside. His eyes were closed. I felt his dick against my stomach. I got turned on and tried responding, but he didn't want that. I got quiet and waited for him to tell me what to do. In a while, he began to feel me, move his hands over my body. At first, the kneading and squeezing felt ticklish and I laughed, but the expression on his face shut me up. It looked like a trance, his mouth falling open, eyes shut tight.

He held me tight in his arms, strong as girders. Then he pressed his hips so hard, the breath squeezed out of me. And once more, and my chest made a wheezing sound, like an empty vacuum cleaner bag. He was so big, two of me at least. I didn't know if I should be scared, if he was trying to kill me. But even though he was holding so tight I couldn't breathe, I was curious what he was doing. What he wanted. The guys want their nut, that's what they want, but that wasn't what Gordon was looking for. And as he pressed and tightened, I felt the power in his body, the power that came from all those years. He smelled like sweat and leather and old man and cologne; I could almost feel the empty, dusty plains he came from, the places he reminded people of, the whole story of all the westerns in the movies and TV shows and fantasies people have of America. And as he humped and pressed and felt me so tight, suddenly I felt like a liar. He was looking for something he thought I had but I knew I didn't, and in a moment he would get inside and find nothing, and know it was all phony and be disappointed. I almost wanted him to crush me so he could see that it wasn't there, that I wasn't hiding anything from him.

Then he came; a sharp gasp, and his whole body shuddered, eyes tight, face twisted. He let go of me and I inhaled air. Leaned up to kiss him, but he turned, slipped me out of his robe and rolled away.

I lay there for a while, trying to get my breath back. Trying to remember who I was supposed to be.

When I could, I got up and found the bathroom. Wrapped myself in a towel and lay down next to him; stayed still until I heard him snoring, a few minutes later, everything dark except the eerie, even flame of the gas fireplace. I fell asleep until I felt this tapping on my side. Some man, in a jacket, standing next to the bed. He gestured for me to get up and follow. Outside the bedroom he had my clothes on hangers, and a cup of coffee and an envelope. He didn't speak. In the cool outside a dark sedan was running in the driveway, a driver in the front seat. I gave him my address and as the sky began turning dark purple, we pulled out of the round driveway and out the gates.

20

And finally I was free. They give you a polyester robe, a scroll of blank paper, and that's that. In the senior picture they pose you so you're looking up and ahead at some wonderful future, but the expression on my face was blank. Momma looked at it in the cardboard folder and said, "Oh well."

After the date with Gordon, Ray acted strange. He'd asked how it went and I said fine; he pretended to be cool about it, but I could feel him chewing his knuckles inside. There were more calls for Kevin but he didn't share them with me. "Screening out the riffraff," he said. I had to get an answering service of my own because guys would call the office and Ray got mad. He said he wasn't my pimp or my personal switchboard – although since he got a chunk of every date from all his models, he really was – but I guess he didn't see it that way.

It turned out Gordon really was a nice a guy. Amanda called a couple of weeks into the summer and invited me to a cookout at his house. He greeted me like we were old buddies, introduced me to his friends and acted like I was someone special. When we were alone, I tried to make it clear I was happy to fuck around again, but he never did. I asked Amanda about him one time when we went to the beach. She was wearing a white floppy hat, big sunglasses, and a long white robe. I felt naked next to her with just a bathing suit, smeared up with Ray's concoction of baby oil and lemon juice.

"It's not you," she said. "Don't worry about it. Gordon doesn't even know what Gordon wants."

"I feel like I messed it up."

"You wouldn't have heard from us again if you did. Don't worry, he likes you. Despite the reptilian manager."

"Ray is not my manager. We're business partners."

"Is that what he calls it?"

"Well, it's sort of a verbal thing."

"Aha. Verbal. What's the split?"

"He pays by the scene. Plus I work in the office."

"Ahhhh."

I leaned close, took the sunglasses off her face, turned them upside down, put them back on. She took the bottle of lotion out of my hand. "What is this? It smells weird." I told her. Ray said it would lighten my hair and darken my skin, so I would pop more on film.

"Does this have any real suntan lotion in it?"

"I don't think so."

"So he told you to go to the beach and burn yourself?"

"It's for the camera. Darker skin reflects light better. It's *optical*."

She rolled her eyes, mouthed it back at me. "So, this guy. Ray," she said. "You don't think he's taking advantage of you in any way?"

"No. I know what I'm doing. Besides . . . I have it under control. Ray thinks he's a hot shit, but he doesn't know everything about me."

"You're sure of that?" I nodded. "Tell me, how old are you again?"

"Eighteen."

"And how old were you when you started with him?"

"I met him a couple of years ago."

"Uh huh. That's pretty disturbing right there."

All I heard was the wind over the ocean, the traffic on the PCH behind us. Motors grinding somewhere far away.

"You know," she said, "I looked at Gordon's porn stash. Those guys your buddy uses in his movies . . . they look pretty fucked up to me. How do you justify that?"

"It's the business. It comes with the territory."

"Is that you talking or him? The whole thing seems kind of exploitative."

"Kind of what?" With the sun behind her head, I had to shield my eyes with my hand.

"Kind of sick and gross," she said. "And I'm sure you know big words. Why do you play dumb? Better for business?" Had to give her that one. "Your buddy, though, he's getting just what he wants. You know, I worked for a lot of assholes before I met Gordon. Even he talks about it. Guys like your friend . . . they eat people to stay alive."

"Ray is not like that. I told you, I have it under control."

She picked up my arm, pressed her finger to make a white line.

"I have thick skin," I said. "I'm very tough."

"They all say that."

"Now you tell me something. What was all that poking and sniffing when I met you guys at the hotel?"

"Oh, you remember? Sorry. I have to find ways of screening the people Gordon meets. You have no idea the creeps we've had to deal with. Blackmail, robbery, guns . . ."

"So I passed?"

"You're okay." She turned her sunglasses the right way and considered me a moment. "So, is it fun? Do you enjoy it?"

"Enjoy what?"

"What you do. Fucking on film." It made me feel a little lonely the way she said it. I thought we were friends but it sounded like I was this alien object to her.

"I don't know. I get paid. People buy the movies. So who cares?"

"That's not much of an answer. Do you like it?"

"It's fine. Ray says I'm good at it. So yeah. It's a turn-on. If that's what you're asking."

"What do you get out of it?"

"Well, money, to start with."

"No, I mean guys in general. You have to help me here. I don't have a dick and, honestly, dicks aren't my thing. But what's the turn on? I mean, you watch a movie of a couple of guys fucking and that's all it is, a movie. So you pound your pickle, then all you have is a pile of goo. What did you get?"

"Well, don't knock it till you've tried it."

"Seriously, nothing comes of it. And so much effort."

"I don't know. Guys are hound dogs. We like sex. We like to fuck. We like watching guys fuck. Plus, Ray says that's the only thing a lot of guys have, out in the boonies."

"I can see that. But the cost is pretty high."

"They're not that expensive."

"The human cost. To you and all the kids who do this stuff."

I leaned closer to her face, almost close enough to kiss. "I know what I'm doing. It's fucking fun."

"Huh," she said. "Let me ask you this. Who are your good friends?"

My mind went to the fake names I used to use, Fred and Harry and Larry. "I have friends," I said.

"I haven't heard you mention any. All I hear about is Ray this and Ray that. Are you even having a normal kid's life outside of all this?"

"Everything is fine."

She laughed, sadly, looked out at the ocean. "What am I even asking you for? What a business this is."

I shook my head; didn't know what she meant.

"Look at what I do. Celebrity assistant. Besides being a maid and psychologist and personal shopper, I'm a procurer. I call up guys like your boss and arrange sex for money. And Gordon shouldn't have to do that. I don't even think sex is what he wants. And here you are, a kid, burning himself up because some asshole told you it photographs better. Then people buy movies of you all burned up and your buddy dopes you all up so you'll keep doing it and not feel anything and not even have any friends. So, really, what business are we in? What is the name for it?"

"God," I said. "Don't get so steamed up. It's not that serious."

She watched me from under the wide brim, behind the sunglasses, inside the flowing white robe. I couldn't see her eyes.

"Aw," she said. "Sweetie," and kissed me on the lips. Then she reached down and pulled her robe a bit. On the back of her thigh, just above the knee, a small, neat circle of pinpoints. I looked at them, soft pink marks in her white skin. I put my fingertips there to touch them and she shivered. It felt electric. I got hard inside my bathing suit. Her skin was suddenly goosebumps. I leaned forward to feel the marks against my lips.

■ ■ ■

So the summer went on, slow and uneasy. Stuff went crazy in the Middle East, we had to wait in long lines for gas, and it felt like drowning in a bath of smog. I did two scenes for Ray, one in July, one in August. The August shoot would be complicated and he took me a diner to discuss it.

"So," he said, "it sounds like you've made fast friends with Hopalong Cassidy."

"Ray . . ."

"I just meant that you get along well when we introduce you to new friends of the company. That's good, isn't it?"

"Just tell me what it is." I bit into a reuben sandwich taller than my mouth. He picked away at a plain salad. It was strange, I hardly ever saw him eat. He usually just pushed the food around on his plate.

"We need to revisit the fellow in the hills. He came back and offered us the use of his estate for a location. Hideous statuary aside, it really is breathtaking. I'd like to do an outdoor shoot next to this big pool overlooking the city. Two California boys, bright sun, LA in the background. It'll be glorious. You know Vincent, from the carwash scene? You'll make a wonderful matchup." I said it sounded okay. "But there's an additional piece of business. In exchange for the house, our friend would like some private time with the two of you."

"Meaning?"

"A little of this, a little of that. Nothing outlandish, no whips or chains. If all goes well, he's willing to invest a rather stunning amount in future projects. This could be a windfall, Harris. We could afford new equipment, studio space, salaries . . . I mean, this is the opportunity I've been waiting for . . . *we've* been waiting for."

"When does he want it?"

"Near the end of the month. We can't do everything in one day so I was thinking a weekend. You boys could do your magic on Saturday then we'll bring the crew up and shoot on Sunday." He told me what I would make for the movie and the date, and it would pay for most of the summer, so I said ok.

"Wonderful," he said, "just wonderful. I'll put everything in motion."

"What's he like? Is he okay looking?"

"Oh," he said cheerily, filling his mouth. "Wonderful . . ."

21

Which is not to say I didn't get hugely fucked up before we went. Ray was very generous now that I proved myself on camera. He had pills when I asked, and pot and coke; red pills, black pills, quaaludes, you name it. If I felt nervous, he had something to cut the edge. If I needed more energy, he had something else, and depending how many you took, how buzzy you got. I experimented, mixing them up, sometimes with alcohol, to find a combination that made me feel relaxed and able to perform whatever I needed to, and not fall over the cliff.

On the Saturday I waited for Ray to pick me up at a corner but he was late. It was hot and I felt nervous and the longer he took, the more I popped, washing them down with a Yoo-hoo. By the time he pulled up, I felt like I was floating on clouds, happy to meet anyone and anything that happened to drive by. He opened the door and motioned for me to get in. At first I thought I was imagining how sweaty and anxious he seemed, which made me lean back and relax even more. "Jesus," he said, and spread my left eye with two fingers, "will you even be coherent this afternoon?"

"What? I'm fine."

"Just your good luck we're not shooting today."

"Well if you hadn't been late."

"It wasn't my fault," he snapped. "Vincent disappeared. I couldn't reach him last week and he never showed up today. I called and called, and got no answer."

"Oh shit. What are you gonna do?"

"Just . . . let's get up there and I'll figure it out." He drove leaning forward over the steering wheel, like someone's cranky grandma. Adding to the sense of confusion, we passed a billboard on Sunset for the season premiere of *Bowman*, with the guy standing in front, the pretty assistant leaning against him, and behind them, arch and judgmental, Margaret Lawson, DA.

We drove up the street with the Mount Olympus sign, then up to this big temple of a house with statues of naked Greek gods lining the driveway. "God, I'm so fucked up," I said.

"No, you're not. This is real."

It looked like an art museum, but the tacky plaster kind with statues of David with oversize dicks. A butler opened the door, an english guy in a real butler suit. He bowed, showed us through a marble corridor with more plaster statues, all these little angel boys with curled-up angel pricks like pigs' tails. It seemed like they were talking to me, saying, Ha ha you idiot, you moron, you stoned numbskull. I laughed back at them, stuck my tongue out. Ray slapped my arm so hard it echoed off the walls. Outside, in back, a deck overlooked the city with someone lying on a lounger by the pool in a robe. I couldn't see who it was, only the big outline of a body. A pink guy, wearing this wild colored caftan and a pair of sunglasses.

"Come on," Ray said, and pushed me. I couldn't help giggling.

The deck was awesomely huge. I looked over the edge. It was on stilts, the whole thing, and the pool way out in the air. I tried shaking the deck with my hips to see if I could move it.

"What is he doing?" the guy said as he rose from the lounger. He was pretty big – tall, very fat, very white skin, the colored stripes on the bathrobe flashing in front of my eyes like a strobe.

"He's a little nervous," Ray said. The guy approached and I saw a cartoon blob taking over the screen. I crouched down.

"This is really your Kevin, isn't it?" He poked me in the stomach and I laughed. "Take off your shirt," he said. I did, tossed it away. He pulled the front of my shorts out and looked in. "Hhhmm. Alright. Where's the other dipshit? There's supposed to be two."

"Ah, yes," Ray said. "He's at the bus stop. He must have missed the first one. I'll go down to pick him up now. In the meantime, why don't you and Kevin get acquainted." To me, he said, "How does that sound?"

I was so floating I just laughed and clapped like one of those monkey toys with the cymbals.

"Jesus," the fat guy said.

Now, I need to say something here. I know people are sensitive about things, but the honest truth is we called him the fat guy. Not all fat people are like him, he's not like all fat people. This guy was just huge, and he seemed to relish the power in space it gave him. So since that was his power, that's what we called him.

Anyway.

Ray left and the guy took me into the house, pulling me by the front of my shorts. In the bedroom, more statues, posing and preening, looking down at the floor, up at the ceiling, all in this rapture. I couldn't take my eyes off them and I imitated one of the poses. "Stoned little shit," he said. He unzipped my shorts and yanked them to the floor. I giggled as he lifted my legs out, then chucked them away like a sandwich bag. He stood at the end of the bed and untied his robe. Before I could say anything, he grabbed me by the neck and threw me backward. It felt like flying. He climbed on the bed, turned me over and pushed my face into this mound of soft little pillows. Then his body covered me completely and I thought I would suffocate. I tried to scream. He started humping and it made these loud farting sounds that were ticklish and then I was laughing and screaming. "Jesus fuckin' Christ," he said. He lifted off me, turned me around, and with his hands indicated he wanted me on top. I climbed up and realized his dick was poking up from down there, like a little pink periscope, and he was trying to navigate my asshole toward it. I reached around for it, trying to get it to the spot, but it was too hard to aim something behind and below me, and I kept missing. He took hold of my hips, swore a bunch of things, and started poking and huffing. I tried moving up and down but each time I went down, his body bounced me back up. He groaned, pissed off, *"Fuck and fuck and fuck and fuck . . ."* I tried to keep his dick in but it kept popping out. Finally, between him thrusting and huffing, and my hand guiding, he did come, and let out a huge gasp and settled down against the mattress, trying to get his breath back. And just lay there for a while. I stayed still, on top of him, not sure what I was supposed to do.

Eventually he slid me off, stood up and went to the bathroom. He took a shower, then came back in, put on his robe and went out to the kitchen. In this high voice, he yelled, "You want something, sugar? I'm famished!"

I felt dizzy and sticky. Went into the bathroom and showered off. More naked angel statues in there, and white bowls stacked with orange and brown balls that looked appetizing. I bit into one. Soap.

I found my way to the kitchen where the guy was making a sandwich, humming to himself, asked if I wanted one. I said no thanks, but he gave me a big glass of water and said to drink it all. I did, and he re-filled it, told me to drink it again. And a couple more. And then Ray was there, with someone behind him. At first I thought it was a mirror behind him and it was my reflection, but it wasn't. It was Marcus, this kid Ray used on a couple of other shoots. He had his shirt off all day and was red on the shoulders, plus he had grown his hair out so it was long and scraggly.

"Oh lord," the fat guy said. "*Fried* chicken. This should be very entertaining."

"How are you two getting along?" Ray asked.

"Peachy keen," he said. "I sure got my workout for the week." Ray smiled, uncomfortable at the whole situation. "You want to do your shoot tomorrow, right?" the guy asked. Ray nodded, and the guy came around the counter to where I was drinking the last glass. "Good," he said. "So I expect to be *showered* with a little gratitude for my generosity today," and he dinged the glass with his pinkie ring. I gulped the rest down then let out a breath. "N'ok," I said. "I'm ready."

"What about you, wonder bread?" he said to Marcus. "Ready for some fun?" Marcus stood there, not sure what he meant. "Then let's go boys, it looks like rain." To Ray, waving him off, "You can go now. We'll call you if we need you."

"You know," Ray said, rubbing his hands anxiously, "you've got two of our biggest stars, and their needs and, uhm, whereabouts are critically important to the shoot. Perhaps, if it's alright with you, I'll just camp out in the driveway . . . just to be sure we get everyone out when you need us . . ."

"Fine, sure, whatever," he said, and pushed us both toward the bathroom. Ray tried to signal me something about Marcus but I was too bleary to pick it up.

This bathroom had mirrors on all the walls and a big oval-shaped, orange tub. "All right now," the guy said, and dropped the robe. Marcus yelled, "Holy shit!" like he just woke up. "You are *one fat motherfucker.*" The guy stopped, gave him a look of death over his shoulder, then lowered himself into the tub, kind of arranged himself, till he was as comfortable as he could be. "All right," he said, "here's the plan. You two boners listening to me?" I looked at us in the mirror. We did look pretty dumb, mouths hanging open, farmer sunburned and stoned. God knows what Ray gave Marcus on the ride up. "Listen carefully," the guy said. "I want you two to come on me first, then you're going to piss, right where I tell you. Kevin, I want you to come in my mouth, and you, dumbhead . . ." Marcus was looking at his reflection. "Hey, stupid," the guy yelled. "I want you to come on my chest. Then the piss. I'll tell you where when we get to it. You got that?" We both said yeah, and he made us repeat it, but we were wrong. He yelled the instructions again, until we could repeat them back right. "Alright boys," he said, "start your engines."

And we did. Jerked off on the guy, and he loved it, smeared it all over himself. But when it came to the piss, he took up all the room in the tub and it ran onto the floor. Marcus seemed half awake, yawned once, trying to aim where he was told. The guy moaned and rubbed himself all over – *oh yes, oh yes, oh yes* – and he wanted it in his mouth, which was a trick, but also sort of fun to aim, like one of those carnival games. In the end, he was happy, and jerked himself to another big gusher, all bouncing around in there. When he was finished, he told Marcus and me to lift him up, but he was so covered with piss and spooj we couldn't get a grip. Marcus said it must be suction; I thought it was just a bad angle. We tried a couple more times but he was too stuck. I went out and got Ray, and the three of us grabbed a hold of his arms and pulled. Ray had sweaty hands anyway and lost his grip, fell backward and banged his head on the marble floor. "Oh! Jesus!" the guy yelled from inside the tub. "If you splatter your brains on my travertine, I will kill you."

"I'm fine," Ray said, and jumped up. We took another hold, Ray said *Heave*, and he came out with a big wet shlooop.

"Dear god," the guy said. "I have *got* to get a bigger bathtub." He had a huge red indent from the spout on his back. Then he clapped. "OK boys, daddy's got a party and I need you out of here, pronto."

■ ■ ■

Then Sunday, and the shoot.

Vincent never reappeared. Since the fat guy wanted to watch the whole thing, and invited some of his friends, Ray had to use Marcus again. Which was disappointing for me. Not just because I was hot for Vincent, but because Marcus was this scrawny, clueless kid. There was something about him I didn't like, and I certainly didn't want to fuck him.

"Not ideal," Ray said, "I understand you. But he's close enough and we only get one chance. So can you be a trooper and guide him through it, please?"

I looked at this kid and I knew where Ray picked him up, it was all over him. The source, the center of it all.

It's funny because Santa Monica Boulevard actually is the physical center of the industry. The studios are arranged all around it, in Burbank and Culver City and Universal City; the prop houses and film labs and storage places line the side streets; the movie stars live to the west so they have to drive back and forth across it. That two-mile stretch between Fairfax and Wilcox really was the center of everything, and by now, I was more familiar with it, I knew what was going on. The boulevard was kind of a parade, with all these guys walking up and down, day and night, with cars slowing down, opening doors. Like all the big streets here, a river. If you needed money, you could stand on this river, take your shirt off, and someone would open a door to you. For a lot of kids, this was where they started, where they ended up. Thrown out of their town because they're gay, they'd get a bus or a train or a ride, and here they were, in Hollywood. Only it's this long, desperate street, with cars prowling back and forth, people rolling their windows down an inch to take a look at you. See how tasty a morsel you are.

If you walked up and down the street long enough, one thing you noticed were the electric poles on both sides, like enormous sailboat masts; old and wood, with four and five layers of wires suspended high into the sky. If you looked up at them, it was breathtaking, astonishing that wooden poles could stretch that far and carry so much. When the air got cool and the fog set in, the electric lines sizzled loud enough to hear from the street.

Santa Monica was also the center because so much came out of it. You could feel it like energy: desire, hope, need, desperation. The people in cars wanted what the guys on the street had; their bodies, strength, vitality. Youth. The guys on the street wanted what the people in cars had: money, food, security, a place to sleep. And there was all this power, electricity, on the street, in the buzzing transformers ten stories above, flowing east to west, pulling the cars along, pulling all the kids from out there, from the desert, from America, into LA. These guys were charged with that energy, in their short shorts and tight jeans and tank tops, leaning into cars, getting sucked into cars. The cars of directors and producers and casting agents and costume designers. And then on Friday night TV shows, you see the happy family, and you notice they start wearing short shorts and tight jeans and tank tops. The center of it all, this road, naked and raw.

Marcus had shown up a year earlier. I met him while I was working at the office and he was waiting for Ray. I could tell he had nowhere to go. He had the look a lot of those kids did, like hungry mice with their ribs showing. I gave him a bag of chips and a Coke and we talked while I swept. He was from some place out in the desert and he ran away from a foster home where they beat him. He said he got to LA a couple of weeks earlier. I asked where he met Ray and he said he picked him up on Santa Monica, and here he was again, a year later. He'd filled out a little, grew the hair out, but still this stick of a kid. Scrawny Marcus. And now we had this crew, standing around under the blistering sun, and Ray and Ozzie, and the fat guy and his friends, with cool drinks and ice cubes, all staring at us, waiting for us to start.

"Well?" Ray said, and again, "action."

There was no conversation or setup in this scene, just two guys banging by the pool. I knew I would have to begin by kissing Marcus and holding him. He didn't know what to do and just stood there like a dolt.

"Start!" Ray yelled, agitated. So, this was going to be some work. And what do we know about that, what have we learned? So I took him and I kissed him. And this dumb, poor kid didn't know anything, didn't feel anything. "Kiss me back," I whispered, and he did. I tried to shield my mouth from the camera, hoped no one read lips, because I had to tell him when to kneel down, when to stand up, how to suck a dick. I could feel him shaking. I put my arms around him and held him tight, whispered in his ear, it's ok, but I thought he might be crying. I asked for a break. We took a dip in the pool to cool off. Half an hour went by and Ozzie started yelling that the sun was moving. Marcus was shivering, even though the pool was warm. I asked him if he could finish. You know, I said, Ray won't pay unless you finish. He nodded, climbed out and we got back to it. I said, just do the motions and get it over with. But this kid was so scared. I could see Ray charging toward us and I stopped him. "He can't if you yell at him," I said, holding his arm. Ray hissed, "It's all shadows now. We're losing the light." And I turned and looked at this kid and I knew we had to get a scene out of him. So what do you do?

I took Marcus's hand, and put my arms around him. I could feel him shivering. And something inside opened and embraced him. I could see how scared he was; but I felt scared too, because I had to let something out I didn't like to. The only way Marcus would get through this was to be loved and cared for, and so, for that hour and a half, someone would love and care for him. There was no other way. I told him to forget about the camera and the people watching, and I forgot about the camera and the people watching, and made him feel as though it was only him and me, and he was the most important person to me in the whole world. As we got close to the end, I felt him starting to cry and I started crying too. I turned our heads away so no one would see. He kissed me, a real kiss, and I put my hand on his cheek. Ray yelled, "Too close! Too intimate!" I lowered my hand, put it on his side instead. And we got through it. Marcus came and I came, Ray got what he wanted, Ozzie got what he wanted. I held onto Marcus, said good job, but we were both trembling. You can't survive very long being that exposed.

When we were packing the gear, I heard one of the fat guy's friends say, "Well I hope it looks better on film because it certainly didn't look very good from here." Then they laughed and went back inside. Ray paid Marcus and we drove down the hill and dropped him off. I watched in the rear view mirror as he walked away down Santa Monica and disappeared.

22

Saturday, and breakfast. Me, Alicia, George, momma, eating in the kitchen with the TV blabbing. The phone rang and momma answered, talked to grandpa for a while, said "Sure," and handed me the phone.

"What?"

"He wants to talk to you."

"Why?"

She shushed me, shook the phone. I mouth *Why?* again and she shook the phone again.

"Hello dear boy," he said, jaunty and buoyant. I heard the dog yapping, probably on his lap. "We should have lunch. I miss your charming face."

"Uhm, ok." I looked at momma. She shrugged, not convincing. "I can come up with Alicia . . ."

"Oh, let's make it a boys night out, just you and I."

"Ok," I said, and made the date. Momma took the phone from me, hung it up. *I don't know* is all she would say.

On Tuesday I stood in front of his big white door while the doorbell rang the whole long tune, up and down. I heard footsteps and fumbling with the knob and he pulled it open, cigarette in hand.

"Well," he said, looking me up and down, "now that's a package worth waiting for!" He leaned out and kissed my cheek. "Come in, come in."

We talked a few minutes in the foyer, grandpa smiling the way he did, some part of him observing from a distance. "You know, Harris," he said, "the old gasbag is upstairs, sleeping last night off. What say you and I drive down to Brentwood and find a place to eat there?" I met him outside as the garage door started up and he backed his huge Mercedes convertible out. In that car, he looked like the duke of something, a bright pink sweater tied around his big shoulders, white hair brushed back. I got in the passenger side, the big door swinging like a gate, and we coasted down the hill.

"How's tricks?" he yelled, over the wind. He drove like always, a maniac, the tires squealing and him seeming not to notice. Just smiling, steering with his right hand, his left arm draped over the door. I had to hold the armrest to stay upright.

"OK," I yelled back. "The usual."

"Wonderful," he said. "Wonderful!" He took in a big breath, the car flying over the rises and turns on Sunset. "I absolutely love the summer, don't you? The smog is so *crisp.*"

He kept smiling, satisfied and delighted with everything around him.

"Say, did I hear your mother mention a job?" he shouted. "Something about diesel engines?"

"Motors," I yelled back. "It's motors for equipment, like pumps and stuff."

"Aha, motors and pumps. That's of interest to you?"

"It's a summer job."

"Pays well, does it?"

"It's ok."

"I wouldn't have pegged you for a factory worker. Must be a very tidy operation, I must say."

"Huh?"

"Your hands. They're spotless! They must keep a very clean house."

"Oh, I don't . . . I don't work on the motors. Just office work, and stuff."

"Ah, well, that explains it."

When we got to Brentwood the tires screeched as he pulled up and stopped hard in front of the restaurant. He'd already handed the keys to the valet and leapt out; I had to jump and follow. Inside, he knew everybody, floating in with his big sweater and turning to each face, saying, Hello! and Hi there! and You look wonderful! as he glided across the floor with me stumbling behind. At the table, he ordered his martini and I asked for a Coke, but he shook his head at the waiter, gave two fingers. An older couple came over and he spoke with them, shaking hands, smiling his broad smile. They talked a few moments, then the waiter dropped us both martinis and grandpa took a sip of his. I looked at mine, glistening and sparkly in the fancy glass.

"Don't be a prude now, drink up," he said, pointing a forefinger at me. I did, and it was good. He breezed through the menu, said the cobb salad was heavenly, and laid it down. Turned to me and turned on that lovely, open face. "So how are you, my lad? The world is your oyster now. Any plans for the future?" Nothing, I told him. He opened the wine menu, put on the half glasses he wore on a chain around his neck, perused the pages. "Anything in the *love life* department?" he said, dropping the words low.

"Grandpa."

"Oh, come now. Not even a crumb for the old dowager?"

I shook my head.

"Ah well, can't blame a guy for trying." He took the glasses off, wiped them with his napkin. "But say, looks like your grandma's the belle of the ball these days." That was true. They had done so much publicity in advance of the third season, we had hardly seen her. "You know, I hear there's talk of a spinoff," grandpa said, "and all about her."

She hadn't told us that. "Really?"

He nodded. "That would be something, wouldn't it?"

"Yeah," I said. "That would be great."

"Yes," grandpa said, let it hang a moment. "Well, enough about that. Let's get back to you. My word," and he looked me head to foot, "what are we to make of this sudden explosion of, I don't know what . . . all *hair* and arms and legs? Quite striking. Quite a difference from last year. Do tell."

"I don't know what you mean."

"You're an eyeful, young man. You must have all the king's horses and all the king's men running after you. Especially with that . . ." and he meant my jeans, which were pretty tight, "rather provocative leisurewear."

"They're just pants."

"They're never just pants," he said, joking but serious. "Any more schooling on the horizon? College or some such thing?"

"No. I guess I'm not that smart. My grades were pretty bad."

"Don't let it worry you. I never liked school myself. Being smart has nothing to do with grades. Perhaps your expertise lies down other avenues."

Then the sound of people eating and talking and clinking their dishes and silverware in this fancy restaurant; the low him of conversation and civility and manners. His deliberate silence and this feeling of what am I doing here, scraggly and out of place. I felt suddenly exposed. As if he could sense it, he put his hand on mine, said, "Well, don't worry," and sighed. "I couldn't remember school if I tried. Germany was such a long time ago, it seems like something that happened to another person entirely."

When he mentioned things like this, I had to remind myself that's where he was born. Because he had no accent you would never know he came from another country. He told us he was an actor when he first came to the US and he had to get rid of the accent or he'd be playing Counts and Nazis his whole life. He didn't like acting anyway. He gave it up and became a producer or something, which is when he made all his money. Somewhere in there is when he met Nana.

"Never told you much about that, have I?"

No, I said.

"Well, I don't know if I should bore you with my old war stories." I looked as eager as I could, hoping he would talk and stop asking me questions. "Oh, all right," he said. He looked at my martini, indicating I should take another sip.

"My father, Jacob, was a rabbi, did you know that? Pious man. Decent as the day is long. My mother was the same. Kind and devoted. They were very close, very loving. Not rich by any standard. His congregation were hard-working people, none of those Wertheim Department Store types. I think it came as somewhat of a shock when they had this son who grew two heads taller than they were, and all this blond hair. Like some alien in their midst. Not what they expected, I'm sure." He stopped for another sip. "Well, Harris, Berlin was a magical place back then. You cannot imagine how much fun it was. Clubs and shows and films and music . . . so much energy. Almost anything went, and we took advantage of it. Perhaps we knew it was too good to last. We wanted to make the best of it before it was too late. Jewish people especially. My parents were constantly worrying about me because I stood out so much. Not just because of the looks, but everything else." He paused, pondered a moment. "Some girlfriends and I worked up an act for the clubs. Just for a scream. I came up with an alter ego. Her name was Fritzi and she was quite a whore. I wore these very short skirts and high heels and we worked up these funny, dirty songs. I was the singer in front because I was so tall, and the other girls were the chorus. We had whole routines worked out, choreography and everything. We became quite popular, all the clubs wanted us. I became very popular too. Right about the age you are now. People thought it was so funny, Fritzi, this sarcastic old beast with a filthy mouth, and then out of the costume, I come along like some fresh-scrubbed schoolboy. Of course, my folks didn't know anything about my life downtown. It would have killed them. *Killed them* dead. They had their suspicions though. So I moved into an apartment with my friends. My mother and father were afraid of me, I'm sorry to say. And afraid *for* me."

The waiters had been hovering at a distance, waiting for a moment to step over and take our orders. They did, grandpa choosing the cobb salad for us both, another round of drinks, then they quickly stepped away.

"At the time I ignored them," he went on, "I thought they were just silly, scared little people, and I wanted to do what I wanted. The club we performed in was very well-known and everyone important came in. Oh, I got calls and introductions . . . wealthy gentlemen wanting to meet the young man behind Fritzi. Goodness." He rolled his eyes. "And I had fun, believe you me." He leaned closer. "A big blonde Aryan, one of them. We had to keep it secret because he was a Nazi. Well. Not actually. He owned a company that did work for the government, and if you had a government contract, you had to be a party member. He had a wife and children stashed out in the country somewhere, but when he came in town for business . . . he wanted the business. I'm ashamed to admit it now, I was so naïve. In the city we were just having fun. I suppose I should have had a clue from the rough stuff this fellow wanted. They all did. Sadistic bastards. Or is it masochistic bastards?"

Sitting frozen, I barely shook my head.

"Whatever it is," he went on, "they liked to get whooped. So I gave it my all. I whooped the sauerkraut out of that son-of-a-bitch. He loved it too, and let me tell you, I was not weak. He loved it so much he wanted to set me up in an apartment, furnishings and all, so he could get whooped whenever he came into the city. But young as I was, even I knew that was a bridge too far."

I realized my mouth had dried up and I needed to finish the drink to be able to swallow. One of the waiters slipped by with the next round, placed them discreetly in front of us. Grandpa started on the new one even though he hadn't finished the first.

"Well anyway, this fellow became obsessed, and I mean all out obsessed with me. He had his assistant come looking for me all over town when he couldn't find me. It was flattering, of course, but this was 1933, and things were heating up. Even a silly thing like me knew that. And you should have heard the filth that came out of this fellow's mouth. The more I hit him, the more he cursed. Oh, the things he called me while I flogged the bejesus out of him. Jew this, jew that, kike, cocksucker . . . the harder I gave it to him, the more he loved it. My contribution to the war effort I suppose."

Grandpa signaled to a waiter to bring the salads over. He laid the plates down, put fresh napkins in our laps with a flourish, and took off quickly.

"Now where was I? Well. All of this came to a head a few months later. I still don't know exactly what happened. When I went to meet this fellow at the appointed time, I was met instead by a very gruff, very grim mid-level employee, a security man or something, who made it clear I was entirely mistaken about such a rendezvous. And how dare I even suggest that Mr. so-and-so would be acquainted with a degenerate like myself. I was advised, somewhat menacingly, to remove myself from the premises, which, by that point, I was more than happy to do."

He started eating his salad, telling the rest of the story through bites of crisp lettuce. Picking away, smiling, looking up, at me, around us, I was aware that anyone watching would assume he was chatting pleasantly about gardening or some trivial thing.

"Don't know what happened," he said. "My guess is someone in the party got wind of his extracurricular activities. Can't imagine he came to his senses of his own accord. Anyway, a few weeks later I was coming home from a night on the town, all alone, down some empty street, and I had the feeling of being followed. Being a bit drunk, I didn't move fast enough and before I knew it, bang, they were on me, several fellows I think. All I can recall is a surge of adrenaline, and whatever survival instinct one calls upon. Somehow, I found the strength to fight my way out and get clear. They pursued me, but only to an extent, and I banged on the door of a friend's apartment to let me in. Well, whatever it was, I got the message, loud and clear. I visited my parents and told them I was leaving Berlin. They were both relieved, I think. Relieved I was finally aware of the danger and taking some steps. My father, kind soul that he was, gave me enough money for the boat and to help sustain me in the US. And I ended up being very lucky. I got out and found people here who helped me get set up." I did have a question, but something behind his even demeanor told me it was not the time to ask. "Anyway," he said, "all water under the bridge. A different time and a different world. And here we are now, so fortunate to be able to share confidences and a wonderful lunch in a beautiful place like this."

I nodded, as sincerely as I could.

"Any thoughts?" he said. "Shock? Incredulity? Makeup tips?"

I looked at my hands, twisting the fancy napkin in my lap. "Are you telling me this for a reason?"

"Goodness, no. Just an old gossip, that's all. Reliving past glories, now that I belong to the Geritol set."

If he was content to let it go, I was too.

"But if there *were* a moral to the story," he said, "though moral decay sounds more like it . . . if there were a moral, I suppose it would be that we think ourselves invincible when we're young. We think we can do anything and nothing can hurt us. Fortunately, we don't have Nazis running after us anymore, so the sentiment only goes so far. But keep it in mind. The things we do have … ramifications."

I made a laugh, maybe a groan.

"What?" he said.

"Grandpa. No one even knows I exist. I'm invisible."

He didn't react, just went on eating his salad. After a moment, he reached across the table and put his hand on the side of my face, very gently. I remembered how he looked at me that first time I met him, like I was someone who mattered. He held his hand there for a moment then let me go.

23

The card was thick blue velvet with a gold logo at the top. I was curious so I picked it up from Ray's desk. The logo was a bunny.

"Nosy," Ray said, and took it back.

"What's that for?"

"Industry event. We're on someone's list."

"Are you going?"

"Lord no. Who wants to hang around Hugh Hefner's vagina party?"

"Can I go?"

He looked at me over his glasses. "I beg your pardon? See the address? Raymond Cicero, President. *Presidente.* Not anyone who happens to pick up mail off someone's desk."

"I think it would be fun to go. You're always saying you have to do publicity. Isn't that publicity?"

"Neither you nor I have the *equipment* to do much by way of publicity at an event like that."

"Well, I think it would be fun." I took the invitation back. "Look. It says 'and guest.' Raymond Cicero and guest."

He put his hands on either side of his head. Just to shut me up I guess. "Alright, alright. But only for the experience. I don't want to make a whole night of it."

So this was on a Saturday. Ray picked me up and we drove into the hills to the Playboy Mansion. They had security guys checking invitations, valets, girls in silky dresses, guys in fancy suits, in tacky suits, the whole routine. It did make you feel like royalty to drive up to this beautiful place and people let you in like you're something special.

I did a little coke before we went so I was pretty upbeat. The whole thing seemed to unnerve Ray; driving up there, I thought of a lobster in a trap rattling the bars with its claws. He actually drank alcohol that night and I couldn't recall seeing him do that. More than one, in fact; he had a couple of whatever he was drinking, wine spritzers or something, and kept mumbling, "This is not my milieu."

We wandered around, looked into all the fancy rooms; outside to the famous yard and the stone pool, the grotto. "*Grotty* is more like it," Ray said. It really made you high, the music, the sexy people, the whole energy. No one spoke to us except the waiters, offering us more drinks and hors d'oeuvres; I was liking it but Ray was getting weirder and more anxious. Less than an hour in, he said he wanted to go. "Oh, come on," I said, "let's walk around a little more." I had a couple more drinks and noticed people giving me the once-over, which at the Playboy Mansion was pretty cool. When they moved to Ray, they diverted their eyes like they looked at a car accident by mistake. I was floating pretty high when we got to this library, a big wood arch leading to a warm, dark room with a fireplace. A security guy asked to see our invitation and I poked Ray. I showed it to him. He waved me in, but stopped Ray when he tried to follow. "But I'm with him," Ray whined. This guy, no-fuck-with-me-big, stuffed into a fancy suit, shook his head. "This is outrageous!" Ray shouted. "How dare you? I'm an invited guest!" Something about the alcohol and the vibe and the warmth of the fireplace pulled me into the room, and I watched myself shrug at Ray as I moved away. "Harris!" was the last thing I heard, and him stomping the floor, before some guys slid quietly behind him, took him by the elbows, and moved him out of sight.

I floated in, and people did start to talk to me; girls with definitely huge boobs, very pretty and very nice and interested in what I was saying. I don't remember any of it, but they nodded and laughed in all the right places. I thought how interesting it was that people acted so fascinated when I knew whatever I was saying was probably crap. It was so much fun to just talk and laugh and not worry about anything. I spotted an empty cushion near the fireplace and dropped onto it, letting the warmth heat my skin. And the feeling of someone entering the space behind me.

"Now, what's wrong with this picture?"

It came from a very deep voice. I looked up and it was a man. Big and powerful, wearing a sleek gray suit, vest, perfect red tie. Maybe thirty-five, forty.

"Not mixing with the ladies?" he said, and I laughed.

"Not my thing," I said, and he laughed.

"Aw, pity. Every red-blooded American boy would give his left nut to be where you are right now."

"Their loss," I said. I don't know why I felt this calm.

"Mind if I join you?" He indicated the round footstool next to me. He was so big he had to spread his legs wide to get onto it. He looked at me with the most intense, curious expression, even more so because his skin was so black, his beard black, with sprinkles of gray around the sides.

"So. What's a nice boy like you doing in a place like this?"

"No nice boy," I said. "Just some jerk."

"That can't be true. You got yourself into the VIP room. You must be somebody."

"It was my boss's invitation."

"That fella they dragged out whining and crying?"

I laughed again, nodded.

"Well then, you're the one who's special, that why you're inside." The guy was a player and you just had to shake your head at someone like him. "So, who do we have here?" he said. "Actor, director, producer? All of you in this town seem to be one thing or another."

"Just an office boy."

"You don't say? They're lettin' office boys into the Playboy Mansion with private invitations?" And he let out this laugh, this deep *bah-hah-hah* that could have opened the ground if he wanted it to.

"My boss makes movies," I said. "I hope he's okay."

"He's fine. Cool his jets a little. But back to you … bit of a curiosity, if you don't mind my saying. Nice young man like yourself, chillin' by the fireplace, meanwhile they carrying the director off in a huff. You telling me the whole story?"

"Sometimes I do movies."

"So I was right. You are an actor."

I shook my head. He leaned closer to my face, this quizzical look. I did the fuck sign, index finger through an O in the other hand. "Ah HA," he said, like a buzzsaw. "*Now* we're getting someplace. Alright then, this whole routine . . ." he made a circle at me ". . . startin' to make some sense. You one of them fancy boys, huh?"

"No," I said, to the inside of my glass.

"You're in pictures, boy, you must be the shit."

"No shit. Just a nobody."

"Aw come on now. We've established you're an invited guest at this event, so someone must have thought you were important. And you're a working actor, in a dynamic and exciting industry. Already I've discovered two fascinating things about you. So this whole I'm-just-a-nobody thing can't be all true, now can it? I mean, can it?"

"Come on," I said. "You're . . . you don't even know me."

"Well, I'd like to. May I do that? May I tell you what a fascinating person I find you to be, after only talking with you these few minutes? May I tell you that?"

I mean you just had to shake your head at this guy. He knew he was playing, and he knew you knew he was playing, but he was having so much fun, you had to let him keep going.

"Sure," I said. "Yeah."

"But you don't believe me, do you? You think I'm giving you a line?"

"Yeah, no, sure. I believe you."

He closed one eye, considered me a long moment. "Now come on, what are you thinking? Be honest. You don't know me, I don't know you. You can't hurt my feelings. What are you thinking?"

"I'm thinking," I said, "why is some big business guy like you talking to a jerk like me?"

He sat back in mock horror. "For the present, let me just say that I've been gratified to have spent these few minutes getting to know you. And if I'm not good enough to enjoy the pleasure of your company, then I'll just take my little old self and find me a place to retire to in this big, scary mansion." He stood and reached out to shake my hand.

"Come on," I said.

He shook his hand at me again.

"Come on," I said.

"Does that mean you'll allow me to get to know you a little better? Would you grant me that gift?"

"Yes, ok. Just please sit down, ok?"

"You're sure?" he said, with that wild, curious look. "I'm not embarrassing you?" Really loud.

"No. Come on." He let out the laugh again, settled back on the cushion. And stared at me. And stared.

"What?" I said.

"Well, it's just manners."

"What is?"

"After all this time? After all we've been through? You don't want to know to whom you've been speaking?"

"Yes, sure, of course."

"Nah, you first. You're the more interesting one of us."

"Why do you keep saying that? What do you mean?"

"Saying what? The truth? Don't you think you're the most interesting person at this whole shindig?"

"Come on. No. Stop it."

"You don't, do you? Now, why is that? Why wouldn't you think you're the smartest, handsomest, most talented son-of-a-bitch at this whole event? And it's just my luck . . . my *honor* . . . to have stumbled across you and been able to spend this time with you. Why wouldn't you think that as your very first thought?"

I mean, what do you say to this guy?

"But you don't believe me," he said. "*Thaaaat's* all right, you think what you need to. I got plenty of time. But you got me hooked now." He leaned forward, like a huddle in a football game. "I gotta know more. Will you let me get to know you some more?"

"Ok," I said, not quite able to meet those intense eyes.

"Ok . . ." he said, and let it hang. I didn't know what he meant. "And you are . . .?"

"Oh. Harris."

"Harris," he said. "My oh my. Rhymes with Paris. Beautiful city. Beautiful place. You ever been?" Shook my head. "Well, we'll have to go some time. Stay at the George Cinq, in the suite I always stay in. Looks out over the Eiffel Tower. Will you do that with me?"

"I . . . I don't . . ."

"Don't what?" This mischievous, delirious expression.

"Don't know?" I said.

"Well, why don't you ask?"

"*What?*"

"Who's inviting you to stay in his suite in Paris, boy. Overlooking the *god-damn* Eiffel Tower. Is that what you mean to ask?"

"Sure, ok."

"Well, hell, I thought you'd never get around to it." He stuck out his hand again and I took it. "John B. Ryan. B for you better believe it. Captain of industry, titan of media." I waited while he kept holding my hand. "Newspapers mostly. East coast, mid-Atlantic region. Based in Cincinnati. Out here for confabs and powwows. And meeting the locals. So it is a pleasure to meet you, sir. I am honored."

"Me too."

"What's that?" he said, still holding, with that smile. I couldn't tell if it was a threat or he was kidding or about to punch me. Raw and dangerous.

"It's my pleasure to meet you too," I said.

"You're *honored* to meet me."

"Honored."

"You bet you are. You tell people that when they meet you. They should be honored to meet you." He poked me in the chest when he said this. Not hard, just enough to give me a stiffie. *"And don't you forget it."*

"OK," I said.

"Ahhhright. You're lettin' this go in one ear and out t'other. *That's* OK. I got all the time." He let go of my hand, sat down again. "Now, tell me.

You have some obligation to fulfill? Some performance to perform? Why don't we get out of this place and find somewhere else to talk."

"But Ray is here. I can't just leave him."

"He got a car?" I told him so. "You got a car?" I told him no. "Then why you worrying? He'll cool down, drive himself home and be all refreshed come morning."

I had to think a moment. "Well . . ."

"What are you, his keeper?"

"No."

"He some incompetent, some mental defective who can't find his way home?"

"No."

"Then why you takin' care of him? Sounds like the man's perfectly capable of getting himself into his own bed. Unless you and he ... " and he made a slurping sound.

"Eww, no, he's just a friend."

"Well then?"

He stood up, this big man in a beautiful silver suit. I looked closer and it wasn't really silver, it was plaid. Little elegant plaids. You think plaid looks like a tacky car salesman, but this was some kind of beautiful material, tailored perfectly to his powerful body. Glen plaid he told me later. Like a second, fine skin I'd never seen on anyone before.

■ ■ ■

His room at the Century Plaza overlooked the city, quiet and humming from this angle. This hotel was famous for its curved shape: the front, where the cars pulled up and the noise and hustle of valets; and the back, broad and open, facing a sloping hillside of dark, quiet trees. Like the long naked back of a person lying on soft grass.

In the room we talked some more and he made drinks from the minibar. The light low in here, the lights of the city sparkling in the distance. I sat in one of the big square chairs against the wall, facing the room. Set my arms on the arms of the chair, and it made me feel like a judge. He did the serious businessman strip-off, kind of a burlesque, except with a suit: shrug off the jacket, hang it neatly on the chair; loosen the tie with a few tugs; take off the vest; unbuckle the belt; remove the tie completely; sit on the bed and take off the shiny black shoes and black socks. I'm sitting watching all this, and I've seen guys do it before. They're trying to impress you with the authoritative way they take off their stuff, but I'm not buying it. Then he unbuckles the expensive belt, removes that, drops the trousers – the coins and thick wallet go clunk on the floor, another thing they want you to notice – and of course expensive boxers. Unbuttons the white shirt. Goes to the bathroom and comes out in the white robe. It's an interesting set-up. We're playing some game I don't know the name of.

"How's your drink?" he says. He does a few more dumb things, looking over papers on the desk, checking something in his wallet. Then he turns off the light and sits on the bed opposite the chair where I've been watching. He's very good. He's rich and powerful, he has businesses and makes decisions in an office in some high-rise with a secretary. I'm nothing compared to him, but he's doing an act now while I sit, across from him, in the chair, watching him on the bed in his robe.

For another moment.

Then I'm launched through the air. Slap against him and my pants are ripped off, the t-shirt off. I want my skin against his right now. His dick is a steel pole, and I have to have it, and mine is free, and he has to have it, like a bomb we have to defuse before it blows up. His hands shaking, tearing his way to it, and my whole nakedness pressed against him, the robe and boxers half off, wrinkled, pushed out of the way. Scuffling, rubbing, we're on the bed, and it's a fight to get to each other, and suddenly, as I pressed against him I came, just out of nowhere, and it felt great, but only the first one, and nothing to stop for. "Oh hell," he says when he realizes, and our mouths are locked, sealed together. The rough scrape of his chest hair and legs make me almost come again and I try to control how intense the feelings are, turn them down so I don't shoot right now.

John is big. Like someone who used to be a football player, now with a businessman's body, all the weight and responsibility. But the desire is still there, and heat, like crazy. He smelled so good. I don't know how long it was but I got tired of fumbling and grasping. I wanted him inside me, I wanted him to fill me up. I got him wet, learned its shape and weight with my mouth then stood up and over and onto it, slow, letting him come into me as I dropped onto him. And once he's all the way in, he's not a mean, I-got-you-and-I'm-gonna-hurt-you, like some guys. Once he's in, there's this shock in his eyes. I'm the one opening up and taking him, but he has this urgency for something, and he lets me see it; surrendering to me, letting me do what I want, showing me what he wants and trusting I'm going to do it, or be it. I used every bit of what I know. His eyes are so big in the darkness. He doesn't speak, his mouth an O. I ride him a good, satisfying, long time, and I can feel when he's ready the first time. I know he's been having little orgasms in there and I know how to push him over the edge, and he does go over the edge, and moans, "oh . . .. my . . .. god." That's my prize, and I feel him filling me and it's enough to bring me over too, and he's moaning and lost in it as much as I am.

When the sensation dissipates, when my breath and his breath come back to normal, I don't want to let him out. I want him to stay inside. "Oh my god," he says again after a few minutes. I know he wants to move, but I know too when he does the sensations will overwhelm him. And they do. He starts to pull out, still hard, and almost cries with pleasure. I'm hard again, and as he pulls out of me, I let myself come again and he whispers, "oh my god," and I roll off him, into the wet, tangled sheets, just breathing, breathing, breathing, and nothing else.

"Mother. Fucker," he gasps in the dark. I feel the terrycloth moving under my body, like a magic carpet flying me away, into exhausted sleep.

■ ■ ■

Half awake in the early morning, before six probably. Him asleep and snoring. Light peers through the edge of the drapes and I can see him, survey him like a landmass. His clothes off, his skin dark and thick. And I feel something under my hand I don't recognize. Ridges and bumps. I move my hands and they're everywhere. Like he's covered with something, but only under his clothes, where people can't see. I pull the sheet slightly;

they're marks, or scabs really, each one the size of a walnut, all over him. They're not open sores or contagious or anything, just healed-up scars of something that happened a long time ago. I look at this ocean of shapes, put my full palm gently flat on his sleeping back. The thickness of his skin, like the bark of a tree. And I suspect, even now, this is something I will never be allowed to know.

I hug closer to him, try to press myself inside. He rumbled a sleepy grumble, the other big arm coming around me.

24

Of course, Ray was out of his mind.

"How could you do that to me?" he shrieked over the phone. "I didn't know where you were! I had to find my way all alone! What kind of person leaves someone at a party like that?"

"Hey," I said. "Am I your keeper?"

"What? No. What do you mean?"

"Are you some mental defective who can't find his way home?"

Silence. Then, "What on *earth* are you talking about?"

"So it sounds like you *did* get home, whether I was there or not. So what's the problem?"

He seemed unsure. "It just isn't like you to abandon someone like that.
. . I find it very suspicious, that's all."

"Well don't."

More silence. Him calculating what he needs to say versus what he wants to. I guess he decides on humble. "Goodness, I don't know what came over me. Only two drinks as far as I can tell. Put me very out of sorts. But still. Those bouncers manhandled me like a sack of potatoes. I thought they were going to throw me into the street head first."

"What happened?"

"They pulled me into an antechamber of some kind. Someone brought me a cup of coffee and some very busty girls brought hors d'oeuvres that were . . . well, now that I think of it, they were rather good. Shrimp puffs I think. And scallops, wrapped in bacon. Went very well with the white wine."

"So there you go. Everything's fine."

"Well, no it's not, Harris. You abandoned me. I was very worried. God knows what can happen in a place like that. I thought you might have been kidnapped or something."

"I wasn't, so don't worry."

"But where did you go? Did you just leave and hitchhike down the hill?"

Oh well, I thought. You have the rip the bandage off some time.

"There was a guy there. I was talking to him."

"Uh huh?"

Silence. Breathing.

"And he was interesting. He was funny."

"Uh *huh*."

"And we, uhm, went back to his hotel."

"Uh huh."

"So that was all."

"I see," he said. "Well," he said. "I'm sure that was very nice for you." Another pause, and I'm waiting for what's coming next. But he only says, "Well, lots of business to attend to, I'll speak with you later," and I can barely say goodbye before he hangs up.

■ ■ ■

John sent a limo to pick me up. Momma was out but Alicia stared out the livingroom window as I got in, her jaw hanging open.

I don't know how John knew when we would arrive, but there he was at the front of the hotel when we drove up. He opened the door for me and put his arm around my shoulder to guide me inside.

"Miraculous day, isn't it?" His voice boomed like he owned the place. He led me to the restaurant, the hostess coming alive when she saw him. "This is Veronica," he said. "She and I had quite an interesting talk about her new boyfriend, Todd." Then lower: "Todd is *quite* the ladies man." Veronica blushed. I could see in two minutes flat he had won her over for life. "Veronica, this is my very good friend Harris. What kind of a spot could you rustle up for us?" She looked at me but didn't see, her eyes starry for him alone. "Right this way," she said, and fumbled with the menus, giggling before she righted them and led us to a window seat. "You're a godsend," he said, and gave her this huge bearhug. "Now," he said, "what will you have? I know. How about everything? Can I get that for you? May I order everything on the menu for you?"

"Come on," I said. "Don't start."

"You think I'm exaggerating?" He snapped for the waiter's attention. "How much of a problem would it be if I ordered everything on the menu for this young man?" The waiter opened his mouth, not sure what was happening. "I would, too," John said, half to the waiter, half to me. "Don't you think you're worth it? Don't you think you deserve someone ordering everything in the whole damn place for you?"

The waiter looked at me nervously.

"Come on," I said, and tilted my head toward the kid. "Stop."

"Well, we'll talk about it," John said, and looked at his nametag. "Bertram. Thank you, Bertram. We'll just consult on this and get back to you." He winked this conspiratorial wink, then Bertram was in on it too. John watched him walk away, whistled loud and sharp. To me, "Mmmm-mmm now that's a tush. Take a look back there, you see? Whoooeee, you all got some good lookin' tushies out here. Not as good as the ones we got in *Ahiya*, but I could get used to these too. You think his tushie was sweet?"

It was impossible not to get caught up. "Yeah. Sweet."

"Not as sweet as yours, though," he almost yelled. "Now that's some *legendary* tushie."

"Oh my God," I said into the menu

"But what do you think? You, me and Bertram, tonight? Get us some room service porter house and mix it up? Three-way and a steak! You up for some of that sweet tushie?" All I could do was shake my head in disbelief, his eyes still just as crazy.

"What?" he said.

"I don't know what to make of you."

"Baby, you can't make anything of me, 'cuz it's already made, and it's perfect."

"Amen," I said, to the menu.

"Beg pardon?"

"I said, Amen."

He looked that look at me – head turned slightly, eyes expectant, like something about to explode. "You screwin' with me?"

"You bet I am," I said to the menu, and the laugh exploded out of him.

"But now there is one thing I want to know," he said. I imitate the look he gives me, over my nose. "Will you allow me to get to know you a little better?"

"Huh?"

"Will you do that for me? Let me get to know a little more about what's going on behind all this mystery and subterfuge?"

"There is no mystery and subterfuge. What you see is what you get."

"Oh, you must have me mistaken for a sucker," he said. "The kind of people you surround yourself with, right?"

"You don't know what you're talking about."

"Uh huh," he said. Considered me a long moment. "We'll see. We will see."

■ ■ ■

Sometimes things happen in slow motion. You're in the middle of a scene and you have to fend off one person with an outstretched arm, another with a foot, like a karate movie. But you can't move fast, you're stuck in molasses. That's what it felt like when the limo pulled up in front of the house. John gave me a kiss and leaned out. He could sense something was off too. "Uh oh. Time to get my face outta this place." He closed the door fast, the limo took off, and the front door of the house flew open and momma came at me. Alicia sitting in the window, watching. And I sensed something behind me, turned and looked, and it was the Grand Prix, parked not exactly across the street but in front of the next house, and Ray sitting inside, watching.

Momma walked out fast, pretending not to. The sound of the limo's engine gunning down the street, leaves and dust blowing behind.

I looked quickly back to Ray, my eyes wide, *don't you dare get out of that car,* trying not to let momma see I'm looking at him. She's got the dish towel, drying her hands like it's a normal morning and she's coming to greet the mailman.

"How are you?" she said, hard.

"Fine."

"Where have you been?"

"Out with friends."

"Your friends have a limousine?"

"Someone I know."

She finished drying her hands. "Get in the house." Her eyes moved to the car across the street. As she watched, I heard the engine start and the car begin to drive away. I'm thinking, You stupid shit.

"Get in the house," she said again.

At the kitchen table, she poured us both coffee. Alicia stood against the counter like a little prig. Momma said, "Go to your room." She did the *Awww* face; momma said it again and she went.

"Look," momma said, "this can't go on."

"What?"

"This out all the time and I don't know where or with who. You obviously have a life you're not telling me about, and I can't have that."

Her hands were shaking.

"It's just friends." I didn't even care what I was saying.

"I . . . I can't have things going on in my own house I don't know about. You've made it clear your life is none of my business and I can't . . . I just can't tolerate whatever it is. And your grandmother ... she's very concerned."

"What does what I do have anything to do with her?"

"I'm just telling you. She's worried. And honestly, I have no standing. She doesn't listen to me if I defend you . . ."

"And do you?"

"What?"

"Do you ever stand up for me? Or yourself?"

And that got her. "I don't want to get into it. I just can't. Everything is going nice and steady right now and I don't need any trouble. I really don't."

"So what are you saying?"

But we both knew.

"Ok," I said. "I'll start looking tomorrow," and I walked out. Halfway down the hall, I yelled, "happy now?"

■ ■ ■

But I wanted to get my own place anyway, so it was really no problem. Ozzie knew a guy who used to model for the company and needed a roommate. His name was Aaron Dodge, but that wasn't real. He was shorter than me, with this very tight, muscular body that looked like it was bursting with power but bound up tight. He had this swagger, and sort of a half-smirk that made him seem like your older buddy who put his arm around you. Super blond hair, mischievous blue eyes, warm and teasing when he was calm, but if he was angry, something entirely different. Then his whole face changed. I saw the same face on a lot of guys; their eyes would narrow and pull back, and they didn't look like people, they looked like foxes or coyotes backed into a corner. I think it was the look of people who had terrible things done to them when they were small – not being treated like a human – and now they had this face that looked like a hunted animal. I would have fallen in total love with Aaron except he didn't have any interest in me and he was pretty much an addict, which might have explained the screaming hot body.

"Yo, Horace Glumbeger," he said, when I called about the room. I liked that he had name for me, but I wasn't crazy about that one. "Yeah, Matty moved out so it's open. But are you still working for that prick Ray?"

I said I was.

"Great, ok, but I don't want everything I do getting back to him. I like you, man, but if you live here, you have to keep it separate, you know?"

"I get it. I have other work too."

"You on a service?"

"No," I said, not sure what it meant.

"Aw, fuck, man, services are great. They take care of everything. Good money, good work. I can hook you up."

"Ok," I said. "Thanks."

"Sure. You working for other studios?"

"Uhm, no."

"Hey, you know, Ojai's always looking for guys. They'd totally dig you. Go talk to Mel, uhm, Grinsom or Grissom or something like that, the guy over there. Tell him I sent you."

"That's great, thank you."

"Sure, man, of course. I mean, anybody's better than that son of a fuck Ray. Honestly."

25

John came back like he said. The next weekend, and the weekend after that. He sent a limo to pick me up and bring me to whatever hotel he was staying at.

I wasn't sure what to make of the probing. He meant it and he liked it and he wanted to get to know me, but I wasn't used to someone asking me things without some other motive. He liked coke too, and he was rich and knew how to get it, and the good kind, which was good because it gave me more confidence to fend him off when he started in on me – like this particular weekend at the Beverly Hills Hotel. He did a couple of lines after I did, humphed it out to clear his head then sat on the bed in his bathrobe. Picked up the newspaper and his reading glasses, read for a minute, then put it down. Then picked up the conversation again.

"So, you met this fella, how? Getting a blowjob behind a convenience store?"

"Close enough," I said.

"And says he's a director and he wants to make you famous?"

"Yeah."

"Well, look at you, workin' that thing. You know just what you're doing, don't you?"

"I do," I said, and kissed him.

"You gonna keep doing it?"

"I don't know. Who cares? It's money and it's fun."

"It is that, I am sure. But how about the future? You got any interests and desires? I mean, besides fucking?"

With John it was hard to know what was a genuine question and what was a criticism. I found that a neutral position was good until I understood. "Maybe. I don't know. Doesn't matter."

"Well, it's your life, it ought to matter. Isn't your life important? Isn't your time important?"

I lay on the bed with my head in his lap, legs to the side, looking up at him. "Who wants to know?"

"Just a question. Some of us have goals. Some of us work for a living. Wish I could just bone all day and get paid for it."

"We can, you know, and it won't cost a thing."

"Boy, you are just a little whore, aren't you?" He pinched my nipples.

"Ow. Yes." I slapped his hand away.

"You ever think about college?"

"Uhm, *what*? How did we get there?"

"Just curious. Not a bad thing, you know. Education."

"I'm too dumb." I reached under his robe to grab his dick. He pushed my hand out.

"There it is again. We ought' talk about that."

"What are you, the guidance counselor? I'm fine. I know what I'm doing."

"You think I'm feeding you a line?"

"I know you're feeding me a line."

"Be that as it may, I'll ask again. Do you think you're worth as much as anyone else? And don't give me the whole *it don't matter, nobody notices me, I'm invisible* thing."

"I do not say that."

"Oh, I've heard you say it. Ver-bay-tim."

"Well, so what? That's the way things are. Some people are important, some people aren't. That's the world."

"Kind of insulting to me," he said, suddenly serious.

"What?"

"That I'm wasting my time, and my hard-earned money, flying across the country to see someone who's not important. Disrespectful to me is all. You think I want to hear that? You think I want to be told I'm wasting my time with people who aren't important?"

"You do just what you like."

"And what am I doing here?"

I grabbed for his dick through the robe and stuck my tongue out. He pushed my hand away, harder this time. "Now, seriously," he said. "That's what you think this all about? That's what I am to you?"

"Well. No." We seemed to have veered off the road and I hurt him. "I don't know what you want. I don't know what you're doing with me at all, if you want to know."

"Eh?"

"I mean, guys like you. They want trophy boys . . . the six-foot supermodels with chiseled teeth. I'm this dumb, scrawny slob. I don't even know what you want."

"Guys like me? What kind of a guy am I?"

"You know. Company car, company suit . . . all that stuff you talk about. How you have to have," and I do his deep voice, *"a fine watch and fine shoes and a fine wallet.* Like those are important."

"Good lessons to learn. You try walking into an office with the raggedy rags you all wear. But we aren't talking about me, we're talking about you. Poor little you and your sad little self."

"It isn't that. I mean . . . it's just how it is."

"So, what are you, worthless?"

"Well . . ."

"Tell the truth. Are you worthless? Is someone else worth more than you? A trophy boy, say. Is he worth more than you?"

I didn't like this conversation at all. I leaned down, burrowing into his robe. "Now . . . stop that . . ." and he pulled my hair.

"Ow."

"Gotta do that, I guess. Feel like you're nothing so you can justify what you're doing."

"What am I doing?"

"Well, that's what I asked in the first place. What do you expect to do after you finish with the fuckin'?"

"I don't know," I said to his crotch. "I don't have a plan."

"First honest thing you said today. Maybe all month."

He looked me over seriously, then picked up his paper again; snapped it open and started reading.

"Well?" I said.

"Oh, you want me to continue? I thought you were through with me for the evening."

"Fucker." I punched his arm. "Talk."

"Ok. Say, you, uh, wanna go pop a couple more of them pick-me-ups before we begin?" I must have looked surprised. "Oh yes, I see what you got stashed away in your pockets. I told you, I am not one of your fools."

I punched him again, harder.

"Ow," he said, rubbing.

"Come on," and I yanked the paper away. He gave me the half comical, half furious look.

"You are one strange white boy. I have no idea if you believe what you say or you're just playing me like you do everyone else."

I sat up. "I don't play anyone. If anyone plays anyone, it's you."

"Ha! You got that Ray fella wrapped around your little pickle."

"What? I work for him. He's my boss."

"He's in love with your ass."

"He is not."

"Is too. I bet you don't even see it. That's what I mean. You don't see anything going on around you a'tall . . ."

"Well not about Ray. That's gross." I got off the bed and opened the mini-bar. Poured out something, one of the little bottles and drank it. Opened a tonic water and drank that. Came back and flopped next to him.

"So what am I supposed to do?"

"You're asking my advice?"

I stared.

"Well, for starters, maybe give some thought to the nasties. You want to be fuckin' on film when you're forty-five? Not a pretty thought. Plus they got some new kind of VDs running around. Don't know about you, but I don't want some ugly bug cluttering up my handsome face."

"I like what I'm doing. It's my life."

"It is indeed. That's all I'm sayin'. So you go back to your fuckin' and gruntin' and gettin' off on everyone watching your pretty ass. And it is pretty," he said, and made a grab. I jumped off the bed.

"Hey! No! Not after that."

"What? I give you a little good advice from the bottom of my heart ... advice *you* asked for . . . and now I don't get no ass?"

"Well I don't know," I said, turned around and pulled my pants down.

"Oh lord. You are an evil little fucker."

■ ■ ■

Amanda called and invited me to Gordon's for Thanksgiving. I was surprised because that's kind of a family holiday. She said he had his on a different day so everyone could be with their own families; this one was just for his friends. "He'd really like to see you," she said. "I would too."

He had it in the big dining room in Encino, with the stuffed antler heads and Teddy Roosevelt guns on the wall. His friends were mostly old, not anyone who looked like they would be associated with cowboy Gordon. Gay guys, some couples, funny old queens, a lot of single people who looked like they had nowhere else to go. I looked around and realized I was the only one of me there – no other young guys, no dates he might have befriended. And the people were pretty nice. No one asked how I met Gordon, only about my life and what I was interested in. Nobody I wanted to fuck though, and at that moment, a high priority.

After dinner, Gordon asked if he could show me something. He took us down a long corridor to the garage, which was a whole wing on one side of the house. We walked past his Rolls, his Mercedes, two Jaguars, custom Jeeps, all with his license plates, Gordy1, Gordy2, etc. We kept walking until we came to the far end, where there was this plain old car covered by a thick layer of dust. Compared to all the others, a piece of junk. It was, he said, a '69 Mustang fastback. Light green – under the dust – and as he walked around it, told me about it, what kind of engine it had, the repairs he'd done. Not restored at all, he said. Just a beauty by itself.

"It's nothing like the others," I said.

"No, it isn't."

He put his hand on the roof and rested it there, like he was trying to memorize it. "But it doesn't fit me anymore. Or maybe I don't fit in it. Either way, we've grown apart."

I didn't know why he was telling me this, and sort of didn't care. "Sorry?" I said.

"Ah well. That's life." He took the keys off a nail and handed them to me. "You keep it for a while. This is a car for a young man."

I was sort of startled. I looked at the keychain with its little kicking horse, and went to give him a hug. He let me, but he didn't like it. I let go and stepped back. He was about to say something more, but the house-keeper called us from down the hall for dessert. He nodded and led us back to the dining room.

■ ■ ■

Ray said we had to go to lunch. I figured we'd walk to the chili stand but he said no, he would drive, and he drove us to Beverly Hills.

"What the fuck is this?" I asked when we pulled up in front. This was the Bistro, and it was fancy. They had premiere parties here, and industry people and Beverly Hills housewives had lunch here, and I hoped no one I knew was inside.

"We're doing very well," he said. "Why not enjoy our prosperity?"

He handed the keys to the valet, who was not at all happy to get into the disgusting Grand Prix.

"Well," he said, once we were seated, "so many changes in our little world, aren't there?"

"I guess."

"Where oh where should we begin?"

I had been dreading this, to tell the truth. Ray had said virtually noth-ing to me in the couple of weeks since I met John, but I knew he had been saving it up.

"I don't care," I said. "Whatever."

"There's a rumor going round the office that you've ventured out on your own. New apartment, I hear?"

"Yes. So?"

"Wonderful. It's good to be out on your own. And you're living with, uh, Aaron, I understand?"

"Yes?"

"Well look, Harris, don't believe anything that kid tells you. He's a chronic liar."

"Ok."

"And an addict."

"You think?"

"He caused me no end of trouble. I'm very concerned he'll do the same to you."

"We're just roommates. I'm hardly ever there."

"Well, watch out for him. He'll pull you into one of his intrigues and the next thing you know, they'll be shipping you to Mexico in little pieces."

"I will definitely not do that."

"I mean it. I do have some . . . concern for you, Harris . . ." I gargled my drink; he closed his eyes until I stopped. ". . . and not just about Aaron. Perhaps I'm jumping to conclusions, but I'm guessing that your sunny disposition the last few weeks might have something to do with Mister Playboy Mansion. Am I right?"

I looked at the plate of whatever chicken this was, with sauce poured over it and marshy vegetables. Stuffed it in my mouth.

"Ya," I said.

"Uh huh. Perhaps you would enlighten me a bit on this wonderful fellow."

"Why do you care?"

"Well Harris, we have a working relationship. You're an integral part of my business. You're as important as Ozzie, or my lawyer or my accountant. I think I have the right to know where my closest associates are spending their time, and with whom."

"No," I said, "I don't think that you do." I thought about what John said, then pushed the thought out fast. "Look, he's fine, so don't worry. He's a business guy. He does something with newspapers."

"What? Delivers them?"

"He publishes them. He works for this company that owns a bunch of newspapers on the east coast. He's a vice president. He travels a lot and he comes here for meetings."

"So, he doesn't live on the west coast?"

"No, he lives in Cincinnati."

"Well, that's quite a haul. So this is a long-distance type of thing?"

I shrugged, kept stuffing my face.

"And how would you characterize Mister Cincinnati . . . does he have a name, by the way?"

"John," I said, through the mouthful.

"Ah ha. Well, Harris, you have a discerning eye when it comes to sizing people up. I'm curious your take on this fellow. How old is he, for starters?"

"I don't know. Older. He's big. Like he used to be an athlete or something."

"Yes?"

"He dresses well. He likes the stuff those guys like. You know, company cars and fancy watches. But he has good taste, not pimpy taste."

He nodded. Pushed the food around on his plate.

"And he's kind of crazy. I mean, he asks all these questions, like he's testing you all the time. Or trying to get under your skin. It's funny, but also kind of interesting."

"Uh huh. Like how?"

"Well, he likes to play these mind games. Like, do you accept this proposition. And if I do, then I have to accept this other one. And he tries to prove things that way."

"Such as?"

I had to think a moment to know how to phrase it. "He asks me if I think I'm okay. I guess he thinks I'm too down on myself. Kind of like a psychologist. They try to tell you everything is okay even if you think it isn't."

"And you think it isn't? What exactly is he telling you?"

"Well, like, I don't think I'm very good looking. I mean, not like Bruce or Aaron or someone. I'm just ordinary. And he challenges me, like, would anyone be interested in me if I was ordinary. Stuff like that."

"I see," Ray said. He took a bite of his food. "What other games does he play?"

It made me smile to think of it. "He challenges my assumptions. Like, if I'm worried or scared about something that's going to happen. Something bad. He says, look at this sweater. Is this sweater here and does it have a shape? And I say yes, and he says, is the sweater going to start unravelling this minute and stop existing? And I say no. And he says, so I must have faith in things being permanent and solid. And so I should remember that and see that things are reliable and don't just fly apart for no reason. That I shouldn't be worried about things like that."

"I see. He proves things to you. With logic."

I nodded.

"Well," Ray said. "Doesn't that sound comforting. And he tells you that you're wonderful and attractive."

"He says I'm ok. I asked him what he was doing with me. I told him what you said, you know, how guys like him like trophy boys. Like what's he doing with a slobby jerk like me?"

"You told him what I said?"

"Yeah. So he tries to make me feel like I'm ok. That I'm making up a story about how bad I should feel and it's just a story."

"Well, my goodness. That sounds like a psychologist I ought to see."

"So that's the kind of stuff. He's funny. Kind of crazy. He puts on this southern country guy voice and people eat it up. They go crazy for him. And he puts it on when he wants to. He can talk like a business guy, like a vice president if he's on the phone or something."

"I see," Ray said. He lifted the napkin off his lap, folded it carefully, replaced it back in his lap. "And *is* he a southern country guy?"

"I don't know. I think he was really poor." I wasn't going to say anything about the scars. "I mean, the way he talks, it's really him. He turns it on and off when he wants to."

"Well, this fellow sounds awfully impressive. What a catch. Tell me, have you visited him in Cincinnati?"

"No, he travels all the time. He has to meet with the different papers. He's hardly ever at home."

"Yes, I get that. How often does he come to LA?"

"Every couple of weeks. I talk to him on the phone every night. He calls me from where ever he is."

"Every night? So this is quite a close arrangement then?"

I shrugged. "For now."

It seemed like Ray was about to ask more, and I thought of saying more, but we both stopped before whatever it was we were going to say. Finally, he said, "Well, it sounds like everything is just fine. You have your own place, and the titles are selling well, and we have a date for the next shoot. And Mister Wonderful sounds just wonderful. So all is fine."

"I guess so."

"Well," he said, his face unreadable, "isn't that fine."

26

I could see why the other guy moved out. Aaron sure kept that place busy. When he wasn't out on a date, he had guys in the apartment and they went at it for hours. It was hot to listen to at first, but it started bugging me because I couldn't get any sleep. A couple of times his friends asked me to join, but Aaron looked doubtful, so I said no. Plus, they did a lot of coke and other stuff in his room; it had this burned, acrid smell, and I found pieces of cooked tinfoil in the trash. But after a while, I guess Aaron decided I was cool, and they started cooking the coke in the kitchen. When they offered, I figured with all the regular stuff John and I were doing, it might be interesting to try. And I did, and it was amazing. Like being a comet and shooting through space with power you never experienced. And when they asked me to come into his room with them, I realized how badly I wanted to feel Aaron's body, and I went, and the sex and the coke were the god's honest brain-and-balls-and-nuts-bustingly hottest experience I ever had in my whole life. I wanted to come and come until there was nothing left, then come some more. I loved every living, fucking minute of it.

And then I got so sick I thought I would die. I couldn't get out of bed for two days.

"Oh dear, that does sound bad," Ray said. He had called the apartment about a hundred times. I told him I had the flu and he fussed about taking me to a doctor. I said I would be in Wednesday. "Alright," he said, but he knew it was suspicious. "Well, I'll see you Wednesday then. And you'll call me if you need anything?" I said I would, and went to throw up and sleep some more. The apartment, I noticed, was empty. Aaron and his friends had taken off, the day or two before, I couldn't remember when we had the fuckfest. I said to myself I needed to think carefully before I did something like that again. The acrid smell filled the apartment, but somewhere, the smoky taste registered in the back of my head as warm and delicious.

■ ■ ■

We did the scene Ray wanted in January. A guy he knew owned a car repair shop so we shot it there, in the repair bays. We had a production assistant with several jobs including makeup, but before we started, Ozzie said something to her and took the makeup kit and came over to me. "Just a little touch," he said, and pulled me to the side, near the metal tool cabinets. He had me sit on a rolling stool while he dabbed a sponge. He sat wide on another stool in front of me. While the others adjusted lights and moved stuff around, Ozzie said, quietly "How are we doing today?" He patted the sponge under my eyes.

"Fine," I said, "and you?"

Half humming, half whispering, he said, "I'm not having my hiney shot in glorious Technicolor this afternoon. Having some late nights, are we?" He made quick, light strokes, like touch-ups, but his eyes scanned my face. "In this business, you go down very fast. I've seen it a million times. Right in the places I'm trying to cover up now. Ray knows it but he doesn't want to bring it up with you."

I didn't have a smart remark. Ozzie found a brush in the kit and ran it over my eyelids. It felt gentle and arousing. He must have seen it and continued brushing, slower. I hadn't been this close to him before, us sitting alone together.

"He likes you, Harris," he said, "and I like getting paid. So, what's important to him is important to me. I thought you were smarter than the rest of them. If you want to flush your life down the toilet, that's up to you. But don't show up to a set of mine looking like this again."

He considered his work a moment, smudged something softly with his thumb on my cheek. Sitting on the stool in front of me, legs spread wide, I could see his package.

"Alright now, ready to be a good little bang-bang boy?" He tickled the end of my nose with the soft brush.

As he stood, I saw the hard rod in his pants. I've seen a lot of them by now, but for some reason, this one scared me.

■ ■ ■

In the dream I'm in the Mustang and it's fast and powerful. I'm on a road I know, and even though it's curvy, the car is heavy and stays put. But something happens. I'm not paying attention and I don't judge how sharp the curve is and the car leaves the road and flies into the air. Each time I wake up, my heart beating, yelling *Help me, help me!* If Aaron is home, he hammers on the wall. If not, I take a pill to knock me out.

"Well, it doesn't take a Ph.D," John said, in another hotel room on another weekend. "What are you going to do about it?"

"About what?"

"Your *trajectory* problem."

This is his routine; he plays the wise older sage who offers advice and warnings about the bad direction I'm headed. But he also loves coke, and getting us high with it, and he loves fucking me and he knows I fuck guys on camera, and that turns him on. So what he's telling me, what he is doing, I'm not exactly sure. One thing I am sure of is I've fallen for him. And fallen is the word. That's what happens. One minute you're standing on the ground, then the ground gives way and you have no control. When you fall, you trust; you put yourself in that person's trust and lean on them, and if you never had anyone to trust before, it feels so good. I belonged to him, and I could just think about him and it would make me feel safe and whole.

"So what am I supposed to do?"

"Well, to stick with the metaphor," he said, "step on the brakes."

"And how do I do that?"

"To start with, why don't you get a real job. Not one that depends on your ass. They have those, you know."

"I work in an office . . ."

"Man wants your ass."

"I don't have any experience . . ."

"You're a kid, you're not supposed to have any. This is when you get it. And you ain't dumb. I know you're keeping it all in reserve. And that's ok. I'm nobody you need to pay attention to. But some day, you might wish you took some of them brains and used 'em, instead of . . ."

"What?"

"Ha. Never mind."

"Snorting them away?"

"Nothin' wrong with a little toot now and then. But what your little buddies are up to . . . I think that's a whole different can of potatoes."

"I can handle them."

He turned his newspaper pages, looked over his reading glasses. "Famous last words."

"I make a lot of money you know."

He grunted. "And what's your cut relative to the take? What's the great director's share?"

"It's his company."

"Yeah, yeah, yeah." He licked a finger, turned a page, kept reading. "We'll see. We will see."

27

Momma asked me to come for breakfast.

"I have some very good news," she said, "but it's secret, so you have to keep it quiet."

"Sure."

"I had dinner with Eva. She told me they're considering a spinoff from *Bowman*. It would be all about her character. It would be her show. They'd call it Margaret Lawson, DA or something. Can you believe it?" She was so excited I thought she might burst.

"That's great," I said.

"Isn't it? She's over the moon! But like I said, it's all in the discussion phase, so nothing, and I mean, nothing to anyone."

"So why are you telling me?"

"Well, she said this is a big risk for the network. Shows about women are a tough sell, especially a crime show. They had Police Woman, but that was Angie Dickinson. This would be an older woman in the lead, not a sexy young thing. They're thinking they can aim for the *Love Boat* audience, old people who remember Eva, and bring in old guest stars, retired actors and people like that."

"Huh. A show about an old lady with old guests. That does sound kind of dumb."

"Right. So the producer wants to throw a big party for the network and the sponsors. They want to sell them on Eva and show her off in a good light."

"Ok. And?"

She winced. "They would like us to be there."

"Why?"

"They want to show off her family. Since there's no husband in the picture, they want her surrounded by children and grandchildren. She said so they can see she's not some washed-up old drunk in a cold water flat. She didn't want to ask us, but there was no choice."

"How come she didn't ask me directly?"

"She was going to," momma said, brightly, "but she hasn't seen you in a while. I thought I ought to be the one to bring it up." Still something coming so I waited. "It's important we look nice. Could you . . . I don't know . . . get a good night's sleep beforehand, clean your fingernails and everything? Maybe you'll let me rent you a suit. Just for the night. This'll be at some fancy restaurant so you'll need a jacket anyway. Would that be ok?"

"Yeah, fine. When is it?"

She told me the Friday in February, two weeks away.

Meanwhile, this guy Evan called me from Aaron's service. I guess the fuckfest convinced Aaron I had more going on than he thought, or maybe he got a commission. Whatever it was, Evan said he thought I would do well with their clients. I told him I wasn't crazy about it – imagining what John would say if he found out –– but Evan said it wasn't a big commitment. "I get it," he said, "you're more *selective*." I couldn't tell if he was making fun of me. "I could pitch it that way," he said. "Better fees." And I thought about what Ray would say, being cut out of the whole thing. Maybe that was what he meant about Aaron. I said I'd think about it and call him back.

So Ray had gone on this shopping spree, buying new all new stuff – furniture, cameras, fancy lights – and the whole hum and energy of the place seemed to change. Like a machine picking up speed, more product being manufactured and packaged and shipped. New people in the back room, and piles of shiny, brightly-colored boxes. I picked one up. It had my picture on it.

"What the fuck is this?" I yelled.

He was on the phone and held up a finger. I stood in front of his desk until he hung up. "Now, what is the problem?"

"You didn't ask me this. You can't use this. You can see my face and everything!"

"Well, of course. Look at the positioning. Front and center. You're the featured player." The truth was, I never saw any of the movies. I didn't want to throw up seeing how ugly I looked.

"You can't put this out. I didn't give you permission to do this."

"Oh my lord, do I have to explain everything to you? Come over here, Harris." He walked me to one of the cushy new couches, sat down next to me. "Now, look. The whole video market is exploding and we're right in the middle of it. We can't even keep up with sales. Kevin is one of our most popular models, so what am I supposed to do, not put him on the cover?"

"But I didn't . . . what are these?" I shook the thing at him.

"It's for the retailers. Everyone's getting a VCR now. Blockbuster and Wherehouse and all these little storefronts need product. And it has to be on videocassette, not film. I found a distributor who'll get us in all of them but they need a standardized format. You see? It has art on both sides and the spine, so you can see it on the shelf."

I stared in disbelief. Bright and clear and shiny, everything secret and private exploded into the real world. I felt my heart pumping. Things I had in my own hands were being taken away and printed and packaged with no way to stop it.

"But this can't go out . . . everyone will see . . ."

"Oh, come now Harris, don't pretend you haven't been itching for this all along. You could have pulled the plug anytime in the last year. You've been riding this gravy train the same as all of us, and now your talent and hard work have paid off. You should be proud of yourself and everything you've accomplished. With my help, of course."

I kept staring at it. "But this is so clear."

"It means success," Ray said. "So be happy. And while we're on the subject, I have something for you to sign." He got some papers off his desk. "We need a more formal agreement, you and I. As you can imagine, I feel a camaraderie with you, Harris, having found you and nurtured you along this far. It's in all of our best interests to formalize that relationship.

I'd like you to sign an exclusive contract with Nu-Man. You'll be our very first. Isn't that exciting?"

All I could see was the box.

"And one more thing. I'm throwing a premiere party for the new release ... Summer Fantasy, or Winter Fantasy ... whatever fantasy, I can't remember ... but anyway, since you're the star, you're the guest of honor, so you'll need to attend."

I asked when it was.

"Two weeks from now, a Friday in February."

■ ■ ■

The first time there's a blip you want to ignore it but it sets off a bomb somewhere inside. When I called John's office, he always called me back within a half hour. But this time he called at the end of the day. Nothing much, I figured. He told me he was flying all day and had meetings. But still. He always called back within a half hour.

We talked, like always, for a long time. The sound of his voice, his deep laugh. I could sleep and feel safe again. But in the morning, I was worried. And when you're alone, you make the decisions you have to make, to do something.

Evan gave me a couple of appointments and they weren't bad. Regular, middle-aged guys who wanted a couple of hours at their apartment or a hotel. They were a better class of guy than the ones in cars. Since they went through a service, they paid good money and behaved decently, but some of them, after they kept their manners in check, would let go. You could see what they were thinking: I paid for this, so I can do what I want. One guy choked me hard and I had to push him off. He was apologetic, asked me not to tell so they wouldn't cancel him. "Don't do it again," I said, and I felt like his mother, wagging my finger at him.

Aaron came back and we got high again. He loves the rush, and he lies back on the sofa, floating. I reached for him, but he laughed and pushed me away. Not angry, more just like that's ridiculous. I felt a stab. Was that time an audition? I wonder if Aaron loves anybody.

And the worry set in and stayed. Who do you trust? What are people thinking but not telling me? The world really is a dangerous place. When pictures of you and secret things about you can be published and sent out without you knowing. If there are contracts you sign then you have to do things you don't know about. I remembered what we were told: watch out for danger, for people looking to break into your house and kill you. So I have to be more vigilant now. There really are monsters. At night when I woke up, the dreams were sliced open by consciousness. I dreamed of those huge towers walking over us. I could feel the deep pounding, the sound those towers make, and their footsteps, slowly, over our houses, carrying the heavy wires on their shoulders.

"What's the rush, honey?" John said when I finally reached him.

"Nothing. But, why didn't you call me back?"

"I'm calling you now."

Do I say you always call me back right away, and this is six hours later? Do I say that out loud? No. I told him my day, what I'm thinking, what I'm worried about. The dangers that exist. The pounding that wakes me up. That Ray is printing and selling things I don't know about. There's a silence on the other end, then he says, "I'm gonna ask you something honestly, and I want an honest answer. Have you been partying with the albino midget again?"

Without thinking I hung up the phone. I looked at it, the handle on the cradle. I didn't plan to hang it up. I didn't think I was mad or anything. But I'm looking at it now and it's hung up, and someone hung it up. Fuck.

28

And then the Friday in February. Eva's party at 7 in Beverly Hills, Ray's at 10 in Hollywood.

I don't remember what I took but it was enough to make me very relaxed. By 5pm I was sitting on the sofa in momma's house in this stupid tuxedo she rented, staring into space, my arms spread wide over the back of the sofa to hold myself upright.

"You're sure you're okay to go?" she asked.

"Absolutely."

Earlier, when I arrived, seeing what I had done, she sort of blanched. The cheap tuxedo was one thing, with the ridiculous fluffy shirt, but the bowtie and cummerbund were too much. I left those at the apartment and unbuttoned the shirt so I could breathe. I thought I should look as incognito as possible, so I parted my hair in the middle, pasted it down, pulled it back into a ponytail. In a drawer I found a pair of big round glasses. The lenses weren't very strong, so I put them on. "Well, that's a look," momma said. Then we piled into her car and drove to Chasen's, where the party was being held. I arranged for one of Ray's friends to pick me up after, at 9:30, on a corner a couple of blocks away. As we drove to the restaurant, I felt my head bobbing side to side as we went over bumps. "All ready to put on a good show for the team?" momma said.

"Ya," I answered. Alicia just stared at us both.

A valet took the car when we arrived and we walked into this place, all leather booths and dark wood paneling. A small band played in the corner, what sounded like old people dancing music. An official looking guy greeted us, some flack from the show. He kissed momma's cheek like he knew her, shook Alicia's hand, said, Nice to meet you, son, and physically pushed us out of the way. Another guy with a clipboard led us to the head table, next to a small stage set up with lights and a backdrop of black and white stills of Eva and the other cast members.

When we arrived, everyone was standing around with cocktails. Eva stood next to a table with a group of men. She was in prime entertainer mode, sharp, well-made-up, listening intently to everyone and laughing heartily when she was supposed to. I watched her put her hand on someone's arm and lean close when telling one story, listening carefully and rollicking with laughter at another. Waiters came by with drinks and hors d'oeuvres. I started on white wines immediately. Momma smiled at me, widened her eyes after a couple of glasses, and I smiled back, raised my glass to her. Eventually Eva noticed us, smiling, her eyes passing over me.

At some point they decided to do pictures and we had to go up and pose as a family. After the photos, we sat down for the dinner and speeches; they talked about how great the show was, and the cast and especially Eva. After the speeches, while we were eating, it seemed to be a free-for-all, with everyone coming up and talking to us at our table, and waiting in line, talking to momma and Alicia. I heard snippets of conversations. ". . . such a great grandma . . . wonderful to the family . . . spunky . . . sense of humor . . ." And a man's voice, somewhere out there. "And here you are, all by your lonesome." It was some guy in a slick three-piece suit with fancy gray hair. Eyes wide and excited, staring at me.

"Yeah," I said.

"Now, how are *you* related to Eva?" His voice was dripping with curiosity. "Well, what a talented family you are." I think I said thanks, and he leered. And wouldn't leave, just stood there, staring a hole through the top of my head. Finally someone tapped him on the shoulder and asked him to move. "Well, I'm sure we'll be seeing you *very* soon," he said.

I looked around the room. All these guys in flashy suits and polyester ties, nodding, talking, shaking hands. Women in flowing dresses, listening, the charming guest of whoever they were with. All these people playing their parts, doing their roles, and perfectly. These were the people who made the shows that everyone watched, that told us what to wear and what to like, and who we should be, and who were the bad guys and who were the good guys. The people in this fancy room made these decisions. What I heard most distinctly was the clinking of silverware and dishes. It's hypnotizing. And I felt dizzy and close to passing out. I looked across the table and Eva was talking to someone, but she's looking at me and I've never seen this expression before, like she's drowning. She's trying to keep her face up, her eyebrows up, but this desperation is pulling them down. She shoots momma a look, and momma looks over at me, jumps up, kneels down next to me. "Are you ok, sweetie? You need a bathroom break?"

"Nah, I'm fine," I said and rallied, sat up straight. "You sure?" she said. Eva's face sinking as she tries to keep it afloat. "I said I'm fine." Momma went back to her seat.

During dessert an interviewer with a cameraman and a bright light walked around the room, speaking to people at their tables. Despite momma trying to waive him away, he came over to me, the bright light in my eyes, his giant ball of a microphone. It looked like a dick with a big head. He shouted in my face. "How do you like your grandmother on *Bowman*, young man, fighting crime and keeping the city safe every week?"

I was completely blinded. "Yeah, it's good," I said, to the blaze, and laughed.

"Tell us, what is Eva Loesch like as a grandmother?"

"She's good. She keeps you in check. No funny business."

"Aha," he said. "So a pretty swell gal to be chief law enforcement officer for a large metropolitan city?"

I looked away from the sun lamp and around its edges, caught Eva's face watching this scene unfold.

"Ya, very good," I'm saying. "Very tough. Lot of crime, though. Lot of bad people. Doing bad stuff. Bad, bad, naughty stuff."

"Oh dear!" this moron said, and kept going. Momma tried to push him away, signaling the cameraman to move on. Eva tried to draw the PR guy's attention without interrupting her conversation, but this guy seemed intent on his interview and wouldn't budge. "What kind of bad stuff?"

"Ohhh," I said, as the lightheadedness won over, this relaxing, uncaring drowsiness. "Naughty stuff, bad stuff no one wants to know. Guys . . . bad guys. Like that guy over there . . . he wants a blowjob . . ."

"And thanks!" he yelled. The light extinguished instantly, both of them gone in a flash. Momma stared at me. Alicia stared straight ahead, trying not to laugh. Eva was listening to someone, nodding as she listened, her face a plaster mask.

■ ■ ■

Momma pushed a cup of coffee in my face. "You need to go. You need to get out of here." She'd pulled me out to the alley behind the restaurant. I swayed while she gnashed her teeth. "This is a total embarrassment. I am humiliated. You've embarrassed everyone, but yourself mostly. What is wrong with you?"

"Ah, it's such bullshit. Liars. Everybody lying."

"This was important. All you had to do was show up and look nice and keep your mouth shut. You know what you are? Selfish. Selfish, selfish, selfish. Can't you think of anyone but yourself?"

"Hey, I don't need this. I'm not yours, you know. I'm not anyone's property. Or a prop. I can do what I want. People like me and they want to know me. You don't even know how many." Having trouble standing up, I was only just coming to awareness how fucked up I was.

"Jesus Christ," she said. "This isn't the place for this. You have to get out of here. I'll call you a taxi."

"I have my own ride," I said. "You think I don't know how to do things? I know how to do things! I have a lot more things than any of you think I do."

Her face was grave. "I can't talk to you anymore."

I waved her off, started walking away. I hoped she would call me, yell my name, but nothing.

■ ■ ■

I don't remember much about Ray's party. I kissed a lot of people, had a lot of drinks. So many guys there. Guys with hungry eyes, glazed eyes, guys with eyes of eager teenage girls. They asked me to sign their video box and kissed me on the cheek. Guys from other studios, guys I fucked. People were saying things to me, but I wasn't paying attention because I was thinking, I'm the star, tonight is all about me. I nod to whatever they're saying, say, Yeah, and move on, to all the other people who want to touch me and stare at me with glistening eyes. Tonight I had the magic and the power, and it wasn't a fantasy, I wasn't standing on a street somewhere. All these people were here for me. And there was music and dancing and guys pulling their shirts off and I pulled mine off too, and somewhere in all of this, Ray was talking to me, putting those papers in front of me, and it was another signature, so I signed, and the papers disappeared and he disappeared and then it was dancing and partying and the night goes and goes and goes.

29

A long, deep sigh on the other end of the call.

"Is this the party to whom I am speaking?"

I groaned.

"English please?" John said.

"Yeah. Hi." My mouth tasted like a tailpipe.

"Guess bright eyed and bushy tailed is too much to ask, huh?"

"Uggghhhh . . ."

"Oh, lord, what have we done?" His deep, husky laugh. "How bad is it, one to ten?"

My head and nose felt burned up. I'd slept most of the day, then drank about ten gallons of water. The phone rang a bunch of times but I hid under the covers. On the second set of rings, I picked up.

He got a huge laugh out of the whole thing. I told him what happened, at least what I remembered. "It's not funny," I said, but I already started laughing as he joked me out of it. And made me feel better. I crawled under the blanket with the phone, wrapped the covers around me.

"So you took a poop on the party?" he said.

"Kind of."

"Well, what they expect? They invited a pony to a dog-and-pony show. Their own damn fault."

"I wish."

"And you got a contract?"

"I guess."

"Is that something you wanted?"

"I don't know."

Noises in the background. I couldn't picture where he was, but it sounded like someone trying to draw his attention. The squishy sound of a leather sofa. "You want my advice?"

"Do I?"

Silence.

"OK," I said.

"My advice is, nip this bitch in the bud. Go over and apologize to your mama. Probably not as bad as your addled brain thinks it is. And if it is . . . well, you'll find out soon enough. But lying around in your own stew isn't gonna fix anything."

"Do I have to?"

He laughed. "You don't have to do *nuthin'*, cakes. You can lie there and wallow and blow yourself up like Richard Pryor for all the world cares."

I listened to his breathing on the other end.

"Hey," he said, and knocked on the phone. "Anyone there?"

"Yeah. OK."

"OK," he said, like he had to go. "You keep them nipples perky now."

"Yeah."

After we hung up I started to cry.

■ ■ ■

When I got to momma's, the Cadillac was parked in front. "Fuck," I whispered.

I drove around the corner and parked. Sat and thought for a while. John was right. I couldn't just hide out. And maybe he was right about me being paranoid and blowing it out of proportion. So I got out of the car – but first a quick snort from the clear plastic bullet Aaron's friends gave me – and walked back to the house. The wood door was open, the screen door shut. I could hear them in the kitchen, their raised voices. "No," Eva was saying, "*I* should have known better. Especially when that idiot showed up again."

"He has nothing to do with this," momma said.

"He has everything to do with this! It's him all over! He even looks like him for Christ's sake."

I moved away from the door so they wouldn't see me, but sat on the steps close enough to hear.

"It's just teenage stuff," momma said. "All the kids are into it."

"*That's* your excuse? All the kids are into it? I should have known that would be the answer from someone with your history."

"Oh, come on . . ."

"And just like you . . . just like you! All messed up, stoned up, whatever you call it. Showing up at a public function in a state like that. What were you thinking? What kind of a person lets a kid in that condition show up to an event . . . and do *interviews*? He was on camera, for god's sake!"

"No one pays attention to anything a teenager says . . ."

"I pay attention! I pay attention! And it's on film now, so other people will pay attention. And what do you think they'll think?"

"It has no reflection on you," momma said. "It was just a kid with too much to drink. They'll throw it on the floor."

"You know something sweetheart, that's why you are who you are. That's why you're in the situation you're in. Because you don't take it seriously. You don't take anything seriously. No wonder you live in such a shithole."

A long silence after that one.

Then, momma said, "You have no right to talk."

"Oh, I have every right to talk. In fact, a judge said I have every right to talk. And to tell the court if I think something is amiss down here. That's what that was all about. Don't forget, this was all *conditional* . . . on you getting your house in order and keeping it in order. And look what's going on now."

"I think you're blowing it out of proportion."

"You, young lady, are out of touch with reality. That was always your problem. You don't see what's going on around you, and you don't take responsibility."

"If it means acting like you, then I'm glad I'm not responsible. I would *never* do what you did. I would *never* do that."

"Ah, you're living in the past," Eva said.

"You can't do that to people."

"That was the court's decision, not mine . . ."

"You got them involved . . .."

"Because you couldn't take care of yourself! Or a child. For god's sake! With the booze and the pot and whatever else you and that idiot were up to. There was no choice. I had to get involved."

"You don't take someone's child away," momma said.

"You could have dropped it in the bathtub and not even known!"

"With your lawyer and your judge . . ."

"It was a perfectly respectable facility," Eva said. "I made sure of it. Those kids went to good families. And everyone said the same thing, too. Good for you, Eva. That child was in danger. I did what I had to do. It was the right thing to do."

"That isn't the reason," momma said. "You didn't care about him at all. You were afraid it would make you look bad. That's why you snuck out to . . . where ever it was . . . Palm Springs . . . where no one would see what you were doing, so you could *dump* him . . ."

"That is not the reason at all. Besides, who paid the bills? Whose job paid for your house and your food? We were all alone, sweetheart. That was a different time. There were things you simply couldn't allow in those days."

"You gave someone away," momma said, like she was trying to explain it to herself. Convince herself.

"Oh my god! They were wonderful, caring people. Besides, it all worked out. And you had another. So, my god, holding onto slights and grievances that don't make a bit of difference. Would you grow up, please?"

"What kind of a person are you?"

"I'm not talking about this anymore," Eva said. "What we're talking about is *now*, and what's going on under your roof *now*. And I'm telling you I won't stand for it. I can go back to the court if I think something is wrong."

"You had no right. Besides, Harris doesn't even live here, he's an adult."

"Yes, but the girl isn't."

Momma said nothing.

"I can't have any more screw-ups from the bunch of you," Eva said. "If you can't get things under control, I will." And as her heavy footsteps headed toward the front door, I took off.

■ ■ ■

I thought I looked better in the photos. Ray showed them to me, he had a photographer at the party. There we all are, laughing and dancing, and my body looked good. I didn't say it out loud but I thought it was the stuff I did with Aaron and his friends. It made you harder, made your metabolism speed up so you got a better body.

"You know," Ray said, "our friend up the hill mentioned he'd like another visit with you. Alone this time."

I sat across from him at his desk while he shuffled file folders, looking for something. Grunted at him.

"Well, no matter what you do with your private life, we have three pictures to make," he said. "And because he's underwriting the projects, he feels some ownership."

"That's not right."

"Show *business*," Ray said. "*Business*."

I cleaned some gunk under my fingernails with the end of his letter opener.

"I heard a rumor, you know," he said. He looked around casually to be sure no one was listening. "That you've started working with that fellow Evan."

I shrugged.

"You're not on the roster, I checked, but rather a special order."

"Dunnuh . . ."

"I don't know what to say, Harris. Since you're not denying it, I have to assume the rumor is true. Is that correct?"

"Whatever."

He took off his glasses, which I hated, put down his busywork and put his hands on the desk. "I hope you know I consider that a great betrayal.

We have a working relationship, you and I. I went to great lengths to put you where you are, then you go behind my back and make a deal for something I know nothing about?"

"How is that even any of your business?"

"It's my business because you are under contract to me now. If you're out making money off the persona I built and I own, then I am entitled to a share in that interest."

The conversation was starting to make me dizzy. I would have got up and left but I thought throwing up on his desk was just what he deserved.

"I'm not even going to do it."

"What? The service? I know for a fact you already are."

"What are you, a fucking spy? Don't you have anything better to do?"

"I do," he said, "and I'm trying to do it right now."

"What money do you want? You don't even have a service."

"That's because I have a product. And I'm trying to protect that product. And if there were service-related activities surrounding that product, then I should be part of the decisionmaking in the aforementioned service."

"You are so deluded," I said, blowing off my fingernails. "Like all the other business guys."

"Business guys pay you," he said, leaning forward, and quite angry. "They make your life possible."

"John is right about you." I didn't look up at him. He leaned back, folded his arms.

"Ah, Citizen Kane speaks. May I ask what he's right about?"

I thought about saying to his face what John said, but I didn't want to cause a shitstorm. "You just want to get money out of me. I'm just a thing you use to make money."

"Ha! And very good money it is, too. At least you know who I am and what I do. I'm not hiding anything from you or pretending to be something I'm not."

"What's that mean?"

"Quite frankly, Harris, I've listened to your stories about Mister Wonderful, and as your friend, I have to tell you, Mister Wonderful sounds rather tiresome to me. I think he's taking advantage of you. And I wouldn't be surprised if he's not entirely candid either."

"Such bullshit."

"Tell me, why doesn't he invite you to Cincinnati?"

"He travels a lot. He likes the weather here."

"So you've said. But you've never seen his house? You've never actually seen where he lives?"

"Ray," I said, "really . . ."

"It's not that I'm not happy for you. But I am older and I have some perspective. I'm seeing this fellow in a much different light than you are."

I stood and put my hands on his desk. "You're just scared he's gonna make me quit the *nasties*, ain't cha?"

He didn't react at all. Just measured what he said next, put his glasses back on.

"I assume you still make some of your own decisions. And I have all the faith in the world in our professional and personal relationship."

But the shine on his forehead said different.

■ ■ ■

I could tell something changed when John saw me at the airport. I went with the car he hired to pick him up and as we walked out of baggage claim, his huge smile seemed tempered by something. But it remained, the smile, and he gave me a kiss, as usual, in front of everyone, which he liked to do, and because two guys smooching in public was still kind of shocking then. He chattered on about what deals he was working on and who he met and what famous person fell in love with him that week. And I felt outside of him somehow.

The driver dropped us at the Beverly Wilshire, where he was staying, then we went out to a fancy dinner. Back in the room, we fucked, then he put on a robe and lay on the bed to look through his papers. I lay down next to him, naked, staring out the window. After a while, he put the paper down.

"So what are you all filming this month, a vampire movie?"

"What does that mean?"

"Means what it means," he said. "I think you better lay off them sumpm sumpms." He pulled the skin on my ribs. "Loose chicken. Not flattering."

I ignored him. He knew not to say anything, let me build up to it, and in a minute, I did. "What's your fucking problem?"

"What do you think is my fucking problem?"

"Well, you're the one with all the games to make people do what you want them to. You're playing a game on me now, so just tell me what it is because I don't know."

He looked down at me from his tower of a body, through the reading glasses. Deciding, I guess, how far to go. He took off the glasses. "We got what they call in the business world a downward trend here. Them dark circles and all this twitchiness is only the tip of it, I suspect. I got a pretty good idea what you been getting up to, and I will tell you, it is not a good direction."

I sat up. "What? You've been spying on me?"

"I didn't say that . . ."

And this shot of adrenaline filled my chest. Like an injection, it spread from my chest to my arms, exploded in my brain. Who is this person? What does he want? Ray is right. I don't know who he is. I've been deceived.

"Yes you are," I said, realizing all of this. "You have people following me."

He stared at me with this level gaze. "Come again?"

"Oh my god," I said, "oh my god. You are spying on me."

"Would you please sit . . ."

I jumped off the bed. I didn't know what to do. My heart racing, pacing, looking at the floor. Trying to think, trying to think. What to do.

"Come over here and sit down." He reached over and took my arm. I pushed him, tried to get out from his grip, but he was much stronger and closed me in a vice. Pulled me to the bed and tried to make me lie down. I wriggled out, used all my strength to get away, and jumped to the other side of the room. I grabbed a bottle of wine off the cabinet and held it high. "Don't," I said.

"Fine," he said, holding his hands up. "Fine, ok. You win." He settled back down on the bed. "What are you gonna do with that bottle of hundred-and-fifty-dollar cabernet? That was a gift . . ." and I threw it and it hit the wall and exploded. He closed his eyes.

"Fuck all of you," I yelled at him, "with your *stuff*."

But I realized this was a standoff I had no plan to get out of. When he launched himself at me, faster than I thought a man his size could do, I didn't make much effort to get out of the way. He grabbed me around the neck in some kind of chokehold, took my wrist and twisted it so I had to follow him back to the bed. He pushed the side of my head down and it felt like a police hold; in some zonked-out conversation he told me once he had been a cop, or maybe I made it up or maybe he lied.

"This has been coming for some time," he said, "and I've been too nice a fella to bring it up. But since you forced my hand." I made a fierce move to escape, but he held like a machine. "Temper," he said. "Temper. Am I gonna have to hold you down to say what I have to say?"

"Fuck you!"

He tightened the pressure on my neck and I felt my face going red. "Number one," he said. "Listening?" I couldn't speak now, just spit. "Number one," he said, "You are not made for the hard partyin' lifestyle, little man. Whatever shit you're snorting or swallowing is already gone past you. I don't know what kind of a rager you're on tonight, but I don't want it in my hotel suite." He pushed hard for a second and I lost all air. He let go slightly so I could breathe again. "Number two. This guy you're in business with is not a fella with a good reputation. I asked around. You could do a lot better with a lot better people . . . if you even want to stay in this line of work, which you need to think about given the diseases and whatnot floating around." Another hard crush and no air, then a release. "Number three. I'm not sure I care to be inside the same hot little ass that anyone with a hundred fifty bucks can buy himself into. Like I said, I don't know what deals you got yourself into, but I have a pretty good idea. And," one more choke and release, "number four. You got no plan, boy. You got no exit strategy. You're facin' the real world here and you're startin' to look downright scary." I was almost unconscious now. "I'm gonna let you up now, and I want you to think carefully what you're gonna say next." And he did release his grip and I gasped for air, coughing, while he sat back and watched me.

"Asshole," I said, when I could speak.

"Takes one to know one."

"I think you're lying to me," I said.

"I *know* you're lying to me," he said.

Then the vat of anger, confusion, drugs, bile, plain old meanness and maybe a vein of what's in our family sprang a leak. I looked at this guy, staring placidly at me, and something was pricked. The predator behind all of us.

"You don't mean anything," I said. "You're just the tag-along. You don't even exist."

He considered this. Looked off toward the window. When he looked at me again it was the same face he always had – excitement, curiosity, anticipation – but behind it, something else. Shock. Exposure. And I realized when you say something like that, you have to be loyal to your words. Even if you hear the cruelty right away, you have to stand by your cruelty. In the split second I saw the scene just as it was: he may be richer and wiser and older at this minute, but I'm the white kid who grew up with everything, and I can say anything I want, and he's the black guy who terrible things happened to, who had to earn everything, who's paying for my meals and my fancy hotel, and if I tell him he's nothing, then no matter who we are to each other, at that moment, I have the bigger knife.

He folded his papers and tightened his robe.

"I don't think I want to talk to you anymore tonight," he said, and went into the other room.

30

Now the stomping came in the daylight too, a daytime dreaming. Lying in bed at night I was sure there was this deep pounding, these heavy footfalls. I even asked Aaron. I went into his room, woke him up, and he said, "Man, what the fuck . . .?" startled out of his own sleep, and "No, leave me alone, get out of here," and I went back and lay down and I could hear it clearly. During the day, I stopped where I was, looked around. Looked at other people to see if they heard it too. Do you hear that, I asked some lady on the street, and grabbed her arm. She yanked it back, walked away fast.

John was gone before I woke up in the hotel. The bill was paid but he wasn't there.

I stepped into the morning but I didn't know where to go. It's a blue gray smoggy day like all of them, like always, and I have nowhere to be, nothing to hang onto. Ray hired more office workers, so now I get paid by the scene, he said, according to my contract. No scenes, no money. I float through the day, pacing myself to the march, the slow rhythm of the stomping. It goes on, moving from past to future, and I can see it, the line of giants behind us, over us, in front of us. They walk in straight formation and I am out of synch with their timing. I have to get in lockstep, otherwise I'm cut loose and I'll float away untethered. Get through the day, get through the week. A date, a night of smoking with Aaron's friends, the week passes in front of me like a strip of film and then it's the weekend and I don't remember what happened every night. How many days it's been since the last one. I stand up from the livingroom floor. I'm asleep on it and I don't remember when I lay down. Then it's bright outside, it's day, and light slashes in between spaces in the blinds. It's the phone waking me up and it won't stop ringing. They don't hang up. It keeps ringing and ringing, all the time it takes me to stand up and move to the kitchen and drink some water and look at this phone that will Not. Stop. Ringing.

"Oh my god, I was so worried."

This voice on the other end I can't place.

". . . when you didn't show up and I couldn't find you."

"Huh?" I said.

"At the Marina. You and Gordon were supposed to go out on the bay," Amanda said.

"Oh. I'm sorry. I must have forgot." I can't make this mouth move like my own.

A gray silence on the line.

"Don't go anywhere. I'm coming over."

I said I was fine, but all the way over the hill, from the valley to Malibu, making the sharp turns and twists in her little Toyota, she watched me with sideways glances.

Gordon had another house in Malibu, off the PCH. Over hills and windy roads to this magic land of rolling lawns and estates. Not tacky like Beverly Hills; this place is green and lush and endless, with ocean all around. You wonder where this world came from. It doesn't seem to be on any map, you don't see it when you drive the PCH north. Gordon and Amanda called it the ranch, but I'd never been there. At the end of a long road we arrive at a tall hedge wall and a gate, covered with vines. She gets out, punches in the keypad and the gates open. Down a driveway to a big, modern house. Empty, like a lot of the houses here. I see white curtains floating gently through open windows in the breeze. In the kitchen she gets orange juice from the refrigerator and gives me a glass. Watches me carefully. I try to smile at her.

"Baby, you're just not built for this," she said. She is so pretty. Careless about her looks, her short hair, like a boy, her trim body, like a boy, her beautiful, simple face with a cigarette hanging. The loose white T-shirt; I can see through it. She is a cuter boy than me. She comes around and puts her arms around me. I can't help it, I have a hardon.

She says, "Why don't we lie down?"

So many rooms in this place. Floors and hallways and wings. It's so modern and I can't understand where we're going. Jutting white angles everywhere. She takes me to a large, simple room with a big bed and double doors to a balcony. The placid ocean beyond. Sheer white curtains ripple in the breeze. I can't take my eyes off them. There's a word that describes these curtains you can see through but I can't think of it. It's goofy sounding, but it means something beautiful. I try to remember, but all I can think of is Gomer Pyle.

This room is peaceful and serene, almost no weight at all. Is this where you go when you die? It's so beautiful here. A different world from hot, dirty LA, the warehouses and backyards where we shoot movies and ejaculate in sweaty back seats of cars.

I realize I'm naked under thick white sheets. Amanda dabs my arm with a soft, wet something, says, "Just to bring you down, honey," and a pin prick and then suddenly, oh, flowing, peaceful floating relief. Oh, I feel so fine now. Letting go and not worrying. I can almost feel myself again in this peacefulness. And with it, the arousal, the power that started all of this. It surges and Amanda is next to me under the soft white blanket and the T-shirt is gone and I'm so hard against her, inside her. My hips move just the slightest, just enough to make her eyes close. And I lie still. The dick is mine but I give her control because I know that's what she wants. I want her to be happy and feel what she wants to feel. That's all I want for any of us. I go with her into this pleasure, this beautiful blue ocean below us.

And the word comes, as I fall into soft, deep unconsciousness.

Gossamer.

31

A weekend in a mansion by the sea in Malibu. Whatever Amanda did.

On Monday I felt like myself again. Somewhat. Enough to think and talk, anyway. The electric towers are stationary and silent, for now. I can't clean up all the dogshit of the last couple of weeks but maybe I can make a start. At least one of the things John was right about. I walked into Ray's office and he gave me that sour face.

"Yeah, yeah, yeah," I said.

"A week! A whole week I couldn't reach you! You know, an answering service doesn't work unless you call and ask for your messages. You know that's how it works, right?"

"I'm sorry. Things are fucked up right now."

"It's that little shit, Aaron. I told you he was bad news. I told you. And look what's happened."

"I'll take care of it."

"I hope so. Because we have some looming deadlines, *Kevin*. We have three films to deliver and at this rate we'll be lucky to get them done in the next six months. You need to be a very busy beaver this year." And he started droning on about storylines and models and I sat there in the guest chair while he rattled; slid lower and lower the more details he piled on, until finally, after a break in the yammering, he's asking, "Well? Well?"

"What?" I said, tuning it all out.

"These are lucrative projects, Harris. You will make some good money. Could you at least *feign* interest in something built all around you?"

"Well, look, that's what I want to talk to you about."

"Oh, yes?" he said, all smarmy.

I looked at the gray metal side of the desk facing me. "I think I need a break. For a while. This is . . . too much." His face unmoving. "Maybe in a couple of months I can come back to it. I don't know. But this is all too fast and out of control."

One of the new office guys was standing nearby, filing papers. Ray waved him away with a vicious hand; when we were alone, he took off his glasses, rubbed the little raisins on either side of his nose. Without looking at me, he said, "That is just not possible right now. We've entered into contractual agreements that require the delivery of certain products by certain dates. And you know what a valuable part of this operation you are. So, no, I just can't allow that right now."

Now I did look up at him. "Well, I don't care what you can allow, *Raymond*. I'm all fucked up and I need some time. I don't want to do this anymore."

He scowled at me, bit into his cheek. "That is not alright, Harris. You made a pledge to me and I trusted you. I made deals and commitments based on that pledge. You can't just jump up and run away. This is the real world."

"You're not listening . . ."

"I am absolutely listening. And let me remind you, you signed a contract. That is a binding legal document that states you are responsible . . . you are *obligated* . . . to deliver three films for this company during the life of that contract. And that is not negotiable."

"What the fuck are you talking about? What are you gonna do, sue me? Good luck. I have twenty dollars."

He seemed to bear down on me. "It has a no-compete clause. I can prevent you from working anywhere else. And I will absolutely sue you for that."

"Are you listening?" I realized I was almost screaming. "I said I don't want to do this anymore. I'm not going anywhere. I just want to stop. What the fuck is wrong with you?"

He stood up from the desk, opened his mouth to speak, but before he could, someone yanked the front door open and sunlight came slashing in.

A man rushed at us with more behind him. A clamor in the storage room, and raised voices, then yelling, and more men came flooding in through the back door. The first man reached Ray and grabbed his wrist.

"Raymond L. Cicero, you are under arrest . . ."

The guy behind him yanked me to my feet, handcuffed me behind my back and babbled something. As he pulled me outside, I saw more cops rushing in, tearing open file cabinets, grabbing boxes from the packing room, filling the place like water. Police cars out front in a blockade, more blocking the alley, cops rushing around to catch any of the back-room guys trying to sneak out the bathroom window. I got shoved into the back of a police car where I could watch it all. Everyone in the office, handcuffed and pulled out, and everything inside there, all the film, files, equipment, everything, carried into the bright afternoon by an army of officers; piling it into a truck, the police lights flashing off the side of the building and the guys from the machine shop standing outside, acting like they don't know anything. People on the sidewalk, on the street, watching, gawking. I looked down at the floor of this police car and the gum wrappers and brown muck on the thick rubber mat. And there is nothing more I can do.

■ ■ ■

Momma and George bailed me out. The excruciating silence between us told it like it was. Momma's eyes were black holes.

They let me go pending investigation. I wasn't on the warrant. But Ray was, and his employees were. It caught up with him, whatever it was. All the things I knew he did and all the things I didn't. It was a major bust. I saw the photographers.

George drove us home. I sat in the back like a kid. None of us said anything as we turned the corner. The Cadillac was parked out front.

Almost like a play, the silent actors perform their blocking: George pulls into the driveway and stops. Momma opens her door and gets out. George opens his door and gets out. Those two move to the front door and go in. I'm left here alone, so I do what I'm supposed to. I open the door and run. Away from this disaster, away from whatever is going to happen. I leave them to their fate and I run into the dark woods alone.

■ ■ ■

By 11am the next day I was standing in front of a tall modern apartment building under a bright Cincinnati sky. I had the address all along.

Last night I couldn't be the good guy. I needed a boost and I needed money, so I broke the padlock on Aaron's door and took what I needed. I knew where his stash was and took that too. Bought a ticket and walked onto a plane; bought a pair of movie star sunglasses at the airport and here I was now, the celebrity from LA, in your wonderful town to start my new life among you wonderful people.

In the lobby, an old man in a dusky brown uniform stood behind a desk. It was a fancy building with modern sculptures and a fountain of black marble and wall-sized abstract collages. I said to the man, "John Ryan's apartment." He looked at me, squinted, said, "Oh, yes, of course." Went to a back room, came back and handed me the key. "Here you go." It was light, a duplicate, with a tag that said 1506. I'm surprised it's that easy, but I guess that's how they do things in doorman buildings.

It was so quiet inside the apartment. I'd never been in one of these high-rises before. All you hear is the hiss of the air conditioner. He has it decorated beautifully. Wood floors and African wall hangings, a wide, glass coffee table, a sculpture of two hands shaking. Dark leather furniture, a chrome wall unit. More sophisticated than I imagined, understated and masculine. I breathe in the air of my new city, my new life.

Something dropped in the kitchen sink.

"John?" I said.

I walked into the living room, imagining the look on his face. Excitement shooting into my chest.

"John?"

Around the corner, into the kitchen, and there was a man with a towel around his waist, holding a piece of toast.

"Oh my god," he said, startled. Then, "Harris? Jesus, you scared me."

He had a nice body, this guy. My height, but thicker and more muscular. Longish blonde hair. It's me, 15 years from now. If you were old, with bad eyesight, you might think we looked alike. I followed the line of solid muscle down his stomach to the cloth around his waist, faded and colorful, a torn beach towel the shape of his hips. I never saw anything that looked so much like it belonged to someone as that towel. He'd put his hand on his chest, I guess I really scared him.

"I wasn't expecting anyone, that's all," he said. He had the slightest southern accent. He tilted his head at me. "*Ohhhhhhh*," he said, and took a bite of the toast. "You were gonna surprise Johnny, is that it?"

I couldn't move.

"Surprise," he sang.

It was so quiet I could hear him chew.

"You want some?" He held it toward me.

I didn't move, just shook my head.

"Suit yourself." He licked jelly off his fingers. Then he laughed, half to himself.

"Who are you?" I asked. My heart was beating so fast it took all the oxygen. I couldn't calibrate my voice.

"Oh, sorry. I'm Corey." He didn't come to shake my hand or anything. After all, I was in his kitchen. "This is kind of awkward, isn't it? But you'd have found out sooner or later. So it's sooner I guess." He smiled. He had these nice, crinkly lines around his eyes, his tan so smooth and natural. I thought, wow he's handsome. I'd want him too. "What would you like to do?" he asked. "You want to wait til Johnny gets home? I don't know when that'll be. I mean, I could call him at the office?" I couldn't tell from the playfulness if he was teasing or I looked so scared he was trying to be nice.

"I've never seen you before," I said, out of breath.

"I know. But I've seen you. And heard about you." Another pause. "So . . . nothing? Coffee, toast?" None of it. "Suit yourself." He licked more jelly off his fingers. "I'm sorry, Harris. You must be tired. Would you like to lie down?"

I was paralyzed. The only thing I could do was shake my head.

He shrugged. I guess it was just too good, because he couldn't help smiling. "Then would you like the whole story?"

I nodded.

"Okay," he said, and took a sip from the coffee on the counter. "Well, let's see, when was it? Last year? Johnny came back from LA when he met you at that party, and oh my god! He couldn't stop talking about you. He was infatuated. I mean, *fascinated*." He chomped some more toast. "He meets people all the time, you know that. He attracts people like flies. But he was just obsessed with you, Harris, I hope you know. He really has feelings for you. I mean, I was jealous. He never did that before. But I figured he was going to have to come clean with you one of these days . . . I don't tell him what to do, you know he makes his own decisions . . . but then I didn't hear much about you for the last couple of weeks, so I figured something must have happened."

I didn't reply. I didn't think we were having a conversation where I was supposed to participate.

"Johnny, you know, he only goes for drama to a certain degree. If things get too wild, he's out of there. Trust me, Harris."

We stood in silence another moment. He had licked all the jelly off his hand now. "Just so you know," he said, "Johnny knew who you were when he met you at that party. We'd seen this video, and you were in it, and he went nuts. I mean cuckoo. He said, *I want a piece of that,* and he bet me he could do it. You know how he loves games."

I did know that.

I looked around this apartment. Never been here before, never would be again. Nothing to do with me. It's the nightmare in real life; you're in some guy's kitchen and you're the one who broke in. You never think you're the bad guy in the story.

■ ■ ■

The plane landed at LAX at midnight. The only way back to the valley at that time was by bus. In downtown, the driver yelled at me to get off and transfer to another. I had to walk blocks through deserted streets, past men standing around fires in metal barrels, to the next bus stop. Slept on a bench till the next one came and honked its horn. In Burbank, I lay down on the last bench and slept again. When the sun came up, the cool mist of morning smog, the massive engine of LA grinding back into life woke me up.

I held my hand on the phone for ten minutes before I had the courage to put the money in.

"Oh, that's wonderful," Ray said. "Just the person I was hoping to hear from."

I had to say it. "You were right. About everything. John … "

His nasal breathing on the other end. I knew enough to shut up, let him think what he was going to think. "Look," he said, "I only got a few hours' sleep and I'm a wreck. Where are you?"

I told him. An hour later he pulled up to the bus stop, looked through the passenger window. "Well, get in already."

■ ■ ■

I lay on the sofa in his apartment all day and night without moving. In the morning, he got up, went out without a word. When he came back, he dropped a white bag on the coffee table with hamburger grease leaking through; pulled a chair up, opened his own bag and started eating.

"So. What are your plans? If I may be so bold."

"Don't know," I said, quietly as I could. "I don't have any."

"Well, in case you haven't figured it out, that was vice. And after what I've paid them over the years. I tried to tell the judge. I told him I wanted my money back. Just for that, he slapped on a contempt charge." He laughed this bitter laugh. "They're drumming up all sorts of outrageous accusations. The lawyer says we can fight but it's going to cost. Plus all the damage to the office and the inventory. Everything is impounded. We're out of business for now. I can't even comprehend it all yet."

"I'm sorry," I said, to the hamburger.

He looked me over. "Doesn't sound like you had much of a vacation .. . where was it, Cincinnati?" I nodded. In the midst of all this catastrophe, in Ray's grungy, dirty condo, a fragment of cease fire, his hostility turned down, at least for the moment. "I'm sorry about that," he said. "Live-in lover, huh?" I nodded. And I laughed, as it hit me. "A trophy boy," I said. We both laughed.

"But look," he said, "we have to start gluing this mess back together. I've been on the phone every minute since I got out. There's a housekeeping task I need you to help me with."

I looked at him. I hoped he could see how destroyed I was. But he went on.

"It's about our friend on the hill. We are . . . how can I put it . . . heavily leveraged to him at this point. And his interest in the business is sitting in evidence lockers for the foreseeable future. We won't be able to turn around what he was expecting in the timeframe he was expecting it, so we need to buy some time and make it worth his while to stay in."

"Meaning?"

"He's giving a party this weekend. A special guest appearance would go a long way to smoothing things over."

"Oh, please no . . ."

"Wait," Ray said, cutting me off. "I told him you were out of the business. I told him that. He just wants to look like a big shot in front of his friends. Maybe a little pinch or two. But I made it clear, this wouldn't be any sort of a full blown . . . anything."

"Aw fuck, Ray, I'm all fucked up. Please. I'm so tired."

"Harris, this is an emergency. The future of our business, and quite possibly my life, is hanging in the balance. We need this fellow on our side and we need to convince him his investment will be returned. If Ozzie or I or anyone else could do it, believe me, we would. But the only face he wants to see is yours. And, quite frankly, since you left me high and dry, you could do me this one small favor, at least."

"Alright."

"Thank you. You won't have to do anything. I'll drive you there, I'll wait for you and I'll drive you back. It's nothing at all."

"Where is it?" I asked.

"Palm Springs."

32

The next day, while the sun set in the west, we drove east. Through the city, past the malls, into the desert. The air turned cinnamon, then purple. Out the window, I watched the scrub brush moving fast, the hills moving slow, the sky moving not at all. I'd never been to Palm Springs and I didn't know how far it was. By the time we left civilization and got to the real desert, it was dark. Ray switched on the radio and hummed along. He was weirdly calm, like he was driving alone. An hour and a half later, we turned off the freeway onto a long, gently curving road in pitch black. Something knocked the car; it felt like we were being blown off the road.

"Jesus," I said, and grabbed the handle.

"It's just the wind," he said.

I squinted to see what could make wind like this, but it was too dark.

At the end of this long, empty road, we came into the lights of the town. The road split into an incoming and outgoing lane, with a block of stores in between. On this Saturday night it seemed pretty busy, an ordinary looking small town with stores and restaurants. People walking on the street, couples holding hands, old people ambling out of a movie theater. Ray turned right, off the main street, craned his neck looking for signs. He fished a crumpled paper from his pocket and turned on the light to read it. Peered at me under the dim yellow lamp.

"In case you feel stressed," he said, and reached into his pocket. He still had some quaaludes stashed away. By now we'd driven into what looked like a suburban neighborhood. All these houses were one-story, modern and boxy, sort of like ours, but much fancier and well kept. Many with high walls surrounding their yards, lit by soft lamps. Straight ahead, rising into the sky above the houses in the dark, something massive and jagged was stretched across the horizon, blocking the stars. A ghost with its arms spread wide, wrapped around this little town. I blinked, thinking it was a hallucination. "What is that?"

"Just the hills," he said.

We drove almost to the foot of the hills, stopped at a wall with a gate across a driveway. It looked like a fortress, with quiet lighting and plantings along the base. No naked plaster boys here. Ray drove up to a speaker and pressed the button and the gate opened. I expected some enormous ranch, but it was just another one-story house. A Lincoln, a couple of Mercedes, a European convertible parked in the driveway. Ray stopped by the front door.

"Now, turn that frown upside down," he said.

"In there?"

He nodded. "I'll wait in town. I'll come back for you in an hour or so. Can't imagine this will take very long."

I got out and looked back as he drove through the gate. I couldn't see him inside. Before I knocked, the big front door was opened by a serious looking guy with a shaved head, wearing a white jacket like a chef. Men's voices in another room; the guy nodded toward it. This room had a high ceiling and lots of modern furniture, a gleaming marble floor. Bee-Gees echoed in the background. Five or six men were sitting on chairs and sofas, and a huge man, like a bouncer, leaning against the bar with a drink in his hand. I was happy Ray gave me something because the sight of the fat guy, sitting on a black sofa, dressed up in pants and too-colorful sweater, made me queasy.

"Aha, gentlemen," he said when he saw me, "look who we have, the man of the hour." I nodded and the men applauded. I felt light enough to do a little bow for them. "Come in, come in young man," he said, "we're all friends here." I moved into the room. "Come, sit next to me." He patted the empty space next to him. "What would you like to drink, honey?" I said a beer was fine and he nodded to the bouncer, who went to the bar and brought me a bottle. He was big, this guy, with nice clothes, a turtleneck and a jacket, trying to look sophisticated. Underneath he was massive. The other guys were laughing and talking, their faces shinier than it was warm in here. On the glass coffee table, squares of folded paper, fine white dust on the glass. "You want to party, honey?" The fat guy gave me a roll, cut a line, and I did it. "Well," he said to his friends, "I've told you all about my pet project, haven't I? I'm a purveyor of fine adult film. What's it called again, sugar, the company?"

"Nu-Man Productions," I said, sitting up, coughing. I had to take a swig of beer.

"Nu-Man Productions," he said. "Couldn't be truer. And Kevin here is just one of the many stars in that glittering stratosphere. Just look at the puss on him, will you?" He squeezed my face hard and they laughed. "Who wouldn't want to invest a small fortune in that?"

He started going on about his other projects and what he paid and what he was making. Some of the movies I heard of, others not. The beer seemed to amplify the effect of the pills Ray gave me and I felt disoriented. I was sweating and I thought another line would clear it. "You go right ahead, honey," the guy said. "Zip that right up." And he kept talking, them all listening to his jokes, the things he was saying. He put his hand on my thigh; I smiled, kept nodding. It got so hot in there. I drank more of the beer. Looked at my wrist for my watch, but I didn't have one. "It's still early, sugar, don't be checking the time on us just yet," he said. "You need a refresher?" He signaled to the bouncer, who brought me another, and took the empty out of my hand. It seemed like only minutes, nodding politely and listening, but soon I felt something soft, and realized I'd fallen sideways into his lap. I didn't have any balance and my legs were too weak to stand. His big arm came over and pulled me into him.

"Oh my, is someone getting tired?" He looked down at me. "Partying too hard?"

"I don't . . . I don't know."

"That's alright," he said, and finished his drink. "Funniest thing about my side project," he said to his friends, "*Nu-Man* Productions. Little did I know, I'm the majority investor. In fact, I'm the only investor!" They thought that was very funny. "And, top it off, you know what they did with that investment? You know what I found out, from the six o'clock news, no less? Why, they flushed it down the toilet! They got busted for, oh my, quite a stunning array of pandering and obscenity and solicitation charges. All of which are awfully unsavory. Awfully unpleasant. And the last thing I need my name associated with." The others didn't seem to be laughing anymore. The fat guy looked down at me, stroked my hair. "And then, to add insult to injury, our sweaty little friend told me you backed out of the business, honey. Is that right?" I nodded. "Aw, that's too bad. But if that's true, then you're not much use to us anymore, are you?" I said probably not and the guys thought that was funny. "Your friend is not very smart, is he?" I said, no, he wasn't, and they thought that was hilarious. "Well, I'm glad we agree on that," he said. "So I need you to do me a little favor, then. I need you to help me show your friend how serious I am. Will you do that for me?"

I said ok.

"I knew you were a good boy." He sat up and my head fell flat on the sofa. In the distance, I heard his voice, that pissed-off tone I remembered. "Jesus, that took long enough. Take care of this, will you?"

The bouncer came over, heaved me up, carried me over his shoulder and threw me onto the cement floor of a room like a garage. All I could see was the one lightbulb in the ceiling.

In the movies, this is where the scene ends. The camera pans up and out a window and you hear the screams from a distance.

It was funny because that's the one thing I could always do, the one thing I had going for me. I was small and wiry and I could slip away from danger. But not this time. Now it was the dream where you can't move and they can do anything they want. They tied a rag around my head and stuffed part of it in my mouth, but it didn't stop the awful sounds an animal makes. Cut right through the drugs. A free for all, beating and beating. Just beating on something because you could, because no one would stop you. The built-up rage of all that frustration, all that power, everyone wanting that nut so badly. I could almost understand it, wanting to let it all out. And they did. After a while no more talking, only guttural sounds. A million miles from human beings using words, just breathing, pounding, beating without even meaning, the pain everything and nothing.

This time we do not endure. Just a thing on a cement floor, a bloody pile of meat in a room with no human beings.

■ ■ ■

It was still dark when they exhausted themselves. Probably three or four in the morning. They threw the body onto an old rug and rolled it up, the taller one carrying it on his shoulder to a car behind the house. Up a long, twisting road in the dark, somewhere so quiet, high above the lights of the city. The wrong side of the hill, because hot wind blew hard here. Two of them went, one to carry the package, one to help. They took the rug out of the trunk, climbed a ways from the road, then snapped it open. What's inside flew out and rolled to the edge, then over and down, rolling and scraping all the way to a ravine where no one will see or know. Coming to rest against a dead bush.

At the top of the hill, the sound of a car driving off, rocks and pebbles crunching under its tires. The moon shines a yellow, waxy light, a million tiny eyes peering with blank expressions. The desert exhales; silence and peace after that rude interruption.

At last, everything is back in its place.

III

SUSPENSION

1

1998

The fog is down again, bending time.

It softens the sound of cars and freeways, soothes nerves jangled by bad dreams and burning days. People open their eyes inside of houses bathed in fog and think the world is hazy. If they could see it from above – if they looked down from high over the city – they would see the clouds snuggled up to canyons and hills like cotton packed around a gift, pressed against the ground. Not where they're supposed to be at all.

Inside the still-gray of early morning, a few restless souls walk up and down the streets, alone, their heavy clay feet trudging the empty sidewalks. Most people in Los Angeles are sleeping, the fog comforting their dreams, soothing their worries. Its tender fingers don't reach these people, though; they roam the streets with dark, hollow eyes and cups of coffee, vaguely recognizing each other in gray clothes. Dreams and fog can't bring them comfort anymore. They've already seen the truth.

At six or seven in the morning, on a Sunday, one of these men walks down a wide sidewalk, the power lines still buzzing overhead. His haunted excuse is a box of white kitchen garbage bags – the two-ply kind. He needs these badly. He sees himself from above, even while he moves along the empty sidewalk; sees each footstep and the pain in the right leg that causes a slight limp; sees the two more blocks to the supermarket, three behind from the apartment.

He can even count the number of steps he has taken so far.

■ ■ ■

On the trip back from the market, the fog is burning off and the real world of cars and people groans into life. As the volume comes up and reality sinks in, I come back to this body, no longer seeing things from above, the camera shooting someone else's life. Which for me is a more comfortable way to see things. But for now, coffee; so before I turn onto my street, I stop at Six Gallery and sit at a table in front to watch the people come by.

It's after eight now. My friend Andre walks by with his dog. He's coming from his meeting and his eyes are bleary. He sits and has coffee with me, the one thing I can have as much of as I want. Andre is handsome, much younger than me. He looks about 23, but his eyes are tired from the strain. To these boys, these kids, I'm a warning, a harbinger of what might become of them if they don't straighten out. They like me, though. I'm a nice guy and they know I don't want anything from them. I buy them coffee and listen when they want to talk. Everyone has a story, but the kids seem reticent to ask me about mine.

I went to meetings myself for a time, but they wanted a commitment I was unable to make. At first I wasn't sure what I was there for. Drugs, sex, loneliness? I couldn't decide. They wanted you to be exposed and raw, tell the truth and be seen. That was way too much for me. So I hid in my cave and licked the wounds in private. What caused the wounds – the physical ones at least – I only have fragments of. Like a plate that was shattered, then Crazy Glued together, minus the pieces that skittered under the sofa. You just live with the empty spaces and stains marked by adhesive. Which is not unlike what my face looks like now.

This is all taking place in a valley. Not The Valley, the place I grew up in, but a valley in time. The 1990s in Los Angeles. A deep breath between the old world and the new.

The twentieth century people who built the city and the industry had gotten old, and retired or died. The studios that once dominated the town suffered a long, slow decline into quiet, empty warehouses, the remaining stages churning out game shows and talk shows, the rest for lease. Riots, fires and earthquakes scared everyone out in the early 90s. The real estate boom that would transform LA hadn't happened yet; September 11 hadn't happened yet; no such thing as social media, hardly any internet. This was a quiet after one storm and before another, like an insulating fog. The refugees, people left over from the old world, roamed the city like Israelites during the forty years, waiting out their time until they die and children re-populate the world, reanimate a dead landscape. Those children, the ones here now, look right through ghosts like me, through the transparency of other survivors. To them, we're phantoms of a past they know nothing about. I prefer it that way. No one looks at me or knows me or expects anything. Just people on the street, looking at each other, for each other, wondering what happened.

■ ■ ■

I work at a restaurant on Santa Monica Boulevard. It has a New Orleans theme: a patio in front facing the street, a courtyard inside with a railing around the second level with shops and offices. It's very cute in a hokey kind of way, and as reliable a place as you'll find. The chubby, jovial guys who meet on Sunday mornings, if you squint hard, you can make out the golden boys with dreamy eyes and sun-speckled tans who came in after hours when the clubs closed in 1975. It's still them, the ones who survived, together eating brunch after all these years. That makes me happy because so much else is transient. So many people died, disappeared, were destroyed. If there is a place the survivors can meet and enjoy their good lives, then I'm happy to be here and bring them eggs and french toast. My tametag says Martin from South Bend, and that's how they know me. Quite ironic that I am now a diner waitress. Once in a great while someone gives a second look, but it fades; he doesn't know what he saw, and goes on with his order. I bring it quickly and efficiently.

My mother still lives in North Hollywood. Alicia gone, to Berkeley, then a degree in biology, living in a condo in Redwood City. She got out, smarter than all of us. She has a good life with a nice guy and a dog and a

Jeep. They laugh at us down here in Los Angeles, the northern California people. I don't blame them.

Momma talks to me only about safe, unimportant things. Tonight it's folding chairs. She asks if I left one at her house; she worries I broke up a set and says she'll bring it back if I need it.

"No," I said, into the phone. Lying in my bed, looking up at the stained, cottage cheese ceiling in this dark apartment. The cloud-shaped stain over my bed has been there since I moved in. Sometimes I wonder how that shape came to be. Something very raunchy, maybe, or sinister, that happened a long time ago. Now only the stain remains.

"It's not mine," I said. "I don't have any folding chairs."

"Well, maybe you could use it. You know, for guests?"

I sighed, no need to laugh. "I don't have guests. It's fine. You keep it."

"Are you sure? I can drop it by any time."

"I'm sure."

We said our goodnights and hung up. We play our game, each playing the part. Then I lie here a while, listen to the cars race up and down this quiet street. I left the hall light on, and get up to shut it off before I'll fall asleep in my clothes again. Passing the round, dusty mirror on the wall next to the front door, I see the face I have now and I'm always surprised. It's some man looking back, someone I don't recognize, with a humorless jaw, sunken cheeks, and the eyes slightly misaligned. If you didn't know him you wouldn't think anything was off. But if you did, you would notice that one eye is slightly lower than it used to be, just enough to make you think it's a different person. Just that slight difference between one person and another.

2

Because there are earthquakes here, I always think of what I would lose if my apartment collapsed. Especially the kind that hits in the middle of the night and you have to run out in your underwear. I took an inventory once; there isn't anything I couldn't replace in ten minutes. What I do have, in my bathroom cabinet, are fifteen boxes of sleeping pills. Some are the prescription kind I collected from friends, others are over-the-counter. Mashed into a paste and swallowed with the right combination of booze and Pepto-Bismol, they will do exactly what they're intended to do, just permanently. The pièce de résistance, when I'm in the mood to consider it, is the electric blanket to wrap the whole thing up in. Make it painless and soothing, like falling into a deep, warm sleep; an intoxicated baked potato. People who have a thing for knives or guns or leaping off tall buildings are just big show-offs, if you ask me.

I have to be sure the pills are fresh because they can go stale. There's nothing worse than reaching the lowest point of despair, swallowing a handful of expired tranquilizers and waking up with diarrhea. I tried that once and learned you have to be a conscientious pharmacist to pull it off. Anything older than three months you toss out and replace.

The white plastic garbage bags figure into the plan as well. There's the old saw about clean underwear; along the same lines, you can't have a messy apartment when the EMTs break down the door. It's just bad taste. Everything has to be neat when they find the body. No piles of crusty food, no starving cats licking tuna cans. The body itself could be a problem, but a note sent by mail the previous day will alert the police before it

bloats too much and stinks up the place. There's the electric blanket question, whether that will make it more or less pleasant to unwrap after 24
hours, all preserved like a turkey in the oven. I don't know enough about
post-mortem anatomy yet, but these are merely logistics, one of the many
details I still have to work out.

■ ■ ■

I got paid on Friday so I went to Robinson's and bought a bathrobe for
Eva. Blue satin with white trim. Her birthday was coming up and I knew
she needed one. With age comes authority, and as momma got older, she
began to impose her own style onto Eva's life. Like cheap clothes. She
went to Mervyn's and bought polyester mix-and-match blouses and skirts,
said, "Look, they're so easy to wash." Eva said nothing, but when momma
left, she threw them in the trash and covered them with coffee grounds.
She did it when I was there so I knew she wanted me to know.

Robinson's was in a mall next to the Beverly Hilton that isn't there
anymore. The quiet, forgotten Robinson's. It sat there, this gleaming
white, beautifully stocked department store, filled with salespeople, and
no customers at all. Like a department store in heaven. I took the wrapped
bathrobe, thanked the saleslady and walked out to the equally white, completely deserted garage and got in my old pickup – a lone red blotch in this
antiseptic world – and drove across Beverly Hills to the house on Palm
Drive. When I got there, the house was quiet. I thought no one was home,
but Mrs. Wyman sat in the livingroom, reading the paper. She looked over
her half glasses when she heard me.

"How are you today?" she said, with her firm, clipped pronunciation.
Gave me the once over, her green eyes penetrating. For some reason, she
wouldn't call me by name. She called momma Carolyn but never referred
to me at all.

"Good," I said. "Well," I said, correcting myself. "How are you?"

"Very well, thank you."

"How's she doing today?" I asked.

She looked at me with distaste. "I'm no judge of character on a daily basis. Why don't you find out for yourself." The exchange, like all of them with Mrs. Wyman, was awkward. The first time I met her, a few weeks earlier, I assumed she was a housekeeper or someone momma hired. But she was dressed nicer and more stylish than Eva, and never seemed to be doing anything a housekeeper would do. The new, green Jaguar parked at the curb seemed to be hers, also nicer than Eva's Cadillac; and Flor, the woman who had come once a week to clean and do laundry for years, was still coming. So I wasn't exactly sure who Mrs. Wyman was. She sensed how uncomfortable I was that I couldn't go until she dismissed me. "You know," she said, "I believe I saw some lemonade in the refrigerator."

"Thanks," I said. "Thank you, I mean." I nodded, almost saluted, and ducked out.

It's funny how the places you always knew turn old fashioned without changing at all. When I was a kid, I thought Eva's Beverly Hills house was the sharpest, most stylish place imaginable. Phil and grandpa's had too much kitsch – frilly print upholstery, phony spinning wheels – but Nana's house was solid and unpretentious. Now, walking up the stairs, it seemed quaint, a 1950s matron's house. The slightest smell of mothballs and dust.

She sat in the big chair next to the bed, her feet crossed delicately on the ottoman. Today a beige skirt, new blouse, professional looking jacket, and spectators. Elegant clothes she bought herself, and she looked ready for work. But there was none, not since the memory problem. It started a few months ago. Age 76, she had no plans to retire, and things were going fine until she forgot a few lines. Nothing big, but they had to do the scene a couple of times and she was embarrassed. She went home and told her agent not to book anything until she figured out what was going on. She visited every professional and did all the tests and they all said the same thing. No sign of dementia or Alzheimer's, just old age, when memory loss is normal. Before they examined her, she admonished each one, "Don't say old age to me, buddy," and they all laughed, thought she was cute, and ended up telling her it was old age.

"Look Harris," she said, and pointed at the TV. "These people are absolutely idiotic. This one, he says the girlfriend owes him money for a diamond brooch he gave her. They broke up and he wants the brooch back or the money. I mean, honestly, have you ever heard such pettiness in your life?"

"Nana, they make this all up."

"No, Harris, the sad truth is it's all real. You see the bailiff . . . wait a minute, there, you see, that man standing in the back? That's Norman Whitlock, he's a friend of mine. I call him every day after this program to find out who these people are, and you know what? They're just as ghastly in real life as they are on TV. Even more, because they have much worse skin. You stay here till the program ends. You'll see. As soon as this is over, I'll call Norman and you can ask him yourself."

"That's OK, I don't need to know."

I leaned down to kiss her cheek.

"How's my bestest starry grandson?" she said. "Still letting those movie star looks go to pot?" She pulled my cheek. "Life is short and you're half way through it. Why are you wasting it visiting an old broad in the middle of the day?"

Scars and limps and other broken stuff leave me nowhere near movie star looks. But we know those are the things a grandmother is supposed to say.

"I told you," I said. "I work nights."

She reached for her pocketbook and pulled out the cigarettes and lighter. Lit one up, said, "Mmm-hhm," then launched into the monologue. "What are you doing with your life anyway? A *waiter*? I don't get it."

"Please, Nana, don't . . ."

"What have you accomplished with all your talent and looks? Those are gifts in this town, let me tell you. What have you . . ."

". . . made of yourself, made for others, made for the world . . ."

"Well, if I keep repeating it, it's because it's true. I mean, I have no choice, I'm old. But you're young. You're in the prime of life. So, you lost your marbles. Big deal. We all have our crosses to bear. But fifteen years, sweetheart? My god, you get back on the horse."

"Nana," I said, looking at the TV. "I don't have a horse."

"Ah ha, make a joke of it. But you know I'm right. It's the truth what I'm saying to you."

She gave me a look like she did sometimes now, like someone looking clear through a window. Then just as quick, the face withdrew.

"Well look," she said, "I don't want to hold you up. What do you want?"

I handed her the box. She turned from the TV, moved the cigarette to the side of her mouth and took it. Broke open the ribbon with that serious expression, pulled off the top, lifted the nightgown, looked at it front and back. "Ya, that's fine," she said, and dropped it back in the box. Success. "Anything else?"

"How's work?"

She shrugged, eyes on the TV. "Brain's still broken. Everything else ok. Just can't remember things. Next week I get a vitamin B shot. They give it to you in the ass, you know. I told them they can stick it right in the head if that would help, but nope. Has to be the caboose. Lucky for me my circulation is lousy. I can't feel anything down there, so it all evens out."

"Well, keep at it," I said. "Let me know if I can do anything for you."

"Don't worry about me, I can take care of myself. But how about you? Can you say the same?" The little jabs came more often. Not quite an incision but something with a duller edge. "Well?"

"I guess I'll be on my way then." I leaned down to kiss her cheek. She kept her eyes on the TV.

Downstairs, Mrs. Wyman looked up from the newspaper. I realized I hardly ever saw them together; Mrs. Wyman seemed to occupy the house in one place and Eva in another, and I thought of those sci-fi movies where the two people live in the same space but different dimensions. Right now, she held me with raised eyebrows, waiting for whatever I was going to bother her with.

"Testy," I said tilting my head toward the stairs.

"Wouldn't you be if you wanted to work and couldn't?"

She went back to her crosswords but I knew she was listening, waiting for me to leave.

"Oh, by the way," I said. "Do you know if there's an electric blanket around here I could borrow?"

She narrowed her eyes like it was the dumbest question anyone ever asked.

3

So, 1998, and we still used a lot of paper. Advertising, magazines, fliers. If you wanted people to know something you had to get it in print. Near my apartment in West Hollywood, near the bars, they gave out these thick, free magazines with news and personals and massage listings. They're stacked in metal racks and men in trucks come every week to refresh the stacks; then people pick up the magazines without thinking, throw them in the street and leave them all over the place, in alleys and gutters, fanned open like fish flapping out of water. Now I'm walking up the street toward my apartment with a bag of groceries, and there's a slurry of soaked magazines forming a little wall of sludge at the curb ahead of me. Someone must have opened a magazine rack and dumped all the new copies into the wet gutter. I step over the mound, looking down at the words and images on liquified paper. I feel a pang of something on the back wall of my brain.

Later that night, I stopped at a Rexall, a Sav-On, a 7-Eleven and my supermarket. More sleeping pills. You have to be careful not to buy too many in one place or they look at you suspiciously. Also, you have to mix it up with things like tampons and Preparation H so the checkout people don't ask anything. Driving out of the supermarket, the little paper bag on the passenger seat crinkled with the air blowing through the open window. Something simple like that, a brown paper bag. It sounded like freedom.

When I got home, the first task would be to neaten up the place. I opened the box of white kitchen bags and stuffed in all the paper cups, frozen food trays and old newspapers. Cleaned up most of the junk, vacuumed the brown frizzled rug. Put the blanket I borrowed from Eva in the bedroom, set it on the floor next to the bed. Tomorrow I'll have to fiddle with the controls, see what temperature settings you use to warm, toast and broil. No shift today at the restaurant and no appointments; I lay on the sofa in the late afternoon and didn't realize it but a wave of exhaustion rolled over me and darkness came up like a sheet. The phone ringing in the dark, after midnight, woke me up. Awake suddenly in the livingroom on the sofa, I searched for the phone in this room.

"Hello?" I said.

Silence. I can make out the breathing.

"Hello?" And nothing. Only the sound of air moving in and out. How weird that in one moment you're alone and the next, a person is there with you, a stranger, in the dark of your room and them in the dark of their own room.

"Hello?" I said, softer.

Then the other phone hanging up gently. It was an old phone, I could tell, by the sound of the handset placed on a cradle of hard plastic. Mine is a cheap wireless. I click it off before I drop it on the carpet and watch the dim lights move across the ceiling, car headlights reflected off some building.

I thought of my pharmaceuticals in the kitchen. On the counter, in their soft paper bag, waiting for activation, waiting to be used. I feel peaceful and relaxed again, just thinking about them. *What's a gun for, Earl?* All of this could have been avoided, I thought, as I felt sleep coming on. None of this would have been necessary if those goddamn hikers had only stayed on the path.

■ ■ ■

The Park Service goes to all this trouble to make trails and mark them clearly, so it's really disrespectful when people wander off the pathway. But they do, and they did, these hikers, on the desert side of the mountains outside Palm Springs, and one of them stumbled across a hand sticking out from a bush. She screamed, afraid it was some chopped-off body part.

Her friends pushed the bush aside, saw the whole body and ran down and called the police.

No one had an ID. Anyone in Palm Springs who knew anything wasn't talking. In the hospital for a while, wrapped like a mummy, not really conscious or having any memory of what happened. When it did come back, I didn't care at all. It was easy to lie and say I couldn't remember who I was and then stop talking altogether. I couldn't have them calling anyone in LA to come out and see this. Back then, 1981, they sent people with no money to a crappy facility out in the desert, short on everything except morphine, which was fine by me, and the best way to keep you happy and zonked out until you were well enough for them to throw you out. You can walk out of the hospital then, but you really do still need the morphine.

I hitched a ride back inside the sheltering mountains. Back to LA and the small, ghostly streets in the heart of Hollywood. Back then, just a checkerboard of cheap, dying hotels with burned-out neon signs, men crumpled and twitching on the sidewalk, the rest wandering with hollow eyes. Rooms for rent by the hour, day, or week, and lots of morphine, as well as much cheaper stuff to get your hands on. I decided to stay in Hollywood, not Skid Row or downtown. Too scary for me. A nice middle-class loser goes to the sad, piss-smelling sidewalks of Hollywood because you won't be seen, and whatever you need you can get – change, or drugs, or an alley to sleep in undisturbed.

Walking up Wilcox one late afternoon, a day in the fall, the cool weather was just beginning. Looking north at the hills, with no place to rush to, nowhere to go, I stopped and just looked – at the low, old-fashioned buildings, the melancholy color of the sun sinking behind the smog in the western sky. There was this quiet then, this feeling of Nighthawks at the Diner. In those orange moments, you could still see the little western town that Hollywood used to be, with shops and awnings for the pioneers who ventured all the way west, away from civilization. Behind the movies and nightclubs and freeways, it's a small and scared place, and this slice of light in the afternoon revealed the loneliness like an x-ray.

Further up the street were the working kids, girls and boys trying hard. They still had hope; that someone will want them and pay for them. I stop here on this street and realize I can't walk up to Hollywood Boulevard, ever again. I have to stay down here, on the side streets, and leave the hope to them. Because I'm dead. Those guys killed me. They meant to, anyhow, and being on the receiving end of that intent, even if it doesn't succeed, is enough. You're a walking corpse, and the fact you can still eat and talk doesn't mean very much.

A few days after I got back, being on the street started to feel familiar. Not cocky anymore, this was very straightforward. You just walk up and ask for money. They say yes or no, and that's it. Lots of disgusted looks, of course, but it didn't hurt my feelings. But even for a dead man, that wasn't enough money to sleep and eat. If I panhandled on someone else's territory, I got punched. So I started watching the shops, the stands, the lingerie boutiques, and made a map of what happened when and who got fired; at a certain point I watched myself walk in and ask for the job of sweeping and taking out the trash. I can do those things well. It paid enough for a room in the hotel up the street with the shared bathroom and the moaning through the night of people in pain, the gunshots outside and sometimes inside, the fights and scuffles. But the view out the dirty window was beautiful. I could lie on this ratty mattress and look at the endless gray Los Angeles sky with no clouds to limit your hopes and dreams. No ceiling at all. There was such a relief in ceasing to exist. Sweeping is the most peaceful of arts.

As I moved along the sidewalk one day with my head down, someone called my name. Kept calling and wouldn't quit. This friend of Eva's who'd known us since we were kids. Bossy country club lady. She actually stopped me, held me by the arm. Eva was so worried, she said, the whole family so upset. How could I do this to them? So then I was found, and they brought me back and sent me to some cushy clinic in Santa Barbara with real medical care. Some bones to be re-set. Bit of addiction. But addiction requires energy; there is still something you desire. And if most of that has been beaten out of you, your body's willingness to hold onto anything is not as strong. Now, really naked, with no character to hide behind, no shield or attitude for protection, I went back.

By then, two or three years after we'd seen each other, momma was living alone in her empty house. Eva was so furious after I got arrested, she petitioned the court for custody of Alicia. Momma had visitation rights, but only with a supervisor. Momma went to the police after I disappeared but the police told her I was an adult and there was nothing they could do. She pushed everyone away; George tried to fill the space, but she pushed him away too.

As for Eva, for reasons never given, they didn't produce a pilot for *Margaret Lawson, DA*. They dropped the idea and Eva remained a co-star until *Bowman* was cancelled in 1984. Right after that, *Murder, She Wrote* premiered – the biggest monster hit anyone ever saw, all about an old lady with old guest stars – and caused a great deal of teeth gnashing on Palm Drive. Eva never got another offer like that, and had to downsize to occasional guest roles and a gruesome period where she did game shows. I saw some while sweeping on Hollywood Boulevard, and was fortunate I couldn't feel much anymore, including guilt. Of course, all this made it harder to meet them again.

At first, they treated me like glass. Talked the way you talk to someone with cancer, thinking everything you say will be wrong. Later I overheard Eva on the phone telling some friend about seeing her grandson who'd gone ha-ha, and I felt better. She had come up with a story that worked for her. Once she saw I wasn't fragile, she started talking about it, calling it the time I lost my marbles. "That's just what it was," she said, "All that potential, just blown up and burst out. Happens to the best of them. Got messed up, ran away, had to dry out in a fat farm."

"It wasn't a fat farm," I said. "They just clean you up."

"Well, you're back and that's what's important. Not easy to do, I'm sure. You're tough, like me. You endure."

By that time it was 1985, and I had no idea what we would have to endure next.

Everyone had begun to die. Young, handsome, strong guys. Overnight, it seemed, they turned into shriveled horrors, like bad movie make-up, and no one said anything about it. TV went on like usual. People watched *Hill Street Blues*, listened to Michael Jackson, while death happened all around us. People you knew, people you loved, turned sick and died, and everyone just ignored them. Everyone was so happy with their big shoulder pads and *Top Gun*, while people were dropping dead in public, and even the President of the United States never said a word about it. One person you knew died, then another, then another, and it was like a dam breaking. They wouldn't stop dying. I did the same thing over and over; visited a house, held a hand, stood by a graveside, not weeping, and waited for my turn.

Gordon had a heart attack in 1987, and the world opened its heart for his funeral. They had to make a big deal to say it was a heart attack and not AIDS because everyone was so crazy that no one could simply die. Then grandpa and Phil; Phil from AIDS in '91, then grandpa, in '94, still big and strong, but dead from a broken heart. I was 33, and stood at his grave, not weeping.

I drifted through jobs until this one. Being a waiter seemed a good fit. I could be around people and then go home and not have to pretend to be a living being, which took too much energy. A year passed, and I watched from inside my sober, dead skin; then two years, then more. I could not believe I was still alive, that nothing had found me and put an end to me too. Unless – and it finally came to me – it already had. That this was all a mistake, an error, because of those goddamn hikers. Still thinking of my soft, crinkling paper bag in the kitchen, that seemed the most logical explanation. Those people had simply wandered off the trail, and it was just a mistake that could now be easily corrected.

4

The next day I came home from the restaurant after the lunch rush. In the lobby of my building, I pressed the button for the elevator but nothing happened; the button lit up, but the motor didn't start. I put my ear to the elevator door. Sometimes this button didn't work, but you could call the elevator from the garage. I went down and around, pressed the button there. Now the motor did start with a clunk, the car coming loose from where ever it was stuck. When the door opened, one of the old ladies from my floor was standing inside, dazed, holding a bunch of keys in her right hand, tied together with a pink, fluffy ball.

"Is this my apartment?" she snapped.

"No, Mrs. Olivo, this is the garage."

Her hair was tied in knots with cloth curlers, her blue housecoat covered with stars and question marks. "Oh, I know you," she said, squinting. "The *troublemaker*." She jangled the keys at me, warding off a curse. I got into the elevator, pushed the button for our floor.

"Am I?"

"Yeah," she said. "It's you they're looking for. Skulking around, knocking on doors at all hours."

"Really?"

"They come by," she said. "I hear 'em, loitering outside the door. Playing with the knob. They tried it on me and I smacked the door with the poker. *Whamo!* You better believe they took off."

"It was probably the manager."

"No, sir. I'm at home watching my programs. I know who's supposed to be there. There's something funny." On *funny*, she jabbed the air at me like she meant to poke my eye out.

"Did you see who it was?"

"No! What do you think I am, a snoop?"

The door opened to our floor, she got out, teetering toward her own front door, keys jangling, muttering, "Don't need any trouble around here. All the characters in this building." She turned around once before she went in, looked at me. "Characters," she said, and slammed the door.

Crazy as she was, I had been curious about the loitering and the phone calls too. As I drove out of the garage later, my pickup coming up the ramp onto the street, I saw this kid sitting on the low concrete wall in front of the building. His head followed my truck as it pulled out. He was skinny, with serious eyes, wearing a ratty sweatshirt. Sixteen or seventeen, I can't tell. Maybe a runaway or lost or broke, sitting here near the clubs, where people who live near the clubs would see him. He watched my truck as I drove to the end of the street.

When I stepped into Eva's kitchen, it looked like some chess tournament in progress. All the grave faces: Eva and Mrs. Wyman seated at the table, across from each other; momma behind them standing at the counter, arms crossed. No one looked up when I walked in. A soft clicking sound, the mahjong tiles Eva and Mrs. Wyman were playing. Even across from each other, in their own world, playing solitaire.

"Well, would you tell me if you see them?" momma said.

Eva shrugged absentmindedly. Momma sighed, came over to kiss me. "How are you?" she said.

"Fine. What's going on?"

"We're looking for some dishes," momma said. "Eva thinks I have them and I looked everywhere at my house. I think they're in a box somewhere here. We're having a disagreement about it."

Without looking up, Eva said, "I know what I know. They're not in this house. I can't remember lines but I know what I have."

"Well, would you look for them anyway?" momma said. "That is, if you can find the time in your busy schedule."

Eva ignored her.

"What do you need?" momma asked me.

"I was just wondering, Nana," I said, louder, "did you send anything to my apartment?"

She clicked a tile against another. "Yes, I did," she said. "I know that. I sent Harris a package."

"What did you send?" momma asked.

"Salmon steaks. From Chalet Gourmet."

"You did?"

"Ya ha," she said, her eyes steady on Mrs. Wyman's tiles. "I'm not forgetting anything. They had a special, so I sent him five pounds. Salmon is loaded with vitamins, you know. Good for everything. Muscles, brain cells, skin elasticity. You can freeze it too. Goddamn miracle food, salmon."

"Do you mean the gifts we talked about for your Christmas list?" momma said.

"No, I don't mean Christmas gifts. I mean a package I sent my grandson two days ago. For god's sake, they did every test they could think of." She lifted a cigarette from the ashtray and took a big drag; watched intently as Mrs. Wyman placed a tile against one of her own. "Why do you ask?"

"Nothing," I said. "One of my neighbors said someone was knocking on my door."

"Well look around," Eva said. "If you haven't got it, then someone else has five pounds of fish with your name on it."

Mrs. Wyman laid one more tile on top of her row, said "Mahjong."

"God . . . dammit," Eva said. Stood up, shook her head. "Well, that's all the punishment I can take for one day," and walked out.

"Anything else?" momma asked. There wasn't, so she kissed me and left herself. Mrs. Wyman stood and began clearing the tiles, organizing them into Eva's ornate storage box. I always liked those tiles, their solid click-click and the antique look; like some kind of fine bone, a game with complicated rules that people like me could never understand.

She caught me staring. "Did you need anything more?"

I hadn't looked at her very carefully, because she scared me. As she looked at me now, I realized it was her eyes, so green and luminous against her dark skin.

■ ■ ■

The phone rang again, right after seven the next morning. Like before, no talking. Warm in my bed, I pulled it under the covers with me.

"Hello?" I whispered. "Who is it?"

On the other end, something like cloth moving over the mouthpiece.

"Hello?" I said again.

A word, beginning, but stopped. I can hear the crackly sounds of saliva on the tongue, the edge of a dry mouth. Then the receiver settling onto the cradle.

It's hot under the covers, but I'm shivering.

■ ■ ■

By Thursday, my apartment was clean as it would be. All the garbage dumped, floor vacuumed, everything hairy thrown away. The electric blanket rolled up and ready in the bedroom.

Late in the afternoon, it was time to manufacture the paste.

Each of the prescription capsules has to be opened surgically with an X-acto knife, all the pills ground into powder. I want a good healthy mound this time, no fucking around. I had no hard schedule in mind, just moving calmly from one task to the next. I figured by the time they're all done, it'll be simple to do the last one. My shift at the restaurant was over for the week, and since I wouldn't be expected until Wednesday, a two-day gap came at the perfect time.

Chopping the pills, dicing up chunks, I felt productive, like a chef making a souffle. Sweating, wiping the hair out of my eyes. I wanted the mound of powder smooth and silky, and by nine it was. I got out a tall glass, poured in the powder, added just enough water to make it drinkable and stirred. Magnified by the curvature of the glass, it made a brown suspension. Good word, *suspension*. Instantly recognizable, but also special, because you don't use it all the time. *Suspension*: something they do in school when you're bad; taken out of work with pay; the root of *suspense*; and this beautiful cloud of pharmaceuticals slowly churning like smoke in water.

It would be pretty easy from here. Get the blanket set up, drink the beverage, go to sleep. Who couldn't do that?

I opened the blanket, lay it on the bed, reviewed the various logistics of the day. A note mailed to the West Hollywood sheriff telling them where to find the body; the last thing I need is some unsuspecting person stumbling in and finding the mess. Having dropped the letter at the post office on San Vicente this afternoon, the sheriff's station should receive it tomorrow.

I switched on the TV, turned out all the lights except the small one over the stove. Picked up the glass to bring it into the bedroom, and the phone rang. I should really ignore it, let the machine pick it up. But the volume is down and I can't hear the message. It could be something important, an emergency, someone needing something.

"Yes?" My voice sounds naked and irritable. "Hello?"

I can hear the breathing, small and tinny. They know I'm listening. It's a standoff so I wait. And wait. Then the line goes dead, a finger ready on the button.

So.

That's the last thing I'll hear. Nothing. Kind of sums it up.

Another look around the apartment, a final check. Now, just pick up the cool glass with rolling sweat, take it to the bedroom, to the open, welcoming blanket, and drink it. Turn off the bedroom light, put the empty glass on the nightstand and lie down, enveloped in the ready, waiting warmth. And that is what it is, an envelope. Ready to slip closed around me and take me away from all of this, at long last.

5

The cloud shaped stain.

My eyes must be open because I see it.

Outside it's day. The same unrelenting Los Angeles day as always.

Suspension on the nightstand. Still there.

I must still be here.

I meant to drink it. I really did. But something happened. Some irritating something. As I come to consciousness, I try to remember. Not as clear as an image, more like a pinprick, just enough to be annoying.

Later in the morning, standing upright in the kitchen, I take a mug from the cabinet. Before making the coffee, I look in and there's this brown, viscous sludge at the bottom. I can't remember when I used it last. Staring into the mug, I wonder if it can ever be cleaned. And I try to remember what it was that distracted me from the task. It was a flash of something, and it meant something, but in the clear light of day, I can't call it up. And so I stand there like an idiot – with the scooper of dry coffee in one hand, the mug in the other, staring at the sludge – and tell myself I will not move, I will not make coffee, I will not do anything at all, for as long as it takes, until the answer bubbles up from down there. And I guess when it realizes I'm serious, it does. At least I remembered where I felt the prick.

■ ■ ■

By now, the gutter down the street had been cleaned. I found a rack with this week's magazines, got coffee, and sat at the coffee house while I turned the pages. Didn't know what I was looking for, I hoped something would cross my eyes. But nothing did. I went through all the pages again. Not a trickle, not a prickle.

On my way out, I passed an empty table with an empty coffee cup and a magazine upside down, the full-page car dealership ad on the back. *We're gay friendly! Buy a Toyota from us!* I turned it over, and it was last week's edition. I paged through, only half interested. Near the back, before the escort and massage ads, a blip. Turned back. There was a section called *Milestones*, a list of old men, old women, famous actors, singers, etc., who died that week. It's a column of little pictures with a blurb under each one. I scanned it, and just before the bottom, so small it was designed to be missed, was a photo of a boy's head, badly cropped and poorly reproduced. Only one line beneath it.

"Kevin" – 1980s porn actor, Palm Springs

6

So, it's discomfiting – if that's a word – disconcerting anyway, to read your own obituary. Especially so close on the heels of having made a good faith effort to bring about that very outcome.

Alone, with no one to bounce this off of, I did go to the mirror and pinch myself; went to the supermarket and forced a conversation with the checkout lady to be sure I could be seen and heard. Once confirmed, I went home and contemplated the suspension on the kitchen counter. The powder had fallen to the bottom of the glass and separated. Now it looked like a pile of brown crap, with none of last night's seductive mystery. I poured it down the drain and made a fresh pot of coffee.

Where does one go from here? I had such a good, detailed plan. I was supposed to be far away by now. Instead, all the aches and scars are still here, and I have to face the reality of last night's abortive event. Pretending that it didn't happen seems wrong; I'll just be at it again when I get my wits back. But sitting here doing nothing feels unbearable. I pick up the magazine again.

In the corner of my livingroom is a small bar, which I gather was the height of sophistication when this place was built in 1972. Three feet wide, with peeling woodgrain contact paper on the front, dark orange linoleum on top, there is enough space to stand behind it, preferably in an aquamarine leisure suit, and serve your guests brandy alexanders. Now, I sit on one of the stools, looking at this magazine, at the grainy picture of that kid's head, with an uncomfortable feeling in my stomach. That's terrible,

I'm thinking, this poor kid died. I wonder what happened to him. It makes me sad.

I don't remember how long I sat at the contact paper bar, staring at the photo.

■ ■ ■

The first thing I would need is this additive for the gas tank. A mechanic told me I had to use it because of some problem with the head gasket. When I asked if there was anything besides the expensive repair he wanted, he recommended this goop. I would need two cans, one to go and one to get back. I knew they sold it at the supermarket. Downstairs, I walked out through the lobby, a tall glass entryway with a decorative scene to one side, like an exhibit at the natural history museum, a big display of leaning banana palms surrounded by painted white rocks coated with decades of dust. We never knew if the plants were alive or petrified or plastic, just another relic of the era, and the inspiration, one assumes, for the building's name, *Havaii Lanai,* spelled out in white cursive letters on the front. Through the dusty glass, I saw that kid again, sitting on the cinderblock wall, squinting in the bright sun. I could tell he was going to try and catch my eye. It pisses me off that I'm a mark to these hustlers; you'd think they'd pick someone who looks like they have a little more money. I walked out quickly, turned left toward Santa Monica. At the car wash, I turned, and there he was, following me. I stopped dead and stared him down, angry as I could be. He got it, averted his gaze, and kept walking past me and down the street.

When I got home from the market, I turned on the shower and the phone rang. At first I thought it was the breather. Then, "Harris?"

"Yes? Nana?"

"Oh, good, I've caught you."

"Yeah." The water was running. "What is it?"

"I've been calling and calling and I couldn't track it down."

"Track what down?"

"What do you think? The salmon."

"Oh," I said, "right. Listen, can we talk about this another time?"

"Well, that's fifty bucks of good food, rotting away on someone's doorstep. I think that's pretty important."

"Of course. But, I'm sorry, I'll have to call you later."

"Wait a minute, what's the rush?"

"I'm taking a trip. I want to get on the road before the traffic starts."

"Oh, isn't that nice. Where to?"

A beat. "Palm Springs."

"Really? What have you got, a golf tournament or something?"

"I'll have to talk to you later." And I hung up.

■ ■ ■

As I pulled onto the 10, the word I thought of was *dissonance*. The distance between this world and the next. I'm not sure where I am along the line.

There's a certain freedom when you realize you're already dead. What you do now isn't all that important. You can let go and stop worrying. And driving out to the desert helps you do that. You really are away from all that confusion. I see why people used to come out here to do evil stuff they didn't want anyone to know about. The sky and mountains are so desolate, there's no choice but to keep your secrets. For the fun of it, I imagine a car following me on this long strip of freeway. A dark Ford sedan, maybe, several car lengths behind, its intentions murky and nefarious. The world is a dangerous place and I accept that. And a curious, comforting thought occurs to me: perhaps I don't need to worry about my pickup making it back at all. Up ahead, in a strange town I only saw in the dark, someone died a long time ago. And now a magazine has confirmed it. So perhaps there is a symmetry to this trip. Perhaps I am one leg of a triangle that needs to be completed in order for the piece to become whole.

■ ■ ■

Meanwhile, some things happened somewhere else that I'll find out about later.

My mother opened her front door to an officer from the sheriff's department. He said they received a letter about a dead body, and when they went to the address, they found nothing. Her name was provided in the letter so they had to ask what she knew. Trying to process it and not panic, she did tell them everything, which was nothing, and the officer asked her to please call if she found out anything more. Before he left, he said they can usually tell the hoaxes from the real thing but this one was concerning. Why was that, momma asked, and the officer said because it smelled suspicious. She said they must be very intuitive, but the officer said, no, he meant it literally; someone left a box of fish by the door.

She called my pager but it was off and I wouldn't have called back anyway. So then she called Eva. In the background, the sound of the television, laughter and applause. A game show, too loud, and Eva eating popcorn from the bowl she kept on the table next to the chair. "Yes, dear?"

"I need to find Harris," momma said. "He's not at his apartment and he's not at work. It's important."

Crunching and swallowing. "Mmm, why?"

"It just is," she said, her voice cracking

"I'm sure it's not that bad. I spoke with him this morning."

"You did? When? What did he say?"

"I don't know, a few hours ago. As a matter of fact, he was quite rude, if you want to know the truth. He hung up on me."

"Oh, for . . . .. *where is he?*"

Eva knew the answer, but she had to wait for it now, like a word in the little window on the eight-ball, appearing from the black water inside. But it didn't come.

"Oh, he told me, I know that," she said. "There was something going on, some noise, I could hardly hear. Like a waterfall or something."

"He was at a waterfall?"

"No, I don't think . . . oh, isn't that maddening? I know I know it."

"Mother, this is important."

"Oh," she said, "doesn't that just beat all?"

"Mother . . ."

"Thank you, dear," she said, trying to wring the word out. "Yes, thank you, I'll speak to you later," and put the phone gently down. She knew the answer. She could see where it was. Hiding behind something, like a wall of rock.

■ ■ ■

I had to pee, so I pulled off to a rest stop in the hot middle of nowhere. It's about here that the wind picks up, a constant blast going west to east. Anything not fairly heavy will blow away. After I came out of the restroom, I sat in the truck for a while, listening to the wind, listening for some idea, some direction. But there was only hot air. At the far end of the parking lot, I noticed an old, faded Datsun Honeybee. I remembered that model; it was called the B-210 but they had a two-door version with stickers of a racing stripe and a little bee along the side. They were orange, and after a while the stickers dried up and fell off. It was still a weird looking car, and I wondered who would take such a rickety old thing out here on the 10 where you can get flattened by an 18-wheeler.

I pulled back onto the freeway. In my rear view mirror, the Honeybee started up and left too, the orange dust the same color as its faded paint.

As you approach Palm Springs, the first thing you see are the wind farms. Beyond them, dry black hills, the wall that protects the town from this hot, blasting air. This stretch is majestic and dramatic. Despite the freeway and the cars and the power lines, it's so massive you feel like you're alone. Moving along the road, the mountains slide gently past, the fields of white towers slide gently past, some of the rotors turning, others stationary, some moving lazily like they're being teased by an unseen hand. You make a right off the freeway in a long, gradual curve around the mountains. With the winds buffeting your car, it feels more like flying. And you enter a kind of a dreamscape, another world unaffected by time. The ground is covered with small rocks, striped black and white, and almost antiseptic. The wind has blown them clean. I have a vague recollection of this arc I'm now driving, being a passenger and following the same route.

As the road straightens out toward the town, spots of life appear. A gas station, an old, abandoned garage. Stores and shops. I spotted a motel and it looked just cheap enough to satisfy me. Not much else around, the sign dilapidated, this place a shambles. The guy at the desk didn't seem to care how long I'd stay; he asked for one night so I gave him the $25, and he gave me a key. I walked down the hall past the lobby; many of the doors didn't have locks, some hung open. Darkness inside each one. Snoring from others, a few zombies moving from one room to another, others with people leaning against each other on the floor. Aha. I see why it's $25. I walked back out, said thank you, got into the truck again. A dark Ford sedan drove past the motel. Since I know it's not the one I imagined, since I know I lean to paranoia, I decide to follow it and indulge my worries. As it moved closer to the center of town, it stopped at a few lights, then turned into the parking lot of a 1950s motel, like a lot of them out here. The sign said *Cactus Flower.* I could tell it would be more than $25, but clearly, you get what you pay for, even where time doesn't count.

I waited at the edge of the parking lot, only half paying attention to the sedan. A tall man in a dark jacket got out the driver's side, went around to the passenger door, and a bent-over, smaller man got out. He batted the taller one away. The small man was wearing an overcoat, even though it was close to 95. From this distance it looked like one of those old tweedy kind that college kids buy at used coat stores. He was also wearing a wool beanie and a scarf. They both walked into the office, the shorter one shuffling, trying to make it without the taller one's assistance. It struck me this is the kind of place where people come to die. Perhaps that's what's going on with those two. And that was good enough for me. After waiting a few minutes for them to check in, I did the same.

This was one of those old googie motels from the 1950s. But this was 1998, and the whole hipster renovation thing was still ten years in the future. Back then, these motels were the living dead ghosts of themselves, still with their original orange and sad wood paneling, everything sagging. This manager did ask me how many nights, so I told him three; gave him my card and he handed me the diamond-shaped keytag. Out the back window, there was a pool and a few families, kids, sunning themselves, diving and splashing. The sounds of normalcy were comforting, while in the distance, those black, craggy hills rose beyond like a backdrop.

There was a restaurant off the lobby. Like many of these motels, the ceiling soars upward, connecting one section to another. It was really a coffee shop/diner, the kind of place that has everything you want, not very good but not very expensive, and they bring it quick and refill the heavy white coffee cups stained the same color as my teeth, if you habituate diners as I do. I went in for lunch, and afterward, started through the lobby to my room. The tall man I saw earlier passed me, nodded, and his companion followed, still in his dusty overcoat, scarf and hat, fumbling with his gloves. As I passed, I meant to nod a courteous hello, but of course could not, because my stomach dropped like it was cut open.

"Oh . . ." he said, he looking up from his gloves, the greasy lenses reflecting the bright afternoon. "Harris . . . I didn't expect . . ."

7

Fortunately, the toilet was Sanitized for Your Protection, because I spent the afternoon vomiting into it. Like some stomach virus, everything just poured out. When I thought my stomach was empty, I started gagging again, making these sounds so awful I was afraid it would alarm the other guests. By the end of the afternoon, I felt about twenty pounds lighter, my entire abdomen sore from heaving. I stumbled out of the bathroom and when my face hit the bed, fell dead asleep.

■ ■ ■

In the meantime …

My mother had driven over the hill and sat in Eva's kitchen, two cups of coffee between them.

"You don't have to speak to me like I'm an idiot," Eva said. "I'm not an idiot, you know. They did all the tests."

"I know that. I didn't say you were."

"And I remembered. So there you go."

Momma tapped the cup with her fingernail. "And he didn't say anything about why he was going?"

"No. I asked too. He just hung up on me. Very rude. What's it to you?"

"There's something wrong," momma said. "I don't want to go into it. A policeman came by. There's something strange going on." Eva opened her purse and took out the lighter and cigarettes. "You're not supposed to," momma said, but Eva blew her off with a yeah yeah, and lit up and took a long inhale. "Sounds like the bunch of you," she said. "Guess it was a little too quiet down there. Had to shake things up for old times' sake?"

Momma shook her head, mumbled something.

"What?" Eva said.

"I said *shut up*. It's really none of your business."

"Sweetheart, you're the one who came over here. And I'm helping you out. So I think that makes it my business. You know, the problem with you, young lady, is you're indecisive. You never know what to do in a tricky situation. When there's any pressure."

"Oh yeah? What would you do? Enlighten me on your grand strategy."

"Well, if something was wrong, I wouldn't sit around a kitchen, kibbitzing with an old lady. I'd get up and go out there and find out for myself. Isn't that obvious?"

Momma stared at her, like she did so many times. Right again.

■ ■ ■

At first I thought it was the flashing orange nipple on the phone waking me up, but it was the knocking. This soft, tentative pat pat pat, so weak and relentless. And it wouldn't stop. I dragged myself from the bed to the closed door.

"Go the fuck away."

"Harris," Ray whispered. "I must talk to you. Just for a moment. I'm .. . I'm so relieved you're alive. I mean, that it's not you. You don't know how much I was worried . . ."

I kicked the door so hard that people in other rooms jumped, some guy yelled *Hey!* Nervous shuffling outside the door and slow footsteps moving away.

After I showered, I sat on the bed again. Drapes closed, door locked. But hiding from messages and door knocking, I'll be a prisoner of this room if I don't do something. I opened the door a crack; no one was there, so I slipped out. The rooms in these motels open to the outdoor balcony. I'm on the second floor so I walked to the end, down the cement steps and out to the lot and my truck. Got in and locked the door.

You don't know what to do if you don't know what you're looking for. I pulled the torn magazine page from my pocket and looked at it again. It's a picture of me. So, who do you ask? What do you ask? I started the truck and let it take me where it thought we should go. It drove us to this short stretch of road where the bars and the clubs are located. The road cuts between the inbound and outbound lanes of the main street in the center of town. Six or seven bars sit next to each other, lining both sides of the street.

There's a fatigue to the daytime crowd. Regulars many of them, they look you up and down as you walk into their territory. I'm no tasty morsel, so the looks don't linger. All the guys at this bar were old. Sorry, older. Spiffy polo shirts, mustaches, well-groomed gray hair; but a resigned posture, arms crossed on the bar, shoulders raised as if suspending their bodies like a hammock. They get dressed up to drink and smoke. There was one young guy, cute in a dorky sort of way, with long brown hair, shorts, and a revealing tank top. He was bouncing from one guy to the next, taking the stool next to each one at the bar. Obviously they knew him. Some said hello and kept drinking, others shook their heads. He seemed unbothered, bopping from one stool to the next. One older guy listened and nodded, but didn't take his eyes from the TV. I ordered a Coke.

This was such an odd grouping, I wasn't sure how to approach them. The way they flicked this young guy away, and his persistent optimism, sort of broke my heart. The bartender caught my eye, watching this. I raised my glass, and he came over, dish towel in hand. "Kind of a strange question," I said, and pulled out the magazine clipping. "Do you have any idea who this is?"

He glanced at it. "Looks like some kid."

"This says he lived around here and he died recently." I pointed to the blurb. He shrugged. I thanked him and went back outside.

This short street was wide. In the afternoon, the front porches of the bars were mostly empty, everyone inside in the air conditioning. The air was amazingly dry, it absorbed the heat in some way that made it tolerable. It might have been close to 100 now, but I didn't mind. Standing in the middle of this wide road, the quiet and the heat and the solitariness reminded me of a scene from a western; the lone gunman in the street outside the saloon, waiting for the gang to arrive. But I didn't know which direction to go, which way the gang would be coming from.

■ ■ ■

"Are you going to light up another one?" momma asked.

"Why not? It's my car."

Eva had made sure the new Cadillac came with a cigarette lighter. I went with her. The salesman looked at me like she was crazy. "She wants what she wants," I said. "Can they add it as an option?" He said they would have to charge her for it and she complained, but she got it.

"I don't even know why you wanted to come," momma said.

"You think your old clunker would make it all the way in this heat? This way, you get to drive a new car that's not going to conk out on you by the side of the road. I think that's a good deal."

"But you didn't have to come. I could do this myself."

"Do what, dear? You didn't even know what to do. And besides, you haven't told me what's so urgent you have to do anything at all. I'm sitting here, totally in the dark, helping you out. So I wouldn't complain if I were you."

"Well, you're not me, you know."

"Don't I know it."

Maybe it was being alone together for the first time in a long time. Or being on a road trip, something they had never done. Or maybe the desert, and the way it can loosen your inhibitions, your containment. Your tongue. "Why is it you have to do that all the time?" momma asked. "Stick me? Does that give you some satisfaction? You have nothing else to do now, so you like sticking pins in people?"

Eva waved the smoke at her. "You don't know what you're talking about."

"I'm not as smart as you or as talented as you, I know that. But you don't have to be such a crab about it all the time."

"You're just hypersensitive. That was always your problem. Someone looks at you the wrong way and you go to pieces. If you had to put up with the things I did . . ."

"I've heard all that. I know that. It was hard and I don't blame you. But this constant jab jab jab just seems . . . unnecessary."

"Ahh," Eva said, and brushed her off. "I'm not going to get into anything like this with you. Just keep your eyes on the road and watch your speed. I don't want a ticket on my record."

"I know how to drive."

Eva smoked in silence and when she finished the cigarette stubbed it in the ashtray. "So, have you given any thought to what you're going to do when you get there?"

"I thought I would play it by ear."

"What do you intend to do? Stand in the middle of the town square and scream? Go to the police station and ask if they've seen your son? Who, by the way, is a grown man, despite his peccadillos. And they'll ask you why."

"I said I don't want to talk about it."

"Suit yourself. I just can't believe how much trouble you all get into, considering how little you do. One benefit of being old is that it's no concern of mine. But honestly. The holes you dig yourselves into." She waited a moment, but momma said nothing. "So this one must be a doozy."

"Just shut up for now, and let me think, would you please?"

"Rude," Eva said, exhaling. "Just plain rude."

■ ■ ■

I criss-crossed the street and hit up four other bars. Some guys turned away like I was begging for money, others just shrugged. Bartenders tended to look like they knew something but were no way talking to some stranger. An hour or so later as I walked back to the truck, the young guy with the long hair from the first bar was crossing the street. I asked if he had a moment and he smiled. I showed him the clipping.

"Yeah, of course," he said. "Old cactus dick."

"Oh my god. Should I ask?"

"Well, you know," he said, and laughed.

"How do you know this is him?"

"He showed me this picture before. From back in the day, when he did the pornos."

"Do you know his name? Do you know anything about him?"

He shrugged. "Everyone knows him, he's been around forever. I went to his place a couple of times, that weirdo trailer. What else did you ask?"

"What was his name?"

He tapped the clipping. "Kevin something. I don't remember if he said anything else."

"Well . . . what happened to him? Do you know how he died?"

This kid had a kind of permanent smile, an innocence that could not afford to be cracked. "I don't know," he said, "ask someone else"

"Who?"

As he walked away, almost skipping, he gestured to the whole street with outstretched arms. "Everyone. The bars, the Rawhide . . . everybody knows him."

■ ■ ■

When I got back to the motel, Ray was seated in the lobby. Still in the overcoat, his head drooping into his lap. I walked quietly past, but he wasn't asleep. "Harris!" he called, and lifted his head. "Wait, please, let me talk with you." I kept going but somehow he had the energy to stand up and catch me. "Wait, wait, please," and he put his hand on the door before I could open it.

"I'm gonna barf on you right this minute if you don't let go," I said.

"Well you may, and well may I deserve it, but please, just hear me out."

Being this close to him again, and the musty smell, I felt like punching him. But he was so frail. The flesh under his skin was gone, only a tissue of Ray laid over bones, like papier-mâché. Disappointed, hollow eyes, and whatever else there was, held together by the ratty coat. I held my hand on the door. "One coffee," I said, and nodded toward the shop. "And that's all."

■ ■ ■

We sat across from each other in a booth. A sickly familiar feeling. The waiter laid our coffees in front of us. A big guy with a red face; white shirt, red bow tie, collar too tight. I imagined he could strangle Ray with one hand. He laid spoons down with a clank. Funny how these old diners were built with ceilings that reached up to the sky, all that space to fly up to, sound to echo in.

"Okay," I said. "Talk."

"Well, first let me say how pleased I am to see you, Harris. And to know you're alive and well … "

I stared with silent rage.

" … and I know what you think, and that's what I wanted to tell you. Aside from anything else. I had no idea what would happen. You must believe me. I was shocked and horrified. I mean . . . I had to leave town myself. I had to disappear and leave everything. My life was ruined."

"I hope so."

"It was brutal, let me tell you. I don't know where to start. I went back that night to get you. You must know that. And they told me what had transpired. Well, enough of it. I almost died . . ."

"*You* almost . . .?"

He held up his hand. "I had to run for my life. I had to sell every-thing. And that still wasn't enough to settle what I owed, plus the legal fees. I ended up having to do some time and when I got out I had to leave town. I could never pay it all back. I had to sell the business, the whole catalogue, everything, for cents on the dollar. It was a tragedy, a terrible tragedy."

I took this all in with no reaction.

"I've been in Indianapolis the last ten years," he went on. "Had to move around a few times, but it's turned out to be a good place to settle down. I teach a course now, you know, at a community center. The history of film. Isn't that a scream? That's where I met Carl, my traveling companion. He's been invaluable to me on this trip. Just invaluable."

I stared, dead eyed. It didn't seem to deter him.

"But then, I heard this rumor and I found that . . . whatever it was, obituary or some such thing . . . in some bar rag. I was flummoxed. I didn't know what to make of it. I thought . . . well, I didn't think you were still with us."

"Thank you so much for your concern."

"And then to hear your voice. I was so relieved. I tell you, Harris, I cried. I really did. But I couldn't bring myself to speak with you."

"Of course," I said. "You shit. So you just harass people on the phone, like a creep?"

He shrugged. "What would you have me say?"

I needed the coffee, the lovely, bitter warmth. "You could start by saying I'm sorry. Or what a monster you are. I haven't thought about you in such a long time. Or any of that. I almost forgot about it. About you. What a . . . horrible thing you are."

He sat quietly, looking at his hands in their gloves. I could see it hurt. And I felt angry that I felt bad about hurting him.

"I haven't had the easiest time of it the past few years," he said. "Health problems and all."

"Good," I said, pushing the knife in. His shoulders slumped toward the table. "But I'm here," he said. "Harris, you must know that I care. That's why I came. To see you once more, and tell you how sorry I am."

I was on a dangerous precipice, about to have a feeling, but something occurred to me. "Wait a second," I said. "Wait just a second. You were the one calling and hanging up on me, right? And now you're here? So, you had to follow me. You knew where I was and you were following me?"

"Uhm . . .yes?"

"So why didn't you apologize and say whatever you had to say in LA? What's with all this cloak and dagger shit?"

"Well, I was curious. I mean, one reads in a magazine about something one created . . . something one had a hand in creating . . . and then to find out someone is using it, absconding with it . . . well, it piques one's interest, that's all."

"What do you even give a shit for? You said you sold it all. It has nothing to do with you."

"Well, I feel some ownership, I mean, of my own property . . ."

And now I did have some reaction. "Who *are* you? What are you *talking* about? You're out of this. You don't even live here. You're just some . . . ratty old man in a ratty old coat from, where did you say? Indianapolis? Where the hell is that?"

"Well, by the same token, may I ask what *you're* doing here?"

And I didn't have a ready answer. "It's different."

"Oh, I think you were curious too. You wanted to find out. Maybe you feel a little ownership in something too, could that be it? You know, Harris, I hope you don't mind my saying this, but you don't look like the happiest man to me. I'm not seeing any of that sparkle and wit that used to light up a room. Maybe you were curious about something lost . . ."

"Hey, who the fuck are you, to even think you have the right to talk to me about *anything*? If I'm not what you expected, it's because of what you did. You know, no one would blame me if I just strangled you right here. You know that, right?"

He held up his hands. "Point taken. Guilty on all counts. But that doesn't change the gist of what I'm saying." He pointed at me with his crooked finger. "You came out here because you were looking for something. Maybe you don't know what it is, but you could have sat in your decrepit little apartment and ignored the whole thing. Instead, here you are. So why?"

I sighed. "It's no business of yours."

And now all these conflicting, nauseating feelings. I really had not thought about any of this, about Ray, in such a long time. One benefit of having your brains beaten out. And suddenly, here he is, or the ghost of him anyway. And I was disturbed by the fact that he mattered. If I could have disregarded this shriveled old man like a stranger, that would be nice. But he was something to me, and I didn't know what to make of that.

8

After they filled up the tank, momma and Eva drove into the town and up to the Hyatt, this hulking brick building that dominates the downtown. In those days, during the summer, Palm Springs was nearly deserted. Most stores shut down for the hot season, restaurants closed, wealthy people moved to their cooler homes, and only the ones who had no choice stayed for the hundred-and-fifteen-degree afternoons. The Hyatt was a good bet for a nice room if you had no reservations; unfortunately, an electronics convention got there first.

"I'm so sorry," the front desk attendant said, with a smarmy smile. "But there should be some very nice motels still open on Palm Canyon. Just drive up and down. I'm sure you'll find one."

Eva stared him back. *"I'm sure,"* she said, matching his tone. To momma, "Wise bastard."

"Mother," momma shushed.

They got back in the Cadillac and started driving. "You know," momma said with a laugh, "it really is so empty here, it's not so crazy to stand on a streetcorner and yell."

Eva watched out the window at the closed stores, the empty dirt lots in between low-slung one-story buildings. "Never liked it here," she said. "Too big. Too spooky. Nothing good happens."

Momma was preoccupied scanning for motels and caught a flashing Vacancy on the back side of a sign as they passed one. "Oh look!" she said, and jammed on the brakes. Then the violent eruption as they were thrown

back and then forth. The sound of plastic and glass shattering and dropping onto the pavement behind them.

"Oh Jesus!" Eva shouted. "Carolyn, my god, what is wrong with you?"

"Oh god," momma said. "Are you alright?"

"I think so." She looked around. "My nerves are jangled but no harm
done."

The car was stopped, the car behind them stopped. Momma got out,
already apologetic. She walked back to look at the damage. The other car
had hit the Cadillac square in the trunk; bumper pushed in, trunk lid
dented, rear light lenses smashed and glass on the road. The other car's
bumper was smashed too, hanging loose, the grill shattered, one headlight
awry like a cartoon character.

"I am so sorry," momma said to the driver. He sat totally still, hands
gripping the wheel. "Are you alright?" she asked. He seemed in shock. A
kid, just old enough to drive. "Son? Are you alright?"

"Yes," he said. "I'm sorry." He looked like he was about to cry.

"Don't be sorry, that was my fault completely. I stopped short in the
middle of the road."

"I don't," he said, and looked up at her. He looked so scared. "I don't
know what to do."

She put her hand on his shoulder through the open window. "Don't
worry, we'll take care of it. We should get out of the street though. Can you
start your car?" He tried and it turned over. "Then let's pull over there and
figure this out, ok?" He nodded, his face flush. "What an interesting little
car," she said, looking it over. "What is that on the side, a bee?"

■ ■ ■

Ray said he was exhausted and had to lie down; talking to me took too
much out of him.

After he left, I stopped at the front desk and asked the guy if he knew
what the Rawhide was. He said it was a steakhouse, just out of town toward Cathedral City, and gave me the address. When I got there, it was
one of these theme restaurants, this one a log cabin with a neon sign of a

horse and rider, the lasso flashing. Inside, wagonwheel chandeliers were suspended over a large room with round tables surrounded by heavy wood captains' chairs. A bar at the far end, and a thick, muscular bartender drying glasses. More mid-afternoon loungers at this bar, slightly less showy than the others. These looked like more affluent retirees, guys who had followed Frank Sinatra to the desert and played golf in the sun too much. I pulled the clipping out again and asked the bartender; he said nothing but thought the owner might know and went back to call him.

As I waited at one of the empty tables, I looked around this room, the muzak humming away – raindrops falling on my head – and all these people eating their late afternoon lunch, their early bird specials, drinking the afternoon away. People who came from somewhere east in the early days and made their mark, achieved their fame in the 1950s and 60s, then retired, or withdrew, into this strange, suspended desert mausoleum. Maybe they thought the dry heat and alcohol would preserve them forever. Only problem being you can never leave.

A man came over and stood next to the table. Pleasant looking, a pastel green polo shirt, his body firmly worked out for fifty or how ever many years he was. The kind of affable, affluent businessman who thrived in these parts. "How can I help you?" he asked. I showed the clipping and told him. He pulled out the chair next to me and sat. "May I ask why you're inquiring?" A controlled, blank expression.

"No reason. I was curious, that's all."

"Are you a reporter?" I shook my head. "Are you related? A debt collector or something?" Again, no. "A fan, then?"

I shrugged. "I guess so."

"I see," he said, and clasped his hands courteously. "Well. I'm sorry, I wish I could tell you something, but honestly, I don't know very much. This was just a sad character with a sad life." And this guy a brick wall, albeit pleasant. "Is there anything else I can do for you?"

"Did know him?"

"I'd rather not say any more," he said, and stood.

"Look, I'm sorry to press, but I really am curious. I came out from LA and . . . it's kind of important."

His eyes scanned me up and down, heat seeking and surveying. "There was a lot of trouble around this fellow. I don't know who you are, but I really don't want any more. If you wouldn't mind leaving me out of it, I would appreciate it. Nice to meet you." He held out his hand for me to shake, which I did, then he walked quickly back behind the bar.

■ ■ ■

After they had exchanged information, the boy looked so shaken, momma asked if she could buy him lunch. They found a restaurant not too far from the accident and sat there now, cooling off after standing in the sun too long. Momma ordered a salad, Eva had a steak, and the kid didn't want anything, so momma ordered him a hamburger.

"Do you understand how that works?" momma said. "You give your insurance company my information and they'll contact my insurance company and we'll pay for the damage. It was my fault so you aren't to blame. If it's my fault, I don't think they put any points on your record. Mother, do you know if that's how it works?"

"Don't ask me, I never caused a collision."

"Well, I think that's how it works," she said. She watched the kid. His serious, considered expression, staring at the hamburger. "How is that? You haven't taken a bite."

"We're vegetarians," he said. "I don't remember the last time I had a hamburger."

"Oh Jesus," Eva said. "Just try it. Trust me, you'll never go back."

He considered a moment, put it down, started eating his french fries.

"Where did you say you were from?" momma asked.

"Agua Dulce. It's north of LA. We have a ranch. My mom breeds horses."

"Oh, that sounds very nice. What are you here in Palm Springs for? Do you have friends here?"

"No," he said, quietly. "I was looking for someone."

"Ah," momma said. She felt concerned; it seemed he was scared more than just because he'd been in his first accident. "Is it some special friend you're coming to meet?"

"I don't know yet."

"Well, be careful out here," Eva said. "There's a lot of creeps and weirdos in this town, come looking for a kid like you. Watch it. I'm not kidding."

Momma gave her a look. "Where are you staying?" she asked.

"I don't know. I haven't thought of that yet."

"Hey, we should go in on a timeshare," Eva said.

"Do your parents know where you are?" momma asked. He shook his head. "Do you think they're worried about you?"

"Probably. But things are kind of strange at home right now. My mother . . . she died in January . . . and everything is messed up."

"Oh, I'm so sorry," momma said. She put her hand on his.

"Wait, didn't you say your mother breeds horses?" Eva asked.

He nodded. "That's mom. My other mother, my biological one . . . she died. And mom is very upset."

"I can understand that," momma said. He seemed not to want to say any more so she didn't push.

"Try the hamburger," Eva said. "We won't tell the vegetable police."

He looked at it and picked it up again. Took a bite.

"I'm sorry, I forgot," momma said, "what is your name again?"

"Gordon," he said, through the mouthful.

■ ■ ■

I had fallen asleep when the phone rang. Those orange message lights flash even when the phone rings and it's jarring beyond belief. Without thinking, I came awake and picked it up.

"I have some news for you," Ray said.

"Oh god."

"I did some sleuthing. Carl and I drove over to the police station. Would you like to know what I found out?"

"No. I don't want to know anything about you."

"Don't be a sourpuss, Harris. I asked about this individual and the officer I spoke to was very forthcoming. At least at the outset. He got a file and he told me it was an overdose. That was the cause of death. I asked a few more questions but he got suspicious and he called another officer. He asked me who I was and what my interest was. I said I used to know this individual and I'd like to pay a visit to anyone still living to give my condolences. But they weren't buying it."

"So what?"

"So they have an unsolved case on their hands. I couldn't get a name or an identity, but it seems to be an active investigation." I didn't feel any need to say anything so I let him hang. "Well, Harris, perhaps you and I . . ." and that was all I heard before I hung up and went back to sleep.

9

Now, here's an interesting story.

In 1930, Ezra Goldberg bought a new Chrysler Imperial. It seemed an odd choice for the owner of a chain of well-known drugstores in Chicago. The salesman suggested he look at a coupe or a smaller car, something that would be easier to park in the city. But Ezra wanted the touring car because, by that time, you could drive all the way across the country, from Chicago to California, on new roads and eat at new restaurants and stay in new motels, all along the way.

He brought the car home and showed it to his wife and eight-year-old daughter, Esther. She thought it was the most beautiful thing she ever saw. He told them that Chicago was too dangerous and dirty, and California was the place to be. Like many others, he saw the movies, with the beautiful streets and palm trees of Los Angeles, and he wanted to enjoy the good life in that magical paradise. The other surprise was that he wanted his wife, who both Ezra and Esther called Mother, to learn to drive the car. Mother thought this was unnecessary, because she was not mechanically inclined. What she was was beautiful. Graceful, tall and radiant, she was a type then known as a Gibson girl: a feminine ideal with alabaster skin, soft hair piled high, flowing white dresses of silk, cotton and lace, and in all ways, not the kind of person who drives a car but who is driven in one. But Ezra was insistent. Day after day, he took her out and practiced until she had it mastered. "All very silly," Mother said, since Ezra would do all the driving himself. But she indulged him.

To an eight-year-old girl, the whole thing seemed like a great adventure. You could get into a big, beautiful automobile of your own, and let it carry you across the entire country. It seemed to her a dream come true, and promised a future she could hardly conceive of.

10

They stepped into the late afternoon as the sun began to set, the air just beginning to cool. Momma said, "You know, Gordon, I'm concerned about you having no place to stay. Are you going to a hotel?"

"I don't know. I might sleep in my car."

"Where?"

He shrugged. "I'll find some parking space. Or camp out in the desert."

"I don't like that at all. I would feel better if you were inside, at least for tonight. You're staying with us." He pulled back a little. "In your own room," she went on, with a chuckle. "I'll pay for it." Eva rummaged in her purse for cigarettes, lit one up. "Sounds fine to me," she said, "but don't you have some business of your own you're supposed to be taking care of?"

"We're just putting him up, mother. He can go looking for his friends anytime he wants."

She brushed her off with the cigarette hand.

"Follow us," momma said.

They got into their cars and drove back to the motel where she had seen the vacancy sign, only to find it was filled. The desk attendant was familiar with the city and suggested they drive a little further from the center. They did that, moving slowly down the Palm Canyon road, back toward the desert, until momma spotted another vacancy sign on the left. She pointed to it through her open window and Gordon followed into the parking lot.

"Looks like a dump," Eva said.

"Well, it's not the Hyatt but I guess we'll have to make do."

They all walked in, momma registered for them, one room for her and Eva, another for Gordon. For one night, she said, to start, and she asked the man to put Gordon several rooms away from them so he wouldn't feel uncomfortable. The man at the counter directed them out the door at the end of the lobby, up the staircase to the second floor. Eva asked if they had an elevator. "I'm not lugging this bag up a set of stairs." He pointed to the door at the opposite end. As they approached, a man stepped in front of them and pressed the button first. Eva, momma and Gordon stood behind him while the very slow, old elevator sank to the first floor; the door slowly opened and they waited as the small man in a winter coat shuffled in. Once packed in, the door groaned shut and they waited for the motor to engage, momma and Eva pressed against the back wall, Gordon in front next to the man. It took a while for the elevator to start upward, and as it did, the man glanced to the side, saw Gordon, and seemed to emerge from his shell enough to stare at him intently, up and down. A lot of motor wheezing, groaning, pulling of cables and other sounds until the elevator stopped on the second floor and they waited for the door to open. Another uncomfortable moment while the man licked his lips, taking Gordon in. Momma stepped between them, smiling tightly at the man, her hand on Gordon, gently turning him away. He seemed oblivious. When the door finally opened, the man shuffled away along the balcony, and momma, Gordon and Eva stepped out.

"I told you," Eva said. "Creeps all over this place."

■ ■ ■

I woke up in the dark. A strange room, a strange place. Those moments of confusion until you remember where you are. When I did, I saw it was nearly midnight. I sat up on the bed in the dark. Wind blowing against the window, the sound of an occasional car streaking by this motel. Other than that, just being a part of this silence, the miles of silence between you and anyone else. Even in a motel, even in a town, you can feel the distance, the living emptiness that makes up that space.

There would be no chance of falling asleep again, so I went out to the truck and started driving. Passed the street with the bars, lit up and active, but that was the last place I wanted to be. Kept driving, past the center, then further, the darkness out here something palpable, pressing down on you. Everything was closed at this hour, only a few ragged men walking the streets. This was the era when the occasional, destitute man with torn clothes and no shoes was called a bum, and only the slimmest of margins separated me from them at this moment: this beat-up truck, the dollars in my wallet, a nearly empty bank account. Still driving, past the grand sweep of mountains on the right, a few twinkling lights way up, the breathtaking hillside estates of the rich and infamous.

On the left up ahead, the Rawhide again. I expected it to be shut, but a few cars were still in the lot, the front door lit up. As long as they were offering, I'd just tie up my horse and belly up to the bar. Once inside, it seemed they really were closed and these were friends who couldn't bear going home. All the chairs in the dining room were flipped on the tables, one guy vacuuming; four guys sitting close together at the bar, talking quietly, the TV on with the sound down. I shut the door and walked toward them, cleared my throat. Several turned to me. Behind the bar, mixing a drink, the owner, the man I spoke to this afternoon. He caught sight of me still halfway in the dark. "Sorry, we're closed," he said. I moved closer. "I know, I'm sorry to disturb you," I said. The men looked me over, examining. Not good, not bad. Just looking.

"You again," the owner said, trying not to sound hostile. "We're closing up, and I said everything I wanted to say."

"What is it, Benny, you got the collection agency on you?" one guy said, and laughed.

"It's something else," he said, giving me the eye to go away.

"I apologize for being a pain." I pulled the clipping out, now with more witnesses. "But maybe since it's not so busy, you might have another moment to take a look?"

"Uh oh, missing persons?" another guy said. "You got him tied up in the basement? They're onto you, Benny boy." More laughter.

I stepped closer, into the light, and held out the clipping so they could all see. "I'm sorry I didn't say more this afternoon. The truth is, I knew this guy a long time ago. At least I think I did. It's pretty strange he would have been living out here and died and we didn't know about it. I'm just trying to figure out if this is the same person I used to know."

One of the men took the clipping, looked at it, passed it to another. They gave each other looks as they passed it around. Ben stared at me, irritated. The last man on the end stood up and handed it back. For a moment it felt like a jury, this group, looking at each other, discussing something without saying it. Another strained moment and Ben let out a sigh, said, "Alright, fine," and nodded to a table away from the bar. One of the guys lifted his glass to him.

He came around and took two chairs down, indicated the one for me. "Can I get you anything?" he asked. I said no. He had his own drink, a gin and tonic, and set it on the table. Judging by the redness around his eyes I guessed this was not the first of the night. He looked at the clipping again. "Crazy how old I am," he said. "He was just a kid in this." He shook his head. "Now, start again. What's the story? You knew him?"

"Yes. In LA. A long time ago. I knew him pretty well. At least I thought I did."

"And what was your name again?"

I told him.

"Ben," he said, and shook my hand. "And what is it you want to know?"

"Well, I guess, what happened to him. We didn't . . . we weren't in touch and I didn't know where he was. I saw this notice and I came to find out."

"I see." He took a long swig. "Well. A sad fellow who had a hard time. I suppose he came to the end of his rope. I honestly hadn't seen him in a while so I can't tell you anything about the circumstances surrounding his death." He said this very deliberately, and took another sip. "He was just another one of the folks who came out for a visit and decided to stay. Nothing more to say than that." And he stared at me with a firmly closed mouth.

I realized I wasn't going any further asking stupid questions like a TV detective. It was so quiet in this place, with us basically alone, the guys at the bar speaking in low voices to themselves. Strangely, I felt my dick come to life. At moments like this, every once in a while, I get this sense of intimacy with another person. It can be someone I know, someone I'm talking to, or it can be someone I don't know, sitting nearby, who I've seen and some kind of unspoken attachment is made. It feels like something opens up in me that picks up a frequency, or sends a signal, and connects to another person. Ben's face reddened. Perhaps he felt it. He looked at me carefully and took another sip. "Maybe I'm too far into my cups to know what I'm doing," he said, "but first, if you don't mind my asking . . . what have *you* been up to? You look like you've seen a few things."

I smiled. He was kind enough not to say banged up. "That is true," I said. "I knew, uhm, Kevin, back in the day. We had some adventures together."

"When he was doing the movies?"

"Oh, yes. It was a pretty crazy time."

"So you know about his past?"

"I do."

He seemed to relax, let down his shields. "OK. So what do you want to know?"

"What was he like?"

"What do you mean? When I met him or more recently? When he first got here, he was a pretty sweet guy. Probably '89 or '90. I, uhm . . ." and he finished the drink. "Excuse me," he said. He got up, went to the bar and chatted with the guys while he mixed himself another, then returned, smiling to himself, settled down next to me. "'89, '90, right?" he said. "Well, I'll have to tell you a little about myself, if you don't mind."

"Of course."

"I'm from Minnesota originally, outside of Rochester. And what I'll tell you about *that* is that it was awful. Growing up gay back then ... people just hated you. Kids beat you up, adults called you names, people threw things out of cars. It was a shitty life. I got a job in accounting so I could hide in a room and not have to deal with anyone. And I thought that would be my life, just this shitty, lonely existence. I figured at some point, I'd probably kill myself, jump out a window or something." He took a sip of his new drink. "Back then, back there, if you wanted to see anything about life outside, you had to look at a magazine or a porno flick. And where I lived, you couldn't have magazines sent to your house. The mailman and everyone would know, and you'd be dead. You had to drive into the city and go to a seedy bookstore and buy a movie and bring it home and watch it, all alone, with the shades pulled down. So that's what I did. And there were a couple of videos, they came from Southern California, LA or someplace, and they had these guys in them that looked like normal guys. Not musclemen or models or anything, just good-looking guys like you'd see around the neighborhood. And you have to remember, back then, everyone told us we were sick and dirty and all kinds of stuff. So to see these guys outdoors in the sunshine, all healthy and tan, was kind of a shock. And there was one particular guy ... he wasn't all that good looking, but there was something about him that got me off every time. He looked so real, like he was having a great time doing what he was doing, without any shame at all. It kind of jumped out at you. I know it sounds strange, but it seemed really truthful. I looked for more videos with him, but there weren't any. They only gave them first names anyway and I couldn't tell which one was which." Another sip. "So, some time after that, I decided to quit my lonely life and get the hell out of there. Didn't think about it, just went straight to Southern California. No plan, no ideas, that was all I knew. And when I got here, you know what? I got friends and I got a job and I got sex and I fell in love, and nobody hated me anymore. All of a sudden, *I* was normal. And happy."

He chuckled a little, wiped the corner of his eye. "So . . . fast forward however many years. I'm tending bar over at Ripples, and this guy comes in, kind of quiet, starts hanging around. He's working, I can tell, and he's pleasant enough. They used to show movies there, and one night they were showing a porno up on the wall, and this guy is sitting next to me at the bar, and he says, that's me, and I look up, and it was one of those movies. I said, *What?* and he points and he says that's me. And I tell you, you could have knocked me over with a feather. He didn't look the same, he'd aged a lot, but hell, there he was. So I started talking to him and I got to know him and he was really sweet. Very simple, kind of lost. I helped him out, loaned him money, invited him to hang out with my friends. And one time I came clean and told him how I'd seen him in the movies and what he'd . . . what it meant to me."

"Meant to you?" I said, kind of unsettled. "What did he say?"

"Oh, I don't remember. I don't know if it even registered with him. Probably everyone says that, you know, you're in porn, everyone comes up to you. But in a way, something about him saved my life. So, I thought I owed him."

"So, you were friends?"

"As much as you could be with someone like him. The poor guy, he was all messed up, he couldn't hold a job. But we all helped him, all the bar owners."

"I see," I said. Watching Ben now, his face flushed, recalling something. The act of recalling it bringing him happiness or pleasure. I watched it with this detachment, like a scientist observing some chemical reaction. It made me uncomfortable and I wanted to move the story along. "And you said he was different later on?"

He nodded. Another sip.

"He lived in a trailer camp outside of town. He had one of those silver ones that looks like a spaceship. He thought it was so cool. Even when he couldn't pay the community fee, he wanted to keep it. So me and a bunch of friends towed it out, way out to some unincorporated land, and we got someone to tap off the electric line so he could run his air conditioner and appliances. He still drove in to get his water and dump the toilet, but once he was on his own with no one to keep an eye on him, he got into trouble." He lowered his voice. "Dealing, selling. I tried to get him into a program. Everyone tried to help him, but it was no use. He was a recreational user as long as we knew him, but once he got into business, it was a disaster. You have to be on the ball to do that kind of thing, and he really wasn't. His behavior got so bad we had to band together, the bars and restaurants, and ban him. We told him, too. We said, look, we're your friends, we'll help you get clean, but if you keeping acting like this, you're not welcome. So he dropped out of sight, and no one saw him, and then one day we find out he's at the hospital and he's dead. The police went out to his trailer, a lot of hush hush, then they came around here, asking a lot of questions."

"And what happened?"

His face flushed again but it wasn't embarrassment. "This is a small town," he said quietly. "Everyone knows everyone and everyone knows who not to mess around with." He took a long breath and a pause. "Look at the time, will you? I think I better wrap this up before I say something I'll really regret."

"Of course," I said, and stood up. "Thank you."

I reached out my hand and he stood and took it, held it; looked at me carefully, considering.

"You know, talking with you reminded me of something," he said. "If you don't mind my sharing one more thing. It's weird, I know."

"Please."

"Well, it was in one of those movies. There was this one scene where he was fucking this guy, and they were going at it, bang-bang-bang, and in the middle of the scene, he reached up and he put his hand on the other guy's cheek, like he really cared about him. It was so tender, that one gesture. You never saw anything like that . . . at least I never did."

I wasn't breathing, holding still to let him speak.

"I tell you what," he said, and pulled out a pen. "There's someone else you might talk to." He wrote on a cocktail napkin. "See what she says," and handed it to me. "No guarantees."

11

In the dark momma thought it was a dream and didn't pay much attention. Only after a moment did she realize she was awake and there was some kind of flowing movement in the room. She sat up with a start. The door opened, and the light from the outside walkway lit up Eva in her dark robe as she walked out.

Momma watched this, saying nothing. Maybe she was going for a smoke. Maybe she wanted ice from the machine. She sat a while longer and when Eva didn't return, she got up, pulled on pants and shirt and went out. No one on the balcony. No one at the machine. The sound of scuffing on the dry sand parking lot below and the dark robe moving away, toward the back of the lot. She rushed down the steps, trying not to draw attention, whispering, *Mother . . . Mother!* Behind this hotel, half a mile of empty scrub, sand and rocks before a settlement of houses in the distance, and Eva moving into that darkness. Momma walked, then ran toward her and took her by the arm when she arrived. *"Mother!"*

Eva stopped and turned. "Dear, what? What is it?"

"Where are you going?"

"What do you mean? Where am . . ." and she looked around. "Oh, my goodness. Where am I?"

"You're in the middle of a parking lot. It's the middle of the night."

"Oh, my goodness, I was just . . . I was dreaming just a moment ago . . ."

Momma tried to see her clearly in the dark. "Are you alright?"

"Yes. I'm fine. But . . . oh, my goodness, isn't that the funniest . . . I was sleepwalking. Oh my goodness!" and she burst out laughing. Momma couldn't help it, she laughed too. "What was I thinking?" Eva said. "My god, you're dealing with an absolute crazy woman."

"Well, you're awake now. Let's get you back."

Eva patted her sides, feeling for cigarettes in pockets, but no such luck. As they turned, Eva took momma's arm and looked upward.

"Oh my god! Carolyn!" she shouted.

"What? What?"

"Look at the sky! Look at all those stars! Have you ever seen such a sky?"

She did look, and it really was astonishing. Inside LA we live under a dome of smog; you can see it from a distance, a purple blanket over the basin with a layer of cloudy sheets underneath. But in the desert, there is no dome. "I just can't believe it," Eva said. "Look at it all." And they stayed a while, looking. A ceiling of lights and colors, sparkling, patterns that appear and rearrange and disappear as you concentrate or lose focus. No barrier between ground and sky.

After a few minutes, momma said, "Mother, seriously, are you alright? Can you walk back?"

"Oh, yes, yes. I feel fine." And they started, Eva holding momma's arm.

"Were you dreaming?" momma asked.

"I thought I was. It seemed like a normal dream to me. You know, the kind you know when you're asleep so all the foolishness doesn't bother you."

"What was it about?"

"Well, hardly anything at all. I was just sitting at home, in one of the rooms upstairs."

"Yes?"

"And I had the feeling that I lost . . . misplaced? . . . no, something was gone, and I had to go downstairs . . . to get it."

"What was it?"

As they navigated the rocks and sand, she thought about it. "It's the silliest thing. I had a box of Cracker Jacks in the kitchen cabinet. I wanted those Cracker Jacks so much, and I went downstairs to get them. But when I opened the cabinet, they were gone." She stopped, the hotel sign illuminating her face a wary tone of green and orange. "And I was so sad. I wanted those Cracker Jacks so much and they disappeared. Someone took them away. I couldn't understand how it could happen."

"Is that what you came outside looking for?"

"I don't know," she said. "I just felt so . . . I can't even explain it." Her face was so sad; in the strange light of the sign, momma didn't recognize it.

"Well, don't worry," she said, "we'll buy you ten boxes tomorrow."

"Yes, of course," Eva said, and smiled. "What a crazy old broad. Good lord. Never have I done anything like that before."

"Maybe it's the vitamin B," momma said.

"Aha, there you go. That must be it."

And they got to the staircase and climbed back to the room.

■ ■ ■

The next morning, I checked my pager. I had the cheap one, the little box that fits in your pocket, with a screen for one line of text. I usually kept it off. When I turned it on, many messages from my mother: *call me urgent.* I called back and the machine answered. I wanted to leave a message but it hung up on me, presumably, because the tape was full or the machine was broken. I'd have to try again later.

I looked at Ben's cocktail napkin. A phone number and a name: Marcy Marcy. When I called, just a beep, no outgoing message at all. This was the time everyone had cutesy messages with music or their kids or their dog howling, so a lone beep meant either a broken machine or something suspicious. I went to hang up, but thought, wait: if I was someone who didn't want to be bothered, that's what I would do. So I left a short message, I said who gave me her name and what it was about, and then I hung up and thought about breakfast. I opened the door and saw the housekeeper had left the big rolling cart blocking the walkway so I couldn't get to the stairs. I went the other way and took the elevator.

Downstairs, Ray had plunked himself in the coffee shop in a booth facing the glass door, to be sure and catch me coming in or crossing the lobby. About the same time, on the other side of the housekeeping cart, momma and Eva opened their door and walked down the stairs to the coffee shop. "Oh god, it's that dirty man," Eva said, when they walked in. "Let's sit on the other side so we don't have to look at him." They took a seat in the area behind him. Still earlier that morning, Gordon had awakened, in the room next to mine, got dressed and grabbed his backpack to leave. During the night, new guests arrived at the motel and others left, and one of those that left took their big camper out of the parking lot, leaving an empty space and revealing the dirt red pickup truck parked behind it. Gordon saw this and promptly sat down on the bench outside the lobby to wait.

Inside, the elevator opened, and as I went toward the coffee shop, my pager went off. Marcy's number. I turned away from the coffee shop and over to the payphone on the far wall to call her back.

"Hello?" I said, after the beep. "Pick up? This is Harris, the guy who called before?" And she did. She spoke slowly, it sounded like marbles in the mouth. Not stupid but something else. She spoke so quietly I had to turn my back to the lobby, hunch close to the phone to hear her and reply just as softly. She said if Ben gave me her number, she would talk to me, and she gave me the address of a restaurant on the other side of the city center.

Sitting outside for so long, Gordon had to go to the bathroom. He walked into the lobby quickly, asked the front desk where it was and disappeared in there. Ray was deciding between eggs benedict and a western omelet when his friend Carl came down to join him, blocking his view of the glass door for a moment as I crossed the lobby and went out to my truck; which was then, when Gordon returned to the bench a few minutes later, gone.

■ ■ ■

The address Marcy gave me was another one of these theme restaurants. This one, for some reason, was supposed to look like a ski lodge. In the middle of the desert. Plastic snow draped off the roof and sides, glowing eerily with dirty fluorescent bulbs. I went in and ordered breakfast, and once the crowd began to thin, I asked for her. A man with a ponytail tilted his head toward the back. As I approached, I heard pots clanking, water running, and one person in the corner, working behind high shelves hidden from the rest of the room. It was a woman, small, wearing a white kitchen apron, a pink shirt and pink stretch pants. She had thick black shoes, the sole of one thicker than the other, and moved with a slight limp, lifting huge pots from the sink onto shelves taller than she was.

"Hello?" I said. She turned, regarded me a moment, then nodded toward a black screen door to the rear parking lot where the employees parked. Outside, there was a picnic table. I waited until she came out and sat down, then I sat opposite her. She took cigarettes from a pocket, offered me one, lit up.

"So," she said, "you're asking about Kevvie." She spoke softly; something in her mouth, maybe misaligned teeth, made her slightly hard to understand.

"Yes. I knew him a long time ago. I was curious to know what happened."

"Huh," she said, and took a long, leisurely puff. "Well, that's a lie." And she let it hang, like the smoke. What was I supposed to do, lie some more? Dig in deeper? "So, who are you?" she asked.

Looking at her, I realized she was a person most people would ignore. Short, heavy, one leg shorter than the other, what they called wall-eyed, one eye looking in a different direction than the other. I didn't know which eye looked at me, whether one was a decoy to watch carefully without your being aware of it. I pulled the clipping, now smudged and starting to rip, out of my pocket and placed it on the table.

"I'm really trying to figure out who this is," I said. She took such long draws off her cigarette, really enjoying it. She sat back and stared at me, the crown of smoke giving her this aura of power and mystique. "Go on," she said.

"This picture," I said. "This little head here. This is not a picture of your friend."

"He gave me that picture. I gave it to the newspaper."

"I'm sorry. I know who this is, and this is not the person you knew."

She considered this a moment. "Well, I wouldn't put it past him. He was a born liar. But why are you interested? Ben said you were from LA. What do you care?"

And asked like that, it was a fair question. In the warm sun of the morning, with the familiar smell of cigarette smoke, this woman watching and not watching, it felt okay to think about it now. She squinted at me like she could tell I was struggling. Her eyes traced my face and I recognized the familiar pattern of movement from the misalignment of my own eyes, down some scars on my cheeks, to the off-kilter jaw. Someone put back together without the original map. And without touching me or saying anything, she had introduced herself, she knew I watched her trace the lines, and something unspoken and unneeded to talk about passed between us.

"Because this is a picture of me," I said. It felt strange to say it out loud. Embarrassing somehow. She nodded and took another puff. "This story said this guy died here recently. And I knew that couldn't be right, because . . . well, this isn't him." She kept looking, the wall eye or the other one. I couldn't look at it, I had to look down into my hands in my lap. And as I spoke, I started to cry. "And this may sound stupid . . . but I tried to kill myself a couple of days ago . . . and I didn't do it . . . and then I saw this ... and I got confused, and I didn't know what was happening. And I didn't know what else to do. I came here and I don't know why I came here. I honestly don't know." And then I cried for how long I don't know. Maybe a minute, maybe five minutes. She smoked her cigarette while I did, took her time to let me finish and waited until I could look up at her again. Then she dropped it, tamped it out with her shoe.

"So, what do you want from me?"

"I don't know."

She smiled. It seemed like the only thing to do. And I relaxed. I felt like a person, for the first time in a long time.

"I don't know," I said again, and laughed, through the last of the tears.

She gave me a moment to collect myself. "Well, I can tell you about my friend. How's that?"

I nodded.

"Well," she said, "to start with, he was pretty clueless, that's for sure. I mean, I had to do everything for him. Fill out his forms, pay his bills ... totally incompetent. But that's why I loved him. We laughed about it all the time. He wasn't mean or clever at all. Not cunning enough to survive in the world. Most people are looking out for themselves, angling for something, but he didn't have the first clue how to do that. So I trusted him."

"Did he tell you where he was before he came here?"

"One time he said he was from Vegas, and LA before that."

"What was his name? Or, the name he used?"

"Kovaleski," she said. I said it quietly to myself. "Doesn't make sense," she said. "Too many K's. I didn't believe him. And I saw some papers with other names too, so I figured he made it up. He was such a bad liar. Just not clever enough to get away with it." She waited then, watching me carefully. "You know, a lot of people come here to escape. They have this idea of what they want to be, and anyplace else, people would pick it apart. Pick *you* apart. But here, no one'll call you on it. Kevvie had his story and I didn't mind." She looked at the clipping again. "I figured something would happen but he didn't deserve that."

"What?"

"I was the one who found him. I called the police. I went out to the trailer 'cause I hadn't heard from him in a couple of days, and there he was. Needle in the arm, he'd been dead a while. It was ugly. The police asked me everything and I told them what I knew. It didn't surprise anyone, but still. That didn't have to happen."

"So, it was an overdose? The police don't seem sure."

She shrugged. "Is it important? He's gone and he's not coming back."

"I guess not," I said. She reached into her pocket, and pulled out a big keyring like building supers carry; rolled to one key and pulled it off. "Maybe you can find something," she said, and gave it to me. "Maybe no one knew what to look for." She told me the address and I thanked her. We both stood and I knew not to try and hug her, though I wanted to. She started moving back to the door.

"But be careful," she said. "When I found him, the needle was in his left arm." I must have looked confused. "Kevvie was a lefty."

12

They left Chicago in the Chrysler in the early spring. Father drove eight hours a day, stopping in roadside motels each night. It was still relatively quiet then. The stock market crashed the previous October, but the fallout hadn't spread too far yet. The dustbowl that would push farmers out of the Midwest and onto the roads to California had not happened yet; 1930 was only the first of five dry years. That spring, the world was still simple and bright.

As they drove west, Esther watched the world change. Cities got smaller and disappeared, replaced by miles of wheat and corn and grass. The sky seemed to go on forever. She lay in the back seat staring up at it. Father and Mother spoke occasionally, clasped each other's hand as he guided them across this wonderful, strange land. After the great plains, the desert began: the endless rows of crops disappeared, replaced by sand and cactus and plants that looked like they came from a cartoon. Esther knew it from the bible. A barren, treacherous landscape you have to cross to get to the promised land. However, Father said, since they were crossing in an Imperial, nothing bad could happen to them.

They kept the top up most of the way and bought cloth bags to fill with water when the radiator got too hot. Esther saw real Indians as they moved further west, kids with big dark eyes sitting quietly in carts pulled by horses. A world completely different from the cold wind off the lakes and screaming steel wheels of the elevated outside the apartment window; a new world of warmth and sun and imagination and possibility.

After a few days, Father announced they had arrived at the last stop before they got to Los Angeles. To get there, they would have to climb one last incline, and the car would need a rest after it pulled them up from the desert floor. So they drove it slowly, up to a town perched on the eastern edge of a slope. From there, they could look back across hundreds of miles and see where they had come from. They could see the clouds hanging over the desert, and bolts of lightning sizzling in the distance, stabbing the ground where they found minerals. Esther couldn't believe she could be so high and see so far. Even the name sounded magical: Barstow.

Father had made reservations at a hotel called the Warrener. This was very grand, like a mansion in Chicago, but with fans on the ceiling and windows open to let the dry air blow through. Rocking chairs on the veranda and old people fanning themselves, rocking slowly. The hotel rumbled as the train pulled into the station next door, and people moving excitedly in and out. It was so curious: this much activity, this many people moving so quickly in such a dire, empty place. The bellman showed them to their rooms – one for Mother and Father, an adjoining one for Esther by herself. She was almost too excited to fall asleep, but she did.

13

The conversation with Marcy Marcy unsettled me. I don't like crying for no reason, or for reasons that aren't clear to me. Honestly, I don't like crying at all. It felt like pieces coming apart. Plus, there really was something dangerous surrounding this guy and his mysterious death, and I was tiptoeing into it, alone. As I drove back to the motel, I had the gruesome thought of Ray, and sharing what I knew with him. And the idea of asking him for help – the idea of him at all – and whatever lid I was prying off, felt suddenly overwhelming. I decided to let the truck do the driving again, and it drove us past the motel and back out toward the 10; like a Ouija board on bald tires, it knew what it was doing, and what it was doing was taking me home. So I let it.

Back at the motel, now passing noontime, momma and Eva returned from having driven aimlessly around town, showing a picture of someone and asking if anyone had seen him. An older guy sitting at a bar got irritated. "What the hell is this, milk carton week?" Momma didn't understand. "This guy bugged me the other day just like you're bugging me now. So bug off all of you." That was as much as they could find, and with no further direction, had gone back to eat lunch. Gordon, also tired of waiting and not knowing what he was doing, went to drop his key at the desk, where he ran into momma and Eva, who invited him to lunch in the coffee shop before he drove home. Ray, not having moved from the seat he positioned himself in, ordered a fifth cup of coffee and a banana split, and waited, with beady-eyed determination, for his prey.

By now I was out of Palm Springs and moving along the wide, gradual curve toward the freeway. Nothing left but miles of black and white rocks, the endless sky, the windmills in the distance. As I approached, I was transfixed by how beautiful they were. I had to pull over and simply stare. Majestic and magnificent, as far as the eye could see. Rows of soaring white pedestals arranged perfectly on both flat sides of the freeway, climbing gentle rises to the north and west. And not just the number, but the precision, how they're laid out in such perfect lines. Thirty stories high, as tall as tall buildings, each with its own set of two, three or four white blades. A whole valley that's intensely crowded and entirely empty.

We did a unit on alternative energy in school. I remember, I did a book report on the windmills. Standing here, in the hot wind, I remembered how carefully I typed that report, the words I found in encyclopedias to explain them. Technically, it said, these are not windmills, but turbines. The turbines are located here to generate power. They do this by capturing wind that is made by the land and the air. This valley is a narrow passageway between the hot air of the desert and the cool air of the coast. When those two climates meet, and the differences in air pressure and temperature force their way through the passage, powerful winds are created and they never stop. The turbines catch that wind and turn it into electricity that gets stepped up in voltage through transformers and then stored or sent over transmission lines to cities and towns throughout the valley and the state. This is the blowing heart of California, the source of all that power.

Standing here, outside the truck, feeling more naked than I had in a while, in this hot, blasting wind that most people hide inside and away from, I remembered that power. That I once had. And lost. And forgot.

And I looked back at the truck. We had to go back. If we went home now, we would have nothing.

I got in and turned around and prepared for whatever was coming next.

■ ■ ■

Which was:

In the lobby of the Cactus Flower Motel.

They had all converged, unaware of each other, uncomfortable with each other, as I pulled into the parking lot. I got out, my stomach aching, head spinning. I pushed through the glass double doors with their 1950s lettering and stencil of, what else, a cactus and a flower, and just beyond, coming toward me, the Offensive Line.

Momma, Eva, and Ray.

I froze. A moment of silence. We all recognized each other, and suddenly, shouting on top of shouting, and the man at the counter jumped, the other guests in the lobby jumped, and finger pointing and demanding and how could yous and who do you think you ares and we were so worrieds and they are all looking at each other and then me, a cacophony of shouting and everyone aware instantly that they don't know what they're doing or who they're with or why they're here. And then one more round of yelling and pointing, and in the middle of this assault, I see behind them the boy who was sitting outside my apartment, and he is such a beautiful kid and he's standing there all alone with an expression I don't understand, and for the second time in one day, I started to cry.

"Now stop!" momma shouted, "stop, everyone, look what you're making him do!" And they did. Stop.

"What is going on here?" the man at the desk yelled at us. "Whatever this is, take it outside, if you please!"

Momma waved him off. "Oh Harris," she said, and walked up to me. "Oh, Harris," she said, and put her arms around me.

■ ■ ■

After the meltdown, I convinced Ray to peel himself away from the party and wait somewhere else. Eva and momma were dismayed, to say the least, that he was part of our entourage and connected to me in any way. "I'll explain later," I said, at least several times, as we all stood in the middle of the lobby. Ray finally, unwillingly, shuffled his way back to the elevator and left us. But still leaving us, leaving me, with the present company.

"I can't," I said, standing in the middle of them, "I can't listen to you all at once. Please."

But by then, my mother had come back to life. "What is *wrong* with you?" she said, and out of nowhere, slapped me across the face.

"That's it," the front desk man yelled. "Outside. All of you!"

"Ow!" I yelled. The pain really hit. "Owww!"

"Now!" he shouted.

Eva leaned in and said quietly, "What do you say we stop making a spectacle of ourselves?" and tilted her head toward the coffee shop. I was shocked into silence and momma too, so we followed her – me, momma, and the kid, past the front desk, mumbling apologies, me holding my cheek – into the restaurant and into a booth, momma and Eva across, the kid next to me.

"That really fucking hurt," I said.

"Well, I'm sorry," momma said.

The waitress, who had been watching all this through the glass doors, dropped our menus and smiled, eager to eat up whatever drama we had to serve.

"Coffee, please," Eva said. "Young man, what'll you have?"

"Water," he said, and Eva nodded, but the girl waited. Eva had to say, *"That's all,"* before she would go.

"Well, I'm sorry," momma went on, "but do you know what I've been through? I've been so sick with worry . . . what kind of a sick practical joke is that, sending a letter to the police about . . ." and she stopped, presumably because of Eva and the kid sitting next to her. ". . . a suspicious letter so they have to come to my front door and tell me something awful? What kind of a thing is that to do?"

In truth, the suspension had wiped my mind clean and I forgot all about it.

"Oh," I said. "Oh wow. Yes. I am sorry. I tried calling you back. Your machine is full."

She stared at me with a red face. Eva lit a cigarette, said to the kid, "We're being left out of this, but I bet it's a pip."

"I was scared to death," momma said, then she started to cry, a little. "I didn't know what to think."

I didn't know either. Both of them were staring at me like high beams, and I was caught in a mess of my own making. All I could think to say was I was sorry, and said it many more times. "I'll explain it all later. When I know what's going on. But you . . . how did you know to come here?"

"Where?" momma said. "This motel? It was the only one open except the Hyatt, and that was full."

"No, I mean Palm Springs."

"You told Eva," momma said. Cigarette bobbing between her lips, Eva said, "I remembered at least one thing that day." The waitress dropped the coffees and the water, stood, waiting for the order. "Give us a minute, dear," Eva said. The waitress sighed and walked back behind the counter where the others were staring and talking about us as well. "Well, look," Eva said, "at this point, does everybody know where everybody is? Have we solved whatever problem it is that no one is talking about? Because I am very confused."

I was trying to knit this all together, too. "So," I said to momma, "you got a call from the police . . ."

"The *sheriff* . . . no, they came to my *house*."

". . . the sheriff . . . and Eva told you I had come out here, and when I didn't return your pages, you decided to drive here and look for me?" She nodded. "What were you going to do, stand on a street corner and yell?" Momma and Eva both shrugged. I laughed. I mean, I had to. "I'm sorry," I said again. "So that explains you two." Then I turned to the kid. "But now . . ."

"Oh yes," momma said. "In all this confusion, I forgot entirely. We ran into this poor young man yesterday. I mean, literally. Well, he ran into us. I was so stupid, I stopped short in the middle of the road and he rear-ended us."

"You did?" I said. He was not looking at me, or any of us. He seemed to be staring at a point somewhere just above the middle of the table.

"Yes," momma said. "He came out here looking for some friends and we pretty much hijacked him. He was going to sleep in his car and I didn't feel comfortable about that at all." To him, "I am sorry," she said, "Gordon."

And, you know, the daytime sky can be full of stars too. I can't tell if they're real or because I have no oxygen.

"What is it?" Eva said

My hand on my face holding the broken pieces together.

"What is it?" I heard again.

Sometimes we wish we could change, and quickly, but we can't. We have to do it gradually. Then there's shock, when something happens too fast and you can't process it all. You remember bits and pieces, but you have to put the pieces together later to make sense of it. Some people never do. We're only soft flesh. Between change and shock, though, is fast change. You're on a toboggan in the winter Olympics and you don't know how you got there, but you're schussing down the narrowest, steepest trench of glassy ice and you can't believe this metal half tube you're strapped into can move this fast. You have no control other than to try and stay upright as this vehicle takes you at speeds beyond comprehension from one place to another. And you don't know what will happen when you arrive at the end.

"Are you alright?" Eva said, and she actually snapped her fingers in my face. That really does work like in the movies.

"Yes," I said. "Sorry. I was just remembering something."

I turned and looked at Gordon. His shoulders held high, like he was expecting a blow, looking down at his hands. I put my hand on his shoulder. What else can you do? "Well, that's very nice," I said. "Maybe I can help him find who he's looking for."

"Good luck to you," Eva said. "This desert heat is making all of us looney tunes. You know, I sleepwalked out of the room last night . . . in my *pajamas* . . . all the way out to the parking lot! Can you believe that?"

"I cannot believe that," I said. Momma nodded, sipping her coffee. "True," she said.

I picked up the sugar container. One of those wonderful round glass bullet shaped things, filled to the top, with the little metal door in the lid that flips open and closed, always working, whenever you want sugar. So reliable. All you have to do is fill it up. I hold its comfortable weight in my hand.

"I have a few things to sort out here," I said. "And if Gordon wants any help, I'll be glad to watch out for him." My mother smiled at that. "So there's no reason you need to stick around. I'm sorry I made you worry."

"Well, it all worked out," momma said. "But you better get in touch with the sheriff's office. They were serious. You might be in some trouble."

"I will do it."

"Now, who the hell is that creepy man?" Eva nearly shouted. All the waitresses at the counter turned their attention back to us. "That is about the most disreputable character I have ever laid eyes on. What kind of people are you consorting with?"

"Oh," I said. "Yes. That is . . . someone I knew a long time ago. He's helping me look for someone. And he *is* a disreputable character, Nana, you're absolutely right." She pointed at momma in triumph. "Don't, uh, have anything to do with him," I said. "I'll make sure he doesn't bother you." Momma and Eva both shifted their glance to Gordon, telling me something. "And especially you," I said to him. "Don't go near that man. That's not a joke."

He nodded.

"So, mystery solved," I said. "You can head home and all's well that ends well."

"Well, Jesus," Eva said, "don't be trying to pawn us off just yet. What if we'd like to enjoy a little desert air?"

"You just said it was making you crazy."

"Yes, but now it sounds like you're trying to get rid of us," momma said.

"I *am* trying to get rid of you."

"Well, it's too late to drive back now," she said. "I don't want to sit in rush hour traffic. We'll go tomorrow. Maybe we can have breakfast with you. That is, if you're not too busy with your *manhunt*."

I smiled at them. Not quite sure on the emphasis. But I had no more interest or ability to deal this afternoon. Momma tilted her head at Gordon again. "You need a place to stay," I said, not quite a question.

"I can sleep . . ."

"No," momma said. "You'll have your room again tonight. I'll talk to the front desk. Oh, damn, we have to talk to them right now, I just remembered. We only had one night for all of us." She got up, kissed me, Eva followed, and they both hustled off to the lobby.

With them gone, I shifted slightly in the booth. Turned to see a bit better.

"Gordon," I said. And he did look at me now.

I held out my hand and he took it.

14

That night, with everyone tucked safely in their beds, I thought I had done such a great job, but no. Ray wouldn't give it a break. And in only a few minutes he had me crazy enough to be imitating him again, while he sat like a moron at the desk in my room.

"Harris I simply must talk to you . . . Harris I simply must talk to you . . ."

"I do not speak like that," he said.

"Oh yes you do. *Harris, I simply must talk to you.*"

"You know, instead of insulting me, it might be wiser to share with me what it is you found out."

I sat on the bed. He was right. Besides, I had already opened the door and let him in.

I held up the now very wrinkled clipping. "This guy told everyone in town this was him," I said. "I don't know why. And he made a good living off it for a long time. And you're right, he died of an overdose and no one is sure how it happened. He lived in a trailer someplace outside of town, and I know where it is. And I have the key." I showed him that too.

"Well, you've been a busy beaver. How did you come upon all of that?"

"Charm."

"And what do you propose?"

"I thought about going out there tomorrow."

"Uh huh," he said. And waited.

"Yes," I said.

"And?"

"And what?"

"Are you telling me this for a reason, or just to show off your investigative prowess? Which, may I say, is impressive. Some of that old fire back in the belly?"

"I thought you'd like to know," I said.

"Well, that's very courteous."

"So?"

He raised his eyebrows.

"Are you interested?"

He pulled his overcoat tighter around his neck. "Are you telling me everything? Because it sounds like there's an *and* here."

"This is what I have," I said. "You want to go or not?"

"Alright. But after breakfast, please. I need my rest these days."

"Let's do it after lunch. I have something to do in the morning."

His eyes lit up behind the old greasy lenses. "Would it have anything to do with that intriguing young man? Do tell. I've been tingling with anticipation."

And then I'm not sure what happened. I did stand up from the bed, and I did walk over to him. And what I remember, though maybe I dreamed it that night, was that I stood over him, and despite his musty smell, despite my wish never to be near him again, I put both hands around his neck, which was so frail it fit easily between them, and I leaned down, almost touching his face and I gritted my teeth so hard I felt them crack. And I said, "Do you think there is anyone on earth who will care if you disappear? Do you know how easy it is to dispose of a body in the desert? Because I do." And I felt the soft, crepey skin of his neck as I tightened my hands until the amusement drained out of his eyes. Then I let go, stepped back and smiled. Just a joke. Or probably I imagined the whole thing.

Whatever it was, he dropped the subject and we agreed to meet after lunch the next day.

■ ■ ■

Coffee shops and their soaring ceilings. Don't know why I am most comfortable here.

Yesterday, after momma and Eva left us, I asked Gordon if he could meet for breakfast. I was, I realized, too wrung out to have any kind of intelligent conversation, and he seemed to understand. And now he was here, sitting opposite me.

"So, Gordon?" I said.

He nodded. I noticed he had a big adam's apple. Or rather, a slender neck. Long and graceful, and narrow shoulders. Taller than he seemed at first. Big almond-shaped dark eyes, a seriousness more than a kid his age should have.

"You were hanging around my apartment in LA."

He nodded again.

"How come?"

He shrugged, looked at his hands in his lap. "My mother died."

"I am sorry."

He nodded, head down.

"Your mother . . .?"

"Amanda."

Now my turn to nod.

"Mom didn't want me to meet you. I mean, Zoe. But Mama . . . Amanda . . . gave me your name and address, and said to, someday."

"When did this happen . . . I mean, when did she pass away?"

"About six months ago. Mom got very sad. She's been really sad. I don't know why I thought of it. I found the paper with your name and I had my learners permit so I thought I would drive to LA. I waited outside your apartment and I figured out who you were."

"How did you know?"

He pulled some papers from his pocket. One of them, a photo, he showed me. Amanda and me at the beach. Her white robe, my skin a faded red, bent forward. "It looked like you were planning to leave," he said. "You were buying stuff and I thought you were going on a trip. I followed you to the restaurant you work at and the supermarket."

"That's not creepy," I said, and he smiled, finally.

"I just wanted to meet you before you left." I took this in. He ate his breakfast, small bits anyway. I drank my coffee. Folded my hands on the table. Looked out the window at the field of scrub brush behind this place. So desolate.

"Gordon," I said. "I don't have anything. I don't have anything to give you. I'm sorry. I'm not very much."

He seemed offended, his emotions transparent on his cheeks. "I'm not . . . I didn't ask . . ."

"I know, I know. I just want to be honest. I'm a person without much to give. I don't want you to have some expectation. There just isn't much here."

He took his time, thinking about it. What he wanted to reveal maybe. "Mama said you were a good person. She liked you a lot. She said you got mixed up with bad people and bad things happened. She didn't think you would want to be reminded of it so that's why she never called you. But she said I should make my own decisions and that's why she told me who you were. She thought I should know you because she said you were okay."

So, what am I going to do, argue with some kid who just lost his mother? I didn't want to consider any of this. "Well, that's neither here nor there. Does your . . . mom . . . know where you are?"

"Yes, I called her."

"You should probably get home. I bet she's worried sick." He nodded and looked down at his hands; or rather, at another of the papers he'd pulled from his pocket.

"Mama told me something. If I ever met you," he said, not looking up from the paper. I could see enough of it, worn and ragged, as though it had been opened and refolded many times. He took a breath, careful to read exactly what was on it. "She said . . . she did some bad things when you were friends, and she knew it. But she hoped that if I found you, and told you, that you might forgive her."

He folded it again, and put it back. Looked at me.

No idea how to answer a question like that.

"I have to think about it."

He nodded.

"Look," I said, irritated, "I don't know what I can give you. I mean, I have nothing. I'm sorry you had to make your way through of all this. I'll give you some money to get home. My mother told you about the insurance, so they'll pay for all that . . . but I don't have . . . anything for you. Gordon. I'm sorry."

"Ok," he said. That expression on his face I didn't understand. "Can I stay one more day?"

"Of course. But I have to do something this afternoon. I'll come find you tonight."

■ ■ ■

When I came back down to the lobby in the afternoon, Ray was already positioned there, overcoat and scarf in place.

"Are you honestly this cold?" I said. "It's a hundred and five degrees outside."

"You don't want to know my problems."

I looked at the address Marcy gave me and asked at the front desk if the man knew where it was. He didn't but he gave me a tourist map and I found it there. Back then, no navigation system, no Google maps. Just you and the Thomas Guide and the grid number. On the map, this road was a single straight line then a dotted line then nothing. Into the desert it seemed to fade out, like they didn't know what happened to the pavement. I started out toward my truck but Ray said to wait, Carl was in the rented Ford with the air conditioner running, and he would drive us. He must have figured out my air conditioner only blew hot.

Ray sat in back while I studied the map and told Carl where to turn. Driving out toward Twentynine Palms was hot, bright and silent, like everything here. As we headed north, the wind started kicking up. To get to this spot, you had to leave Palm Springs, cross the 10, go north and then east. When we arrived, the map was right, the road seemed to fade out. I thought we'd gone too far until I saw a metallic reflection in the distance, like a UFO crash landed. Nothing else around.

We pulled up in front, just off the road. The trailer sat in a dirt yard. Behind it, an old green Pinto wagon, the back window smashed out. A piece of yellow police tape on the ground, under a rock, flapping in the wind. In this eerie brightness an Airstream looks like it's bending light, the sand and sky a curved reflection in the bullet-shaped body. This one was dilapidated, dirty and loose at the seams; a sad TV aerial snapped over on top, the spliced power line drooping from the electric wire on a tilted pole.

"Could this be any more pathetic?" I said.

Ray stood behind me. "Never mind. Open up. Let's find out who our mystery man is."

I pulled out Marcy's key and put it in the lock.

"Hey, do we have the right to do this?" I asked.

"What?"

"This is someone's home. Someone's whole life is in here, all his stuff. Should we be doing this?"

"Harris, please, the man is dead. We're a thousand miles from the nearest toilet. No one gives a shit about this individual. Open the door, I'm choking from the dust." But I felt guilty. Like a violation. Here I was, years later, with Ray, doing something that felt familiar and unsettling. "Give it here if you don't want to," he said, and practically pulled the key out of my hand.

"*I'll* do it," I snapped, and he stepped back. "Jesus." I turned it one way and nothing; the other way and nothing. Ray looked like his glasses were steamed, but really just the same film as always. Through them he was staring intently at the lock. "Oh, for god's sake," he said, and turned the knob. The door opened. "So much for keys."

Inside was a stinking tunnel. Weeks since fresh air got in. The police had torn it apart, papers and books everywhere. Or vandals, or anyone coming through and ransacking what they wanted. It was a single room with a kitchen at one end, a hanging printed cloth at the other, and a bed, a cot really, behind that. The floor inches thick with junk: old magazines, water stained and wrinkled, newspapers, checkbook registers, all kinds of paper. Under the table, a cardboard box stuffed with more. I pulled one from the bottom. An electric bill from 1993. "A giant wastepaper basket," Ray said.

A table sat across from the cot with empty square shapes in the dust, probably where a TV and VCR were taken away. Anything of value had been stripped. A small air conditioner in the back of the trailer, over the bed. Ray reached up, had to stand on his toes to get to it. I said, "You don't think that really . . ." and it groaned into life with a sickening metallic scrape. It didn't do much cooling, but at least the air moved around and made it tolerable to stand inside.

Neither of us spoke as we walked through the sea of paper. It seemed to be stuff most people throw away. Yellowed receipts from ten years ago, stacks of junk mail. Near the sink I found a pile of pictures that looked like they had been dumped out of a box. I sat on a stool and looked through them. As invasive and intrusive as anything one could do. As I looked at these pictures of someone else's life, it hit me how little I felt. This was Marcy's friend's home. She probably spent a lot of time here with him. She loved him and he was gone, and here we were, sifting through the remains.

"Aha," Ray said, and pulled something from under the cot. "The stash." A pile of magazines, mostly old. He scanned through them, tossed each one aside, until he got to one he wanted. "Aha," he said again, and held it up. "Smile pretty now." I went over and he handed it to me.

An eerie, disorienting feeling. Pictures of someone doing things. Mostly grainy black-and white, a few color shots. I felt no connection to this person at all. Just sad and heartbroken. He was just a kid. I looked at Ray as he pored over the other magazines. He was the photographer, he knew what he was doing. A professional, he told me. I was impressed. Here's the evidence. Such a mix of emotions. I thought of something that made me laugh.

"What?" he asked.

"He's not as ugly as I was."

Ray shook his head, kept waffling through magazines. "What have you got there?" I showed him the stack of pictures. "Let me see," and he snatched them. He peered at each one then tossed it away, rifling through the pile at lightning speed. I forgot his nervous energy when he was focused. In a moment, he held one up and said, "This must be him. He's in most of these. Look . . . the hair gets thinner, but the face is the same." Ghostly and gaunt, as though he was somehow outside of each scene: if everyone looked tanned and in focus, he was pale and blurry. Ray took off his glasses and sniffled. "Anyone you know?"

I shook my head. He was silent, looking them over again, inspecting with watery eyes. He sniffled hard then, and broke into a coughing jag that wouldn't stop. I waited for him to calm down, but it got louder and phlegmier. Then I got worried and patted him on the back, but he waved me off, coughing harder. His eyes watered, and he couldn't get a breath; the sallow skin turned blue and I decided to get him out. I took him under the arms to the door, slung his arm around my shoulder and stepped down. He felt no more than ninety pounds. Carl saw us and helped me set him in the back seat of the Ford. In a few moments, in the better air, he got control of himself, breathed, took a revolting gray handkerchief from his pocket and coughed about a pound of mucus.

"Mmmm, goodness," he said when he got his breath back. "Terrible air."

"You gonna make it?" I asked. He waved, shook his head yes. "But let's go back. There's some medication I take when this happens."

I went back to the trailer and shut off the air conditioner, looked around for anything we might have left, and closed the door.

15

Back in their room, Eva was patting her neck with a moist towel, Momma sitting on the bed, thinking. "Gordon," she said.

"That kid? What about him?"

"Any thoughts who he might be?"

"He's someone you let smash into the back of my car, that's who. And I am not happy about that. I hope you told them you were driving because I am not having my insurance rates go up on account of you."

She closed her eyes. "I did, mother. I'll tell them again. I'll pay for everything. I'm sorry."

"I hope so. Never have I caused a collision. Never."

Momma lay back and stared at the ceiling.

"Gordon," she said again. "You didn't notice any . . ."

"What?"

"I don't know. Familiarity?"

"What's that supposed to mean? He's some weird kid driving around in a jalopy that now we have to pay to fix up. If anything, he's a lucky kid because he happened to be driving behind *you*."

Momma sat up. "Why do you have to tear everyone down? What does it get you?"

Eva looked like she'd spat in her face. "What are you talking about? It's just a comment."

"It's strange," momma said, almost to herself, considering. "As though there's only room for one of us. If you're here, I can't be. If I'm here, you make me smaller. If I don't get small, you crush me."

"Oh please, don't start caterwauling about this." She went for a cigarette, lit it.

"This is a nonsmoking room," momma said.

"I'm the one smoking, not the room." She pointed the lit cigarette at her. "You were always responsible for you own behavior. I never made you do anything. If you screwed up, you have no one to blame but yourself."

"Maybe so," momma said, and lay back on the bed. "But there was no room for mistakes or experiments. If it wasn't perfect, it was no good?"

"You have to have standards, sweetie, I'm sorry. I couldn't go in and say I didn't feel good today or screw up my lines and say, oops, mistakey-poo. They'd fire me and I'd be scrubbing floors. Then where would you be? Would you have a house and food and everything you need?"

"I know. But let me understand. Because life was tough for you, it has to be tough for everyone else? There's no room for flexibility?"

She blew smoke with a laugh. "Oh, yeah, *flexibility*. I tried flexibility, look where it got me. Your father and his merry band of pranksters."

Momma sat up. "He regretted hurting you. He said it over and over. He hoped you would have forgiven him."

"Eccch. Some things are unforgivable."

"Like what? He told Harris about you two when you were first married. He said you sounded like a real fun broad . . ."

"Oh, what a wise mouth on that kid! There's another one. *Your* son. All the crap he put us through. Put *me* through. That's some nerve to say a wise-ass thing like that."

"Really? It sounded very nice to me. What's wrong with being a real fun broad?"

"This is an idiotic conversation and I am not continuing it with you," she said. "I came out here to help you with whatever it was you were so worried about. And here we are, in a crap motel, my car smashed in, all kind of accusations and grievances from decades ago being hurled at me, and still I'm here. All told, I would say I've been a pretty good mother. If I vent an opinion now and then, that's my own business. The world is a tough place and you never seemed to understand that."

"The world is different now."

"Not that much," Eva said, firm.

"Well, anyway," momma said, lying down again, changing direction, "about that kid. I'm sort of curious . . ."

"Hey, you know what? I don't want to talk about this anymore. Get over it. Move on." Pressed into a corner, she seemed like a lion licking a wound, holding a cigarette with its other hand.

"I'm sorry," momma said, surprised by the sudden touchiness. "I won't bring it up again."

■ ■ ■

Marcy Marcy took a break for me. We sat at the picnic bench again.

"Yeah, this is Kev," she said. I had taken one of the pictures from the stack in the trailer. "Here I am." She pointed to her smiling face next to him, her head resting on his shoulder. I took the clipping from my pocket, now almost rubbed clean and laid it on the table next to the picture.

"And everyone thought this person," I said, pointing to the clipping, "and this person," the photo, "were the same person?"

She shrugged. "Why not? Guys get old, they don't look like when they were young. He said it was true so it was true."

I understood. And told her I didn't know anything more. I also gave her the key back and told her the lock had been broken sometime before.

"I figured. Weird shit happens out there."

I drove back to the motel and checked on Ray. He was lying down in his room, the TV on.

"I'm much better," he said. "It's dust and sand that gets me. And heat. The desert is the last place I should be. So you see, Harris, the sacrifices I make for you."

"Oh please."

"But there are still some pieces floating around here I'm not tracking. Tell me again about this girl with the key?" And I did, what details I could recall. "And, again, how did you find this girl?" And I told him again about Ben from the Rawhide, and what he told me. "I see," Ray said. Then he closed his eyes and I thought he was thinking, but he started to snore. I turned off the TV and tiptoed out of the room.

■ ■ ■

I had arranged with momma and Eva to meet for dinner downstairs at seven, so I knocked on Gordon's door before and asked if he'd like to join me first. When he opened the door, the room was spotless, as though no one had been there. His backpack sat on the floor next to the bed but otherwise it looked unoccupied. It seemed like he had been sitting in there, not touching anything, waiting for me.

In the coffee shop, I asked if he knew who he was named after. "Her friend, the actor," he said. "She was his assistant once. She said he was a nice man."

"He was a very nice man. I miss him a lot."

"Mama told me I met him when I was little but I don't remember. It's funny to see him on TV but not know him."

"That must be strange," I said. "But he was the same on TV as he was in real life. A really good guy, through and through. That's probably why she gave you his name." A few things I never asked to recall came back to me. "He gave me a car once."

"Oh wow. So you knew him very well?"

"No. I don't think you could know him very well. He kept himself pretty guarded from people."

"Why?"

"He was famous. Everybody liked him. And a lot of people wouldn't have liked him if they knew things about him."

"Bad things?"

"No, not at all. But, you know. Personal things." I didn't know how much Amanda had told him.

"You mean that he liked men?"

Ok, well, never mind.

"Yes. And when he was famous that was a big no-no. He didn't have a choice, he had to be discreet about it. All the famous gay people had to back then."

"Is that how you met him? Did you sleep together?"

"Wow, no secrets in your household, are there?"

He shrugged as if it was nothing. And he was right, it was nothing.

"Uh yes," I said. "Just once and it didn't mean anything. We were friends mostly. He was very kind to me when kind people were hard to find. So was your mother."

When he looked at you, his eyes were so penetrating. He might be shy about certain things, but when not, he had a real presence. I was happy to see that, because it must have come from Zoe and Amanda. If I had been around, he'd be a mess.

"Who is that man you're with?" he asked, just as directly.

"Oh, Ray. We worked together a long time ago. He's helping me look for something that had to do with our business."

"When you did the porn?"

I looked into my coffee mug and wondered if it was bottomless.

"Yes," I said. "Your mom. Something else."

He smiled, and sort of blushed. Because I was blushing. "What's wrong?" he said. "Is there something wrong with that?"

"No, I guess not. I just . . ."

"Were you good at it?"

"I have no idea."

"Did you like doing it?"

It hadn't been asked that way in a long time and I thought about it with a clear mind. "I suppose I did. But I don't think this is a discussion I should be having with . . ."

"You're so red in the face," he said. "I mean, if you were good at it and you liked it, then what's wrong with it?"

"It was another lifetime ago. Another person. And things ended badly. It's not something I want to talk about."

He shrugged. "If I was famous and people liked me, I would he happy."

I closed my mouth more often nowadays because I heard Eva's voice coming out of it. Had I not closed it, I would have said, "Well, you're not me," but I didn't. "Anyway," I said, "Ray is here because there was this guy living here, and he died, and from the obituary it looks like he was telling everyone he was me . . . which is weird in a whole other way . . . so we're trying to find out who it was . . ."

"You know, he likes you very much."

A coffee spit-take occurred here. I had to wipe my chin. "Beg your pardon?"

"That old guy. I can see the way he looks at you. Did you sleep with him, too?"

"You know, you have an interesting way of saying whatever comes into your head. But you're a kid and I don't think you know everything you're talking about."

He brushed it off. "So, he's helping you find this person?"

"Yes."

"That's very sad."

"What is?"

"This guy you're looking for. That he was pretending to be someone else. He wasn't very happy being himself."

"No, he wasn't."

Gordon looked at me a long moment, considering. It didn't last, though, because momma and Eva joined us at the table. We slid over to let them in.

"This looks very cozy," momma said. "What are you boys talking about?"

"Fan belts," I said, flat.

"Gordon, I take it you're staying one more day?" she asked, looking into her menu.

"I don't know. I should probably get home."

"Your mother must be worried," she said.

At the same time, he and I said he called her already.

"Ah," momma said. "Great minds. Mother, what would you like?"

"Salad," Eva said. "I have no appetite."

"That's sounds good. What about you two? Tonight's on me."

We ordered and momma asked Gordon lots of things about his school and his home life. He told us how he was having to work more on their ranch with Amanda gone, and the depression Zoe fell into. Eva grew irritated with the direction of the conversation and seemed fixated on the accident.

"You know, cars today are all made of plastic," she said. "If you get hit, it's bent out of shape. They can never put it back together again. You have to buy a new car."

"I don't think that's true, mother," momma said. "If a reputable body shop does the repair, they have to do it to standards." To Gordon, she said, "I used to do books for a body shop. They do good work if you pick a decent one."

"Well, you better pick a decent one," Eva said. "In fact, I want to pick it. The insurance company will try to cheap us down, and you make *lousy* decisions."

"It will be fine, mother, I promise."

"I still can't believe you did that," Eva said. "In my car. After I was generous enough to lend it to you and let you drive it, you go and do a dumb thing and now I'm the one who's sorrier for it. Dumb, dumb, dumb."

Silence at the table, until Gordon spoke. "That's not a nice thing to say."

Eva's water glass stopped halfway to her mouth. "Beg your pardon?"

"It was just an accident," he said. "I'm not mad and it was my car. You're saying very mean things to her."

Eva's jaw dropped. "Who is this kid? What a fresh mouth. How dare you say that to me? How dare you?"

"I'm only saying what's true. You shouldn't talk to your daughter like that."

Eva looked like what she used to call *cross*. Sharper than angry, more like outrage. "I *never* . . . Harris, who is this person?"

Momma and I concealed our smiles by staring at our laps. I couldn't figure an exit from this, but I didn't need to, because a large presence approached the table. A man's voice behind my head said, "Excuse me, don't I know you?" Fear gripped my stomach, but when I turned, he was looking at Eva.

"Probably," she said, snapping into recognition mode. "What's left of her."

"Well, what a treat this is indeed," he said. It was a man, sixty maybe, over six feet, wearing a double-breasted blazer. Stylish for fifteen years ago, but still immaculate; gray dress pants, soft, shiny loafers. Thick black hair, slicked back. "It's an honor," he said, and he literally took her hand and kissed it.

"Oh my, how ga-*lant!* Where were you fifty years ago?"

"What a privilege to meet you in person," he said, stationing himself at the end of the table. "Tell me, dear, are you staying in town?"

"We have been, yes. This is my daughter, Carolyn, and my grandson, Harris."

The man looked at me. "Oh, really? Harris what?"

"Goldberg," Eva said, too loud.

"A pleasure to meet you," he said, his hand a slab.

"And this kid," she indicated Gordon, "I don't know who he is, but he has a smart mouth." It didn't faze him at all. "And you?" Eva said to him.

"Oh, just a fan. Tell me, dear, are you staying here?"

One of the waitresses appeared, smiling at him, her eyes darting from him to us. "Can I get you something?" she asked.

"No, I'm fine," he said. I opened my mouth to ask for more coffee but she skittered away. "I've enjoyed all your pictures," he said. "Tell me dear, are you in town for long?"

"You know, that's a good question. We came out on the spur of the moment. For sunshine and relaxation."

"Well, we have more of that than you could ever need," and he laughed and she laughed with him. She was just smitten with this guy. "There are some lovely shops, even in the off-season. I'm sure the front desk would have a guide if you ask."

"I certainly will," Eva said. "If the heat doesn't kill me first!" They both laughed again. Momma met my eyes.

"Are you much of a golfer?" He had this unplaceable mid Atlantic accent that people used to cultivate in order to mask whatever accent they came with. He pronounced it *golfah.*

"Oh, I adore it! Years since I played, though. Years!"

"Well, our courses are the best in the world. You owe it to yourself to play a few rounds before you leave. You'll be coming back again and again. Now tell me, is this a family vacation?"

Eva said, "Well, I'm here, and these two are here, so I guess, yes, it seems to have turned into a family vacation."

"Any other plans while you're in town?"

"Dear me, no," she said. "Just sun and relaxation."

"Well, you look wonderful, dear," he said. "Absolutely wonderful." He scanned all of our faces, still smiling. "I won't impose on you any further." The bow again. His manners were so precise. "It was such an honor to meet you. I hope you enjoy your stay. All of you."

"The same to you," Eva said. "Mister . . . ?"

And then, nimble in his loafers, gone as quickly as he appeared.

"What a charming man," Eva said, taking a sip of coffee.

Momma shook her head. "I don't know what to make of you."

"What? I can't be courteous to a fan?"

"You," she said. "The most suspicious person in the world. You just let him pump you for every piece of information he wanted. That man knows everything about you now. Who you are, who I am, where you're staying. And you don't know a thing about him. He wouldn't even tell you his name."

"Oh, poo," she said, her cheeks still pink from the hand kissing. I looked at momma, who was looking at me.

16

Desert winds blow at night. They power the turbines, working in darkness and silence. They blow across the desert floor, across states. They blow away the sense of time.

At the Warrener Hotel in Barstow, strong winds blew against the outside walls, but only a gentle breath inside the rooms, which were shielded. Esther could feel everything drying out. Moisture in cotton clothing, the skin on her hands. The desert air removed it, silently, and you could sense things that held together in other places would come apart here, come unglued.

She sat up in bed, seduced by the warmth and softness. Like a wave flowing over her, it changed everything as it passed.

At the Cactus Flower Motel, wind blew from the northeast; the glass in the windows shuddered. Only for a moment, because the gusts don't last. But the shaking was enough to wake Eva up. She got up and dressed in the dark room, careful not wake momma. Then she went outside, down to the Cadillac, and drove away.

■ ■ ■

What woke me up was the phone ringing, and that annoying nipple flashing when it rang. "My god, what is it?" I grumbled into the phone; looked across at the clock radio. 6:30am.

"That fellow you spoke to," Ray said, "at the Naugahyde."

"The Rawhide."

"*Rawhide*. What was the film the mystery man said he was in?"

"Uh, what are you talking about?"

An impatient sigh. "You told me the Rawhide fellow said he used to be a bartender. And our mystery man in the trailer told him he was in the film they were showing on the wall at the bar. What film was it?"

"I don't think he said."

"Find out."

"Why?"

"Find out! Good lord, do I have to think of everything?" And he hung up. I looked at the nasty phone in my hand.

I would have fallen back asleep except for the pounding on the door a few minutes later.

"Wait til I get up, asshole," I yelled.

"Harris," momma said from outside. "Open up. Eva's gone."

I put on whatever clothes I dropped nearby, opened the door.

"She's gone. Her keys are gone, her car is gone."

"When?"

"Some time in the middle of the night."

"Maybe she went home?"

She looked at me like I was an idiot. "Without saying anything? Without saying goodbye? What if she has a concussion from the accident? What if this is dementia?" As she spoke, she made herself more overwrought.

"Just . . . ok, calm down. Let me get dressed and I'll come over."

And a few minutes later, we sat in her room, her bent forward on the bed, kneading her hands. "I should have taken it more seriously. Wandering out in the middle of the night. What is wrong with me? What is wrong with me?" She punched herself in the head. I grabbed her hand before she did it again.

"Stop. It's not important. She seemed fine to me. Stop."

"Oh," she moaned, "what should we do?"

I called the police and told them what happened. The officer asked me some questions and I told him about the sleepwalking and the memory stuff. He listened, sighed, said it wasn't enough to do anything official unless she had disappeared for 48 hours. But, he said, he would alert his officers and they would do a lookout. "If she hasn't broken the law, and she's a licensed 76-year-old driver, we don't have anything to pick her up for. For all we know, there may have been a disagreement and she just drove away. Let me tell you, old people get irritated when their children get antsy."

After I hung up, momma said, "I better go looking for her," but then we remembered she took the car. "Oh my god," she wailed, "she could be cracked up in a ditch somewhere, bleeding to death!"

A tap on the window and Gordon's serious face. "I heard talking. Is everything alright?"

For some reason, I wasn't overly worried about the whole thing. Probably I'm irresponsible and careless, but it wasn't giving me the anxiety attack it seemed to be giving my mother. "Your car works, right?" I asked him, and he said it did, just the headlights were out. Aware of the floodgate that might open, anyway I suggested he and momma get in the beat-up Honeybee and do a drive-around; at least it might calm her nerves. She seemed pleased by that, so off they went, and I went down to get coffee and wake up.

■ ■ ■

Around 9am, awake as I was going to be, I didn't want to wait around for Ray to find me, so I got in the truck and drove back across the sleepy town. When I got to the Rawhide, it was closed, but a well-tended, older Mercedes was parked out front. I went in, found Ben sitting at the bar, working through last night's receipts. I asked him what Ray asked me, but he couldn't remember. He asked for my number if he thought of anything and I thanked him and left.

Ray was indeed up and ready when I got back. For some reason, when I saw him bundled up in the coffee shop, some of my anger and hostility had drained away. It felt like the wind changed during the night, and whatever new air swept in blew out the stagnant air from before. I sat across from him.

"Well, good morning," he said. "Aren't we chipper?"

"Not particularly." I opened the menu.

He watched me carefully, staring through the grease. A person back there, at least for the moment. "Any news?"

"No. He doesn't remember."

"Ah well. I was so overcome yesterday I forgot to take what I meant to. All those magazines. There must be some clue in whatever he was keeping. And if not, they're probably of some value. I could sell them to vintage collectors and recoup some of my cost for the trip."

"God, what a piece of work."

"So let's make one more visit, shall we?"

I shrugged, looking at the egg dishes with names of European cities.

When we got back to the trailer, nothing had changed. Out here, each day the same: light, heat, sand, dust, wind. Only daytime and nighttime, and inside this tube of an Airstream, with the curtains drawn, no real way to know the difference. A time capsule that shoots you from youth to old age, and all you have to do is sit here and do nothing. That's what happened to this guy. That's what happened to me, under my cottage cheese ceiling. We're not so different.

Except, I realized.

Except I'm here and he's not.

Standing in this hot room, this tiny chamber under an infinite sky, I could sense him, I could smell him. He was just here, not long ago in the scheme of things, just a millisecond in desert time. This was all his stuff, the things he loved and held close. He made himself out of these things. And here I am, rifling through them like they're trash, and it hit me that one of the reasons – and I have to sit down because it might be the heat getting to me like it did Ray – one of the reasons I'm here, or maybe the only reason, in fact, is because of this guy. If it weren't for him, I wouldn't be here. Or anywhere.

"Oh, Harris, not you too," Ray said, seeing the water running down my face. "There must be mold spores or something in here. Grab those magazines and let's get out of here."

I thought I was getting dizzy too, but it was the pager buzzing in my pocket. I pulled it out. On the tiny screen, a phone number with a Palm Springs area code, and a message.

Had a pool

I stared at it.

"It had a pool," I said. Ray looked at me. "The movie," I said. "It had a pool."

And that old energy came right back. His eyes lit on the stack of photos I dropped yesterday and he scooped them up; then, stepping neatly over piles of junk, the child-catcher of yore snatched one magazine from the floor and with a lick of the finger, whipped to the page he wanted: the scene on the fat guy's back deck. Ray took a photo from the stack and laid it against the magazine page. Pointed to the nose on the photo, then the nose in the magazine. The other face, not mine.

"Oh," he said, like the air coming out of a bag. "Of course."

17

In the morning, Mother didn't knock on the door to wake Esther up. She got up by herself, went into the bathroom and washed her face, came out and dressed. Mother had still not come in. After what seemed like an hour, Esther knocked on the adjoining door but there was no answer. She waited a bit longer, then slid the door open.

Mother was there, alone, dressed in her usual, impeccable white. Sitting on the bed, her face in her hands. An envelope on the bed, open, with a letter and a thick stack of bills wrapped with elastic bands. Esther went in and sat next to her on the bed. And waited.

She couldn't remember how many days they stayed after that. Mother closed herself in the room, sleeping through the daytime. The counter man looked at Esther suspiciously as she crossed the lobby, going up and down the wide staircase to bring Mother her meals on a tray. Esther watched the other guests too, some having been there before they arrived, the ones who looked like they lived there. They sat in rocking chairs on the patio, their bitter, parched faces looking back over the empty desert they had come from. They were exhausted and could go no further. She realized they would sit here forever.

She walked to the front desk and told the man they were checking out. He looked over the counter at her, a child. She had to convince him she meant it; she went into Mother's room and took the envelope and counted out the dollars and walked back downstairs and paid the bill. Then she told the bellboy to take their luggage and put it in their car, and when he ignored her, she peeled off a bill as she had seen Father do and handed it to him to make him do it. And then she sat with Mother, and talked with her, asked her to get up and continue the trip. Mother seemed vague and sad, so then Esther told her that she had to get up. She collected the rest of their things and guided Mother to the car, into the driver's seat, and reminded her what Father had taught her. The maps already there, laid out on the seat. There was no more time for waiting or sadness or standing still; if you did, the desert would cover you.

"Start the car, Mother," she said. Then, firmer, "Start the car now. We have to go." And Mother did. She drove out of the parking lot, to the top of the hill, and over, and there below, as promised, was the new world. Endless and bountiful and welcoming, stretching gloriously from the desert to the edge of the ocean. As they started descending the long, slow grade, Esther had to temper her excitement with the knowledge that the world they were entering was entirely new, and she would have to be entirely new to meet it.

■ ■ ■

In the hot air of the Honeybee, momma sat in the passenger seat, fanning herself. "What about that street?" she said. Gordon made the turn. In truth, she had abandoned the mission an hour before. Trying to drive down every street in Palm Springs in search of a pushed-in Cadillac, she realized, was futile and ridiculous. Plus, this was the second time she was scouring the roads of an unknown town for an unknown reason.

"I'm awfully sorry to hear about your mother," she said. "That must be very hard on you."

He nodded. "I loved her very much. I love Mom too, but, you know. Mama was my biological mother. So it's different."

"I understand. As hard a time as it must be, it's good to hear you talk about her in such an honest way. It seems like you really know how you feel about her."

"Well, I guess. Isn't that how everyone is?"

"No," momma said, laughing. "You must be able to tell what an odd

bunch our family is, even after a few days. With us, it's more about performance than honesty."

"There can be an honest performance," he said.

"Oh, smart kid, you got me there."

"Mama didn't want us to have anything to do with show business.
That's why she moved out to the mountains. She worked for a lot of famous people when she was young and she said it burned her out. She said
it burned out . . ." he paused a moment, pretended to wipe something off
his chin. ". . . uhm, Harris, your son. A long time ago."

"Ah," momma said, slowly. "So, your mother knew my son?"

He nodded in the stiffest way.

"Well, that's certainly a coincidence."

"Yes."

"Now Gordon, remind me again . . . you came out here to find some
friends? Was that it?"

"Yes."

"Uh huh."

Nothing more from him.

"So," momma said, "did your mother have other children?"

"No, just me. She was already with Zoe when I was born and they
raised me together."

"And your mother? What was she like?"

"She was a very honest person. She wanted me to be too. And to do
that, she said you have to ask a lot of questions so you know the truth. She
didn't let you get away with anything."

"Well, one up on me already."

"And she cared about us a lot. Me and Mom and the animals. She
wanted to make sure we were happy. She said she wasn't happy before I
was born and she never wanted us to feel that way. So it's hard because I
don't know what to do to make Mom happy now."

"I'm sure just being yourself and being there is what she needs the
most."

He nodded. It seemed as though he was less focused on scanning the
streets too, and only making the turns to continue the conversation.

"Does, uhm, Zoe have parents? Your grandparents?"

"No. They were angry when she was young and she fell in love with a woman. She said they hated her and cut her off completely. I don't know anything about them. Maybe someday, but right now, I'm not interested in them."

"I understand."

Gordon cleared his throat. "You said your family is all about performance. But it seems like you all care about each other very much."

"What?" momma said, and laughed. "What show have you been watching? Oh my god, if you knew the crap these people have pulled over the years. Inconsiderate, disrespectful, you name it."

"I can tell. Your mother says mean things. But you're here, and she's here, and you all seem to look out for each other. And no one hates anyone. That's pretty good."

"Well, it's not as rosy as it looks."

"But no one leaves anyone alone."

"And that's just the trouble! No one leaves anyone alone!"

He pulled to the side and smiled. She heard it too, and laughed. But he had pulled over because of something he saw over her shoulder. "Is that the car?"

The Cadillac with the pushed-in bumper, its rear end facing them. Parked at the end of a street. The collision had pushed the back down and the front up, so it appeared to be kneeling on his hind legs, peering upward. And it was peering at the field of white windmills in the far distance.

They got out of the Honeybee, approached the car, tentatively, not sure what they would find. But it was just Eva, sitting in the front seat, smoking.

"I was wondering what you would do," she said, nonchalant, as momma approached the open window. "And don't bother with the metaphors," nodding at the field, "because I'm not tilting at anything. It's just beautiful, though, isn't it?"

"Mother, this is very erratic behavior. We were worried."

"When I go crackers, I promise, you'll be the first one to know. I just felt like some time away. From all of you. Is that so wrong?"

"You could have told me," momma said.

"Why should I? You're a grown-up. So grow up. Maybe there's nothing wrong with my brain at all. Maybe it's just telling me it's time to take a rest."

They stood by the car as the smoke wafted gently out, snapped up and carried away by the wind toward the field of silent giants.

"I tried to take care of everything," she said. "But nothing is as simple as you'd like it to be."

18

Ray and I sat in the same booth I did last night. Only cups of black coffee before us now, steam curling from the heavy mugs. We sat through two refills so far.

"I see how it started," Ray said, "the misunderstanding between this fellow Ben and Marcus. He said that was him on the screen and Ben thought he meant you, and he let him think it."

"Why wouldn't he say, no, the other one?"

"It's it obvious? He wanted to be the important one. He wanted to be the one who was loved."

It made me shudder. "It was all just so gross and stupid."

"What was?"

"Everything. The movies, the drugs, the hustling. What a stupid waste of life."

Ray had lifted his coffee to his lips but set it down. "Is that really what you think? After all this time? Well, I am disappointed. I expected more."

I stared at him, uncomprehending.

He leaned forward, eyes coming into focus. "All of that was a long time ago and I grant you, times are different. But that was good work, Harris. A lot of people enjoyed it and got off to it. We were . . . pioneers of an earlier age. I'm proud of the work and you should be too."

I didn't want to dredge this up. I didn't want to think about it. It had all been too confusing. Good, bad, evil, kind, cruel – the boundaries were too mushy, too hard to understand. A world where the only thing that mattered was how good the show was, how good you performed. After all

of it, the only thing I could do was retreat into the cottage cheese apartment, and even that, up to a few days ago, seemed too much for me.

"Look," I said, leaning forward, "what you did was unforgivable.
Those kids like Marcus were poor and living on the street and you took
advantage of their suffering to make money and get your rocks off. I don't
have to remind you where you and I met."

"No, you don't. Because you were there before I was, selling your ass
and making money before I ever got there."

"That's *different*. That was for *fun*. I wasn't starving like those kids who
did it to survive."

"I paid them well, Harris. I never did anything they didn't want to do.
And the work I gave them was much safer than hustling on the street. And
don't shake your finger at me, all holier than thou. You wanted the fun
and the money and your rocks off as much as anyone. You worked just as
hard, and you helped me do it. You have no right to grill me over for what
terrible things I did to anyone else. I only helped you get what you want.
Don't blame me if you didn't like what you wanted."

My mouth felt like it was full of ashes. I didn't have anything ready to
hit him back. He knew it and sat there, smirking. "Now, if we're finished
throwing acid on each other, there's something more I'd like to say." I
shook my head. "I really do wish you were proud of the work. I regret so
much I don't own the catalogue anymore. For all we know, those films are
sitting on the bottom of the Hudson River. But," and he stopped, took a
moment to actually think what he wanted to say. "You were something
special. I know you never thought so. You always talked about how plain
you were, how you thought I was just a dirty old man looking to suck your
cock. Which, may I say, was very nice and probably still is. It's disappointing to see how you've closed yourself off from the world. I don't know why
you want to destroy yourself and everything you did. But the work was
good. You gave a lot of people a lot of joy and a lot of pleasure, and that's
the best gift anyone can give." Then the lousy rat had to stop and clear
his throat, his eyes wet. "And I'm very sorry," he said, looking down at his
hands. "I didn't invent you or make you or any of those things I said. You
were always who you were. The best one of all."

I sat back with my arms tight across my chest, as far from him as I could get.

"Now, about the other matter," he said, wiping his nose. "I can think of one other reason Marcus might have taken on the role. Once upon a time, we paid him to do it."

"I beg your pardon?"

He asked for a refill and drank a good bit, keeping me waiting, until he was ready. "You know," he said, finally, "I used to keep a gun in my desk at the office. We had so much trouble back then. Actors on drugs, lawyers threatening us, people accusing me of every crime in the book. I always worried when someone I didn't know showed up at the door. But one day I had a very interesting visitor, a distinguished older gentleman. Very charming, very rich. He said he had a problem only I could help him with. It seems that his ex-wife was an actress of some repute. Her career had been in the doldrums for some time, but now a very good offer was coming their way. However, they'd gotten wind of a story about to run in some scandal sheet, the Inquirer or something … about a close relative of this lady, who was appearing in *pornographic films*, and with other men, no less. There was a snappy headline planned for the story … Naughty Granny or something like that … and pictures of this young man, *in flagrante*, which they intended to print next to one of this wholesome old gal with her braids and her dirndl. It was just a dumb, salacious story for page 25, but still, in those days, enough to put the kibosh on a career. Well, as this gentleman explained it, he was confident this magazine had made a mistake. That's why he came down to speak with me directly. He asked if I would be so kind as to provide paperwork to show that the model in question was in no way related to this lady. I might even be called upon to produce the model, in the flesh, to support the claim. With all that evidence, he planned to threaten the magazine with a lawsuit for slander and defamation. If they sent a reporter down to verify the facts, which they might have to do, they would find everything in order to prove, beyond a shadow of a doubt, that they were indeed mistaken. My compensation was very generous, and I was more than happy to oblige, especially, as he put it, as a friend of the family. So, when I thought about who to cast as the doppelganger, you can guess who came to mind. There was a decent enough resemblance and, given the fact that most people back then wouldn't look too closely at man-on-man action, enough reasonable doubt to go around."

I could hear myself breathing.

"As it turned out," he said, "things never went that far. The magazine backed down and you know what happened to us. But Marcus was paid, and he'd been standing by to step into someone else's jockey shorts if the need arose. So, one is left to assume, at least in his own mind, the need arose. He liked the role and decided to keep on playing it."

And this I did have to let sink in.

"So, we're all in this together," I said, mostly to myself. To the table. To hear it echo off the ceiling.

"I'm sorry Harris. Nothing is as simple as you'd like it to be."

19

Back in the room, the orange nipple was flashing again. This time I did answer. It was from my mother, telling me they found Eva and brought her back to the motel. That crisis solved, I drove to Marcy's to tell her what I found out. It didn't seem to surprise her very much.

She tapped her ash on the ground after I finished, the picnic table already hot from the mid-afternoon sun.

"Marcus," she said. "You think that was true?"

"I don't know. That's the name he used when we knew him. He was pretty young, so I don't know why he would make it up. But then, I don't know why people make things up in the first place."

She nodded. "So then . . . *you're* Kevin?"

"No," I said, and had to laugh. "I made that up."

"Why did you do that?"

I shrugged.

"So you guys are all bullshitters?"

"We are. That's what your friend wanted." I thought about the trailer. "He wanted to be the one who was loved."

"I loved him. I guess it wasn't enough." She took a puff off her cigarette. "So you got your answer. Are you heading back to the big city?" I said I was. "What are you going to do next?"

The question caught me by surprise. "Why do you ask?"

"Well, you showed up here, all hot and bothered to track down some big mystery that seemed important to you. You ruffled everybody up around town, waving this picture in everyone's face."

"I thought I was being very discreet."

"So, you happy now? You get what you wanted? 'Cause honestly, I didn't need to know this. He's still the same person to me."

I said I didn't know.

"You told me something pretty rough, you know. What you were planning to do before you came here. That was a lot to dump on a stranger."

"Oh god, I'm sorry. I didn't mean to . . ."

"It's okay. It got you what you wanted. Can I ask, are you still thinking about that?"

I had to think about it again.

"I'm not really in this world," I said. "Something was broken and I don't know if it can be fixed."

"Do you want to be in this world?"

I had no answer.

She took a deep drag on the cigarette. It was almost done, but for some reason I nodded at it, and she gave it to me. I took one, delicious puff, and handed it back. She took the last one then stubbed it out; stood and walked past me toward the door. She put her hand on the knob.

"I lost my Kevvie and I really miss him," she said. "It would suck to lose another."

Then she went inside and closed the door behind her.

■ ■ ■

Back at the motel, a most unsettling sight. Momma near the front desk holding a bag of potato chips, and Ray next to her, chatting away like she was his best friend. She was leaning as far from him as she could without falling backward.

"How are we all today?" I shouted, approaching them.

Momma winced. "Just talking with your friend here . . ."

I said, "I thought I asked you to give us some space."

"Well, it was just a coincidence," Ray said, "us all coming down at the same moment. Your mother is delightful. I was enjoying hearing all about you as a young man. Goodness, what sort of adventures did you get yourself into?"

"I'll fill you in on all of it," I said, and stepped between them. "Momma, why don't you go upstairs and I'll knock on your door in a few minutes."

"Thank you," she said, relieved. "Nice to meet you, uh . . ."

"Raymond."

She nodded and headed for the stairs.

"What an asshole," I said to him.

"I was just curious to put names to faces. After all, we've all been on this grand adventure. And I had a thought. Why don't we all have a big going-away dinner tonight? I'll get Carl and we'll make a party of it."

Marcy had said her friend wasn't cunning or clever. He could never survive in the world. Thinking about it now, there was one big difference between him and me. "I'm not sure that's a good idea," I said. "We had a visitor last night."

"Oh?"

"Yes. This big guy. Very big. And slick. I mean, slicked back. He came over while we were eating dinner and he asked a lot of questions. Like, who I was, what we were doing here. He pretended he was a fan of Eva's but he wouldn't tell us his name and he was obviously scoping us out."

Ray's knitted his brows. "Why didn't you tell me about this?"

"I'm telling you now."

"What else haven't you told me?"

"Well, the consensus is . . . Marcus wasn't a self-inflicted overdose. His friend Marcy got to the trailer before anyone else, and she found him with a needle stuck in his left arm. And she thought that was suspicious because he was a lefty. And Ben told me that Marcus was dealing drugs, and he messed up, and he *implied* that the people he was dealing with were not the kind of people you should screw over."

Ray's ashen face turned white. "You kept this from me?"

I nodded.

"So, they've probably been watching us this whole time?" he said. "You let me step into a drug deal gone wrong and didn't tell me?"

"I'm not sure. I'm telling you everything I know."

"And you think these people ...?"

I nodded again.

"Well, that's . . . oh no, that's no good at all. I can't get mixed up in anything like that again. Oh no, no, no. I almost died! They almost . . ." and he started babbling to himself, a running commentary of what could happen, what had happened. "How could you . . . how could you not tell me? You of all people?"

I shrugged. "What can they do to me?"

"Oh god," he said, and gathered his coat around him as he went for the elevator. When he got in, he turned to me and pointed his pointy finger, speechless.

"Bye now," I said.

The doors closed and lifted him away.

But he wasn't wrong. If Marcus crossed the drug people and they thought we were related or had money they could recoup, I guess they could come after us. But I was right too. I didn't care. If they wanted to break my kneecaps, they could have them. I've been worse places than that. Which gives you some kind of strange courage.

■ ■ ■

I wanted to talk with my mother alone, finally. Although the same delicious, malicious intent that sent Ray packing might have been at work, it struck me, with all our group's pairing up, unpairing, re-pairing, that sending Gordon off with Eva would clear the space for me to sit down with her. Momma dispatched herself to his room to ask if he would take her out for ice cream, and in a few minutes, we all met up in their room.

"What is this?" Eva asked, hackles fully raised. "Putting me out to pasture?"

"No," momma said. "It's just so hot and we'll probably drive back tonight. It seemed like a nice idea to get something cool before we go. And Gordon might like to hear some Hollywood stories. Or anything you'd care to share."

"I don't want to get into a car with the kid who rear-ended me. That's not good driving."

"It wasn't my fault," he said, irritated.

"He's right," momma said. "So you're safer driving with him than me."

"How about I just drive my own car, how about that? I have the safest record of any of you."

"That sounds fine too," momma said. "Ok with you, Gordon?"

He said it was.

"Who is this kid, anyway?" Eva said. "What are we doing, adopting someone else's children?"

"He's the son of a friend of Harris," momma said.

I turned and looked directly at her.

"Gordon mentioned it," she said to me. I turned and looked directly at him. He looked at the wall.

"You lost me," Eva said. "This kid here . . . with the fresh mouth . . . who smashed into us in the middle of nowhere . . . is the son of a friend of yours? Well, I find that very suspicious, don't you?"

"Stuff happens," I said.

She looked at all of us. "I don't know what's going on here, but if that's the way you all want to play it, that's fine with me. No one needs to tell me anything. After all, who am I? Just some old bag. But listen," she said to Gordon, "we'll go in *my* car and *I'll* drive. And I don't want any guff out of you."

"I don't know what guff is," he said, matter-of-fact.

"Jesus, a smart aleck." She gave him a nice, hard pat on the cheek.

Pairing, unpairing, repairing.

"So," momma said, when they were gone. "Anything *you'd* like to share with me?"

"I think you know everything."

"Nice looking boy," she said.

"He is."

"And your musty friend?"

"Gone."

She sat on the bed. Let out a big sigh.

"I haven't done a lot of things right, Harris. I'm sorry. But I'm happy to help you," she nodded toward the door, "with anything you need."

"Thank you," I said. "You did fine. You beat yourself up too much."

She looked down at her hands.

20

"I don't want any ice cream," Eva said, as she drove. Gordon sat next to her. "I only agreed because they obviously want to get rid of us. They won't tell me what's going on, and I've been here for three goddamn days."

"Me too," Gordon said. She pushed in the lighter and fished around in her purse for the cigarettes. "Smoking is bad for your health," he said.

"Don't I know it. But here I am, and the only thing wrong is a broken brain. I know it's probably good genes and I'm not advising you to smoke, but don't tell me what to do."

"What do you mean a broken brain?"

"I've been forgetting things. Lines of scripts, what happened when. Very disconcerting. And I had all the tests, you know. All they say is old age, and I'm not that old."

"Maybe it's psychosomatic. Have you had a big shock lately?"

She turned and looked, mildly amused. "Psychosomatic? Kiddo, you have no idea. No, I have not had any big shocks lately."

"Maybe something is bothering you that you don't want to remember."

Silence in the car as she inhaled the cigarette. Gordon put down his window to let the smoke out. "You really are a wise-ass for a kid. Where do you get the nerve to talk to an adult like that?"

"I'm not being disrespectful. I'm only asking a question."

She gestured toward him with the cigarette, thought for a moment. "You're right. Good for you. You know the problem with people nowadays? They're either too scared or too nasty. No one with the guts to carry on a decent conversation. Where did you say you were from?"

"Agua Dulce."

"Never heard of it. But someone up there did something right. You've got brains and you're not afraid to say what you think. That's a good trait. I wish my kids were like that."

"Carolyn seems like a very nice lady."

"Eh. She's alright." They came to what looked like the end of town. Palm Springs was a big square back then, and the roads just ended at the perimeter. To continue, you had to turn left or right, and follow that road, not too long, until it came to an end too. She turned right, to continue the conversation. "You know the only person who ever stood up to me ... that I respected? My ex-husband. A real bastard and the most wonderful man. Very hard when they're the same person."

"Is he dead?"

"He is now. Couple of times I would have done it myself. But we had a parting of the ways long before that."

"What happened?"

"Well, some things I can't tell a kid your age. But he was something else. A real character."

"How?"

It was easier to talk and drive than talk alone. Something about the driving distracted her enough that she could let the unimportant things go. "Well, he was hard to describe. Brilliant man. Witty, good-looking. Funniest son-of-a-bitch I ever knew. You know how we met? A nightclub act. We didn't plan it, it just happened. One night I was out with some friends at a club, and this guy comes to our table, and he asks me to guess what's in some lady's handbag. They turn the lights on us, and he had me stand up and put on a blindfold. Right there, in front of everyone. He feeds me these lines, stupid little things, like, something the cat dragged in, and I thought dragon, and I said, is it a dragon, and that's what it was, some charm bracelet with a dragon. And we went on like that. He'd say some innocuous thing and I'd get it. Same wavelength, I guess. Everyone loved it and they asked us to come back and do the act again. And I said, what act? I don't even know this guy. And he introduced himself and that was the beginning."

Gordon seemed to be listening, thinking.

"Kept you on your toes, that's for sure," she said. "I had this picture once, a big musical, but a bad director. The whole thing was falling flat, and I thought, Jesus, this is gonna flush my career right down the toilet. I called my husband for help. He'd been in theater when he was young. He came down, and he looked at this thing, and you know what he said was missing?"

He didn't.

"Me. He said the whole thing rested on me and I wasn't there. I said, sweetie, that's all there is, and he said no it's not. So we came up with a bunch of business, he and I, like the magic act. Unbelievable the things we thought of . . . all these gags, people shooting out the wazoo . . . absolutely atrocious stuff, but oh my god, the laughs. Up to then, you know, I didn't think I could do comedy. In fact, I didn't think I was much of an actress at all. But he poked me and joked with me, and he showed me I was funny too. Saved the picture, that's for sure. And the thing was, he didn't give me anything I didn't have already. Just showed me what was there. And that's an awful good gift."

"You miss him," Gordon said.

"When you get old you get used to it."

"Did he love you?"

She needed to savor the cigarette for that one. "Good question. My grandson said he did. They talked. Pissed me off, if you want to know the truth. But yes. I believe he did." She looked at Gordon. "He didn't take any guff either."

"Did you love him?"

He watched her think about it, and the way she did, taking him seriously, was enough of an answer.

"So, why did you break up?"

"Oh, we were too different. He liked . . . well, he didn't like me. As a wife. There are some things you just can't finagle."

They had come to the end of the city again, the pavement disappearing into the sand. "Jesus," she said, and turned around to look as she backed up. "You can't get out of this place, can you?" Turned right on the intersecting road and started down that one. "But we had a good time. An awful good time. Sad that you forget the good times after you've been hurt."

"How were you hurt?"

"Well, there's no point going into all that. It's water under the bridge. If you do, you get bogged down and you can't move forward. You can't get away."

"From what?"

And now she did look at him. Maybe it was the heat, or lack of sleep. The memory thing. Whatever it was, she felt a trust with this strange kid, and the questions he asked. He really wanted to know. Something about his face; something about the nose and chin.

"It's painful when someone leaves you," she said. "It's hard to make sense of it. You don't know why, and it can destroy you if you let it. And you have to survive. You have to. When you love someone. When you're young. Otherwise, it's unbearable."

Gordon's eyes filled suddenly with tears. "My mother is gone . . ." he said, and he started to cry.

Eva pulled the car over. Looked at the kid.

You have to make choices in life. You do what you have to do. And she was tough, she knew this. She ought to tell this kid to buck up and push it away, be tough and endure, like her. She could say that. But this kid's heart was broken. And that's all it was. How much he loved someone and how much it hurt. She could tell him to be tough. Or she could do something else.

She took him in her arms. "I know," she said, "I know, sweetie. I'm so sorry."

And he sobbed and sobbed while she held him and made him feel safe, and loved.

■ ■ ■

"You know," I said to momma, "since we're in the middle of nowhere, and there's a lull in the action, there's something I've been meaning to ask you."

She raised an eyebrow.

"A long time ago, I was eavesdropping on a conversation between you and Nana. You two were arguing about something . . ."

"Imagine that."

". . . and you said something about her dumping a kid out in Palm Springs. You said she gave a child away . . . to a home or something."

She let out a breath. "You heard that? I'm sorry. You didn't need to know about all that."

I waited.

"That was a very bad time," she said. "For both of us, George and I. We were young and stupid. We were experimenting with all kinds of things. I don't know what to say about that time. If go into it, I'll start criticizing myself and I'll sound like her."

"That's ok. But what happened? Did you have a baby she made you give away?"

She chuckled, sadly. "Yes and no. I hated her for a long time for that. I thought she did it for her own reasons, for her career. But now, I can see she was trying to do the right thing. And maybe she was right. I couldn't have taken care of a child at that moment." She took a long breath. "Back then, if you were rich and famous, you could get away with anything. She got a fancy lawyer and they gave the baby up for adoption. And, of course, they did it far away, so no one would see what they were doing. But George found out and he wouldn't allow it. He got his own lawyer and we came out and took you back. It wouldn't stand up," she said, and took my hand. "And we wouldn't leave you alone." For some reason, that made her smile.

"What?" I asked.

"The place she went to . . . it was all a blur but it was somewhere around here . . . at the edge of town. Where we . . ." and she stopped.

Now it was my turn to smile.

"Who knows?" she said.

■ ■ ■

That night, after they all drove home – finally – I walked out of the motel and sat on a big rock at the edge of the parking lot. The sun had slipped away, the sky the color of perfect golden toast, the magnificent show of stars slowly revealing itself. This is the time the night lets out a breath, exhaling the heat of the day, and I do too.

Marcy asked what I was going to do next, and I don't know. I've been inside the home of someone who left too soon, and it felt so bad. I wish Marcy had her friend back. I wish I could tell him I loved him for real and thank him for my life. He lived and died inside an airless chamber, surrounded by lies and stories he told himself in order to survive. Looking up at this wondrous, limitless sky, I thought of my own cottage cheese existence, the brown stain floating over me, and we are not so different.

What did Ray say? *I don't know why you want to destroy yourself and everything you did.* A good question. But do we listen to monsters?

One answer is that a lot of things happened. A lot of bad things. I can't remember them all or know what to do with them. But there were some good things too, and some good people who gave me a lot. And I suppose if you're so shielded to protect yourself, in your desert trailer or your cottage cheese apartment, then you miss the good things when they come. The armor that protects you seals you in as well.

I look up and the stars are brighter now, the show coming alive. The first cool breeze off the desert. I can feel it behind me, and the turbines catching the wind. Making power out of nothing, out of air.

So, what am I going to do next? Well, for one thing, Gordon asked me a question, and I have to stay around long enough to give him an answer. And all these moving parts have to come to rest. So for now, maybe I'll just go home and sleep. And in the morning, say, wake up. Wake up and come into life.

www.ingramcontent.com/pod-product-compliance
Lightning Source LLC
Chambersburg PA
CBHW061937130726
47909CB00013B/2024